What Can Be Done?
Making the Media and
Politics Better

Edited by

John Lloyd and Jean Seaton

Blackwell Publishing
In association with *The Political Quarterly*

Editorial organisation © by The Political Quarterly Publishing Co. Ltd
Chapters © 2006 by the chapter author

BLACKWELL PUBLISHING
350 Main Street, Malden, MA 02148-5020, USA
9600 Garsington Road, Oxford OX4 2DQ, UK
550 Swanston Street, Carlton, Victoria 3053, Australia

First published 2006 by Blackwell Publishing as a special issue of *The Political Quarterly*

First published 2006 by Blackwell Publishing Ltd
1 2006

Library of Congress Cataloging-in-Publication Data

What can be done? : making the media and politics better / edited by John Lloyd and
Jean Seaton.
    p. cm.
    Includes bibliographical references and index.
    ISBN-13: 978-1-4051-3693-8 (pbk. : alk. paper)
    ISBN-10: 1-4051-3693-6 (pbk. : alk. paper)   1. Mass media–Political aspects. I.
Lloyd, John, 1946- II. Seaton, Jean.

P95.8.W49 2006
302.23–dc22   2006013201

A catalogue record for this title is available from the British Library

Set in 10.5/12 pt Palatino by Anne Joshua & Associates, Oxford
Printed and bound in the United Kingdom by The Alden Group, Oxford
Front cover image: © 2005 Martin Rowson, Design by Raven Design

The publisher's policy is to use permanent paper from mills that operate a sustainable
forestry policy, and which has been manufactured from pulp processed using acid-free
and elementary chlorine-free practices. Furthermore, the publisher ensures that the text
paper and cover board used have met acceptable environmental accreditation standards.

For further information on Blackwell Publishing, visit our website:
www.blackwellpublishing.com

What Can Be Done?
Making the Media and Politics Better

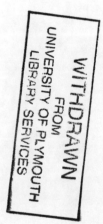
University of Plymouth Library

Subject to status this item may be renewed
via your Voyager account

http://voyager.plymouth.ac.uk

Exeter tel: (01392) 475049
Exmouth tel: (01395) 255331
Plymouth tel: (01752) 232323

Publishing

Contents

Notes on Contributors

Steven Barnett is Professor of Communications at the University of Westminster and the author of several books on the media. He is co-author of *Westminster Tales: the 21st Century Crisis in Political Journalism* and is currently writing a book on television journalism.

Georgina Born is Fellow in Social and Political Sciences at Emmanuel College, Cambridge, and a Reader in Sociology, Anthropology and Music at the University of Cambridge.

Suzanne Franks is a former BBC TV current affairs producer. She is now working on volume 6 of the BBC official history, funded by the AHRC, and writing a PhD on foreign news reporting at the University of Westminster. Her previous books include *Dished! The Rise and Fall of BSB*.

Tim Gardam is Principal of St Anne's College, Oxford. He was formerly Director of Programmes at Channel 4, Controller, News and Documentaries at Five, and Head of Current Affairs, and Editor of *Panorama* and of *Newsnight*, at the BBC. He was a member of the Burns Panel, appointed by the DCMS, that reviewed the BBC Charter in 2004–5.

Jürgen Krönig is UK Editor of the German weekly *Die Zeit*, and writes for TV, radio and printed publications in Britain, Germany and Switzerland.

John Lloyd is a Contributing Editor for the *Financial Times*. He is a member of the editorial board of *Prospect* magazine, and of the Moscow School of Political Studies. He has won several top journalism awards and, in addition to TV and radio work, is a past editor of the *New Statesman* and of *Time Out*. With others, he is creating the Reuters Institute for the Study of Journalism at Oxford University. His most recent book is *What the Media Are Doing to Our Politics*.

Don Redding is a former journalist who has worked for international charities since 1991. In 2001 he became campaign coordinator for 3WE, the Third World and Environment Broadcasting Project (www.ibt.org.uk/3WE), a coalition of leading international NGOs working for better TV coverage of the developing world. 3WE helped found Public Voice, the leading voluntary-sector coalition campaigning for citizens' interests in relation to communications (www.politics.co.uk), which he also coordinates.

Peter Riddell is Chief Political Commentator of *The Times*. He has been writing about politics for nearly thirty years: first, on the *Financial Times*, until 1991, and since then on *The Times*. His latest book is *The Unfulfilled Prime Minister—Tony Blair's Quest for a Legacy*.

Michael Schudson is Professor of Communication and Adjunct Professor of Sociology at the University of California, San Diego.

Jean Seaton is Professor of Media History at the University of Westminster and is on the board of *The Political Quarterly*. Penguin recently published her *Carnage and the Media: the Making and Breaking of News about Violence*.

Martin Woollacott is a former foreign correspondent, foreign editor and foreign affairs commentator for *The Guardian*. He continues to contribute occasional pieces to the newspaper and its websites.

Introduction

JEAN SEATON

Distractions

MODERN societies suffer from a collective attention deficit disorder syndrome. With much to do, many amusements to occupy us, in a world flooded with opportunities for information and endless capacity to communicate with others, all at any time and in any place, with improved reporting from the heart of disasters, and a cornucopia of sources of knowledge—the problem is to get us to concentrate. In particular, we have apparently become increasingly difficult to interest in politics. Moreover, it may be about to get harder. A two hundred year old compact between the media and politics is about to be turned on its head, as new technologies re-engineer the relationship between how views and information are exchanged, judged and assigned significance, and how public opinion is formed. Democratic political institutions will be re-made—they always are—by these changes in communication.

Alexis de Tocqueville observed, of the United States early in the history of democracy, that the press played a vital part simply in organising and editing the novel floods of information and opinion that formed on every issue. 'Newspapers become more necessary,' he wrote, as societies become more equal, and a multitude of individual opinions more diverse and less deferential. 'I shall not deny,' he observed, 'that in democratic countries newspapers often bring about very inconsiderate undertakings in common. But, if there were no newspapers, there would almost never be common action. The ill they produce is therefore much less than the one they cure.' He pointed out that in democratic societies many people have different opinions, which get lost in the crowd, but that when newspapers hold such ideas up for all to see, 'All are immediately directed toward that light and those wandering spirits who had long sought each other in the shadows finally meet each other and unite.'[1] In a shrewd comparison, he was suggesting that the media had become a vital substitute that organised opinion, perhaps just as the authority of ruling elites had done in pre-democratic societies. The newspaper had brought the diverse members of a highly individualistic society closer together. De Tocqueville's acute insight into the role of the press also held for broadcasting, which has also extended this power to focus audiences' fickle attention on things that matter to it (as well as all the other stuff). But this trick has already become harder to pull off—and it is about to get even more complicated to concentrate public attention, let alone on political issues.

It is against this background that the media's relationship with contemporary opinion forming and politics has taken a new, savage, twist. This book considers the messy, raucous, incestuously intimate yet often

Published by Blackwell Publishing Ltd, 9600 Garsington Road, Oxford OX4 2DQ, UK and 350 Main Street, Malden, MA 02148, USA   1 sour contemporary relationship between politics and the media, and rather brazenly suggests that nevertheless, despite all of the swift changes, things could be done to improve and sustain a difficult relationship in the interests of democracy. It also suggests that the emergent communications revolution makes it urgent that we begin to be more self-conscious about the role of the media in democracy, because there is also much to be lost if we are not more careful. The problem is how to advance the capacity of all these novel technological and social opportunities to hold open new arenas in the interests of citizens.

The public is, of course, already busy exercising new tastes, building new networks, doing new things, establishing new tones of address and making new markets. But this calls for prudent policy to protect these developments, imaginative institutions to interact with them creatively and new means of explaining and judging reality—which is what, so far, reporting and respons-ible editing have done for us. The market for the media has always been both rumbustiously carnivorous and yet separated out from the mainstream of the market for other goods by all sorts of protective and exceptional policy devices—on the grounds that the market in opinion was too vital to be left to the vicissitudes of business alone. From the US First Amendment, which protects freedom of speech (somewhat oddly now), to the creation of the BBC as a 'public service' broadcaster (so far, a triumphantly mutable but mostly a steadily public-interested institution, dependent on a licence fee), to the postwar restructuring of the German broadcasting scene (which was rapidly regionalised and de-Nazified), to the financial arrangements that made Al Jazeera possible (a very considerable capital 'gift')—at every turn the media have been made an exception of. They have been developed in ways that advance their public, political role, and indeed could not have survived or thrived without such considered interventions. It is important to realise that although they all blossom best under competitive pressure, nevertheless, making sure that the combat is about things that matter—quality of reporting, engagement with audiences and standards of editorial intelligence—cannot be left simply to any abstract 'market': useful competition often requires special conditions. The point is that all of those media that have helped keep political systems decent have had something beyond market pressures that has influenced them. When they have functioned in this way, they have indeed been a tremendous democratic weapon. It is this tradition and the principles that underlie it that we need to hang on to—not particular forms of communication. But it may not be easy.

The truth shop

One aspect of the changes that have recently taken place is an alteration in the trading terms between the media that deal in politics, politicians and political institutions. Of course, politicians have often moaned that the media are mean to them and journalists have often denounced the sly ways of politicians. Yet, what is happening now is not just another round in a long-running and essentially cooperative mud-slinging match between political actors, some in the media and some in political roles of various kinds, an essentially benign and enjoyable public sport with a jousting edge for the players. Nor is it just another sequence in a familiar argument that somehow, now, things have got more vulgar or bad tempered. John Lloyd's path-breaking book, *What the Media Are Doing to Our Politics*,[2] acutely clarifies the ways in which the news media have, almost casually, helped to establish a culture of contempt for politics, while crowding out politicians' own voices from the arena. The contemporary media, he suggests, have become a threat to democracy rather than a means to democratic deliberation. Meanwhile, the political will to protect news and information as a public good has weakened, at least in the US and much of Europe. Whether media coverage is a cause or a symptom of a novel public attitude towards politics, the changes over the past twenty years are clear, measurable and perturbing. The public votes less and less and distrusts politics more and more, and despises politicians (if it thinks about them at all) even more than it used to.[3] There has been a distinct generational shift: whereas in the past people used to 'mature' into an interest in politics as they grew older, they appear to no longer do so. This trend is replicated in different forms all across Europe and in North America. People who drive on roads mended by politics, have their hips repaired and babies born as a consequence of politics, who go to schools that have evolved as a result of politics, and have the very air they breathe cleaned up or polluted by politics—Why are they not merely indifferent, but hostile to it all? Nevertheless, evidence shows that people increasingly fail to make any connection between these things that affect their lives and the political institutions that manage them. While the media are certainly not solely responsible for this attitude (education, the nature of public services, the moment of history and many other factors contribute), the way in which we discuss in public what matters to us (which is what the media facilitate and probably shape) is one important component of the brew.

Politics is also responsible: not only have some political strategies eroded public trust, but some proposed solutions seem wilfully blinkered. On the one hand, the answer has been seen as a series of 'technical' innovations; on the other, we have developed a series of institutions that are based on a suspicion of politics and politicians. Thus, one answer to higher voter turnout, for example, has been seen as an issue of making voting 'easier' to do—e-voting and postal voting are considered to be remedies: but while this may be desirable, it is far more likely to be what a vote means to voters that really matters. As Alex Keyssar has pointed out in the US, 'The danger is that those who write the rules of the voting competition win. The public vote ratifies a decision already made elsewhere.'[4] But, while we have sought to avoid this danger in the UK, through the good offices of the Electoral Commission, this is itself based on a premise of a kind of suspicion and hostility to politics. Meanwhile, the media have been happy to go along with the culture of 'transparency' for political actors, though not remotely prepared, with the exception of public service broadcasters, to expose their own decisions, predicament, choices or finances to any public scrutiny at all.

However, what makes thinking in the area of the media and politics all the more unsettling is that there is no comfortable perch for us to settle on: we want simultaneously to demand that the media scrutinise politicians and political structures more vigorously, and yet worry about the impact of the audience-hungry media show on institutions that matter. If the media have been increasingly aggressive and dismissive (in ways even the most responsible of them fail to grasp), then the politicians have also often cavalierly debased aspects of political life. But the problems will not go away because both sides blame the other and shout loudly. The aim of this book is to take stock at an interesting moment and to begin to think about what could be done to make things better. Indeed, if we acknowledge how dysfunctional the relationship seems to be in parts now, the goals of more strenuous reporting and a desire to secure greater public absorption in the matters that affect them are not incompatible.

Above all, there is a distinct smell of paradigm shift in the air. At the same time as something is happening to politics, a revolution is also gathering pace in the media that we have traditionally relied on most to communicate politics: their traditional forms are all in trouble. They face declining circulations, difficulties in attracting audiences, problems with advertising revenue shifting to other new media and increasingly insecure futures. Audiences are fragmenting, disappearing, dissolving. When interviewing top broadcasting mandarins and newspaper executives, the dominant worry is the same: how they can relate to individualised audiences who spend more time communicating with each other, and less with the established media. Of course, audiences are still out there, but they are configured in new, mobile ways and they are more difficult to engage. A series of interrelated technological and social changes are creating new political and media landscapes (and consequently economic ones) that will have dramatic democratic impacts. The technologies of communication have altered more rapidly in the past five years than since the beginning of broadcasting; and, critically, an abrupt shift in the model of communication has occurred. The dimensions of the revolution are only really just becoming clear, but it is so profound that it is not only affecting politics, but all other—for want of a better term—producers of culture. There is a real sense of tectonic plates being about to shift across many sectors. Driven by technology and changes in how they live, audiences want personalised communication, their own downloaded entertainment (portable), they want to compose their own video clips, express their own views and take and distribute their own pictures. The public has become more fragmented and less secure in its habits. We live in more varied ways (and more and more of us live alone). We are more comfortable, want to be heroes in our own story and are perhaps hungrier for more highly charged fun than before. We want to choose what we think in the same way that we want to download our own music selection on to our iPods. Much of this, of course, we know how to do because we have learnt from the media—and just like the music on our iPods, we compose our personalised selves out of mainstream media material. Nevertheless, there is a simultaneous expansion of the possibility of democratic engagement with this new power. However, everywhere from music to publishing, from movies to games, from newspapers to broadcasting, there is an acute shared anxiety about the ability to go on engaging audiences—who want to perform, not merely observe.

All of this can be a fruitful leap for an intelligent public, but the new dimensions of society pose new problems for the relationship between the media and politics. Thus while we have been rather good at representing our multicultural self to ourselves, so that screens and indeed other institutions have put on show a multicommunity theatre of Britishness, and this is no mean achievement (one in which the BBC, together with the very remit of Channel 4, for example, have actually taken a critical lead), nevertheless we have failed to understand the inner life of some of these communities whose representatives we watch in public life. We have also failed to display our common life persuasively to many of our citizens. The modern fragmentation of the media, with particular tastes and particular groups all sold just what—and only what—they are interested in is one driver of this occasionally blind splintering. While there are still great waves of common public feeling, they pose quite new challenges. Of course, some things do not change: despite pious sociological encomiums about the 'globalised' world, the British public, for example, 'is not interested, won't watch, will turn off, very, very fast any comedy, soap opera, entertainment programme that is about any foreigners who live abroad – except Americans'. 'It is,' observed Jon Plowman, the Head of BBC Comedy Entertainment, 'an iron law.'[5]

Indeed, there have so far been three responses to the new media revolution. First, newspapers have become increasingly opinion led. If you cannot deal in information any more, perhaps you can deal in views. These views have also broken away from the older political regimentation of party politics—as Colin Seymour-Ure has demonstrated, none of the parties can now rely on any organ of the news to reliably represent its views: the commentariat is perplexingly politically promiscuous.[6] Who would have thought *The Guardian* a natural political home for the excellent but hardly *Guardian*-esque Max Hastings and Simon Jenkins? Or that the ultra-conservative *London Evening Standard* (which even in its social columns only covers right-wing parties) might be a home for progressive Nick Cohen, or *The Times* for David Aaronovitch? Like some game of political musical chairs, they all seem to be in the wrong place: but that is part of a deliberate attempt by all the newspapers to cover every base of opinion. This twenty year old press trend has, however, also been followed by television news, which has become more opinionated in a narrow sense too—now celebrity reporters ventriloquise politicians. Thus, as Andrew Tolson has shown, we used to hear Chancellors of the Exchequer on budget day on the news, but now we hear and see engaging economic reporters telling us what the Chancellor 'would', 'will' or 'might' say, but not what he has actually said.[7] Such developments in news reporting do not 'just' happen; they are the consequence of scrupulous research into how to engage audiences, as the problem for television news—just like the press—is the fleeing public. The result has been a more fluid, chatty, cheeky, opinionated, fast, performance, but one which by definition seems to put reporter and audience in a conspiratorial community—against the politicians.

The second response has been that of broadcasting: faced with acres of channels because of the new technology, it has been forced to produce permanent twenty-four-hour news, but it is a sadly repetitive, empty, format—except when there is a crisis, or a vehicle for what is really current events. The third response has been to pursue stories into their micro-hearts, aided and abetted by the odd contemporary conventions of invasive rights; stories are often propped up by an incremental detail. This is not the 'investigative' journalism that went away and dug and sifted reality; it is different. It is often based on the assumption that any discretion is a lie, and it uses circumstantial detail to construct apparently authentic stories, which are frequently quite false.[8] Meanwhile, newspapers have begun to broadcast comedy shows, while broadcasters—or at least the BBC—have taken the place of newspapers, with huge hungry newsrooms: the BBC increasingly publishes reports, and surrounds broadcast programmes with acres of written online material. There is much gain in this. News is sourced and produced highly professionally on the main channels, but there are savage contrasting pressures to make each item a miracle of compression—which must surely frustrate knowledgeable journalists who take increasing risks to bring us the news, and which cannot seriously explain such a complex world to preoccupied audiences.

However, the most important driver of this situation is that newspapers and commercial broadcast news organisations are in economic difficulties everywhere (except in the developing world, where they are, perhaps, in a different stage). What newspapers really sell is audience attention: they sell it to advertisers, who buy it to sell products; the revenues then subsidize what we, the punters, buy. The commodity that has kept all of the important democratic stuff flowing is the manufacture and trading of audiences' attention. The only exception to this is public service news, which also depends on audience attention, but which 'sells' it for its own legitimacy and for the public good. Public service news, like the BBC, is sustained by a political will, but its market situation is as fiercely competitive as that of any commercial producer. However, not only are there now many more reliable and cheaper ways of harvesting audience attention than news, especially among the elusive young (celebrity stories, online chum reunions, games, mobile-phone downloads), but our long-term dependence on the traditional form of the news subsidised by advertising means that we are unfamiliar with its real costs, and seem not prepared to pay for the more expensive online model.[9] We have become accustomed to getting our news on the cheap: which served democratic purposes well—but, as it were, accidentally. Now, news as it has been traditionally produced and financed, especially in newspapers but in much broadcasting as well, is in commercial decline, and may, like the dinosaurs, be about to hit an evolutionary catastrophe. Indeed, it is the news vehicles that traditionally have provided the democratic glue, that depend most on adjudicating evidence and least on shouting, that are most threatened by the swift delivery of information on the Internet. Of course, new kinds of reporting are emerging, from participants ever closer to the heart of dramatic events, to concerned communities and partisan groups, but for the time-starved modern citizen, reliable adjudication of events may be increasingly elusive: the market—as it works at the moment, at least—may not deliver such values.

The single most troubling problem in reporting, felt acutely in all those news organisations that attempt accurate, realistic scrutiny of contemporary life, is objectivity. In older, less fragmented political systems, broadcasters often hid behind 'balance', claiming to report somewhere in the middle of a couple of competing ideologies. But this is no longer sustainable. In the US, 'balance' and fear of political attack has driven much reporting down increasingly bland and misleading paths. Being in the 'middle' between competing views on global warming, when the important, authoritative evidence is on one side, is to tell the public a lie. Nevertheless, finding a new version of 'balance' remains a key task: in a diverse society, how to attract and represent all the viewpoints is more important than ever. Yet, at the same time somehow, we need media that *arrive at a just view* of events. Indeed, 'objectivity'—or the attempt at it, which is after all what we need—is a process: it is how you worry, it is how you balance judgements, it is the criteria you use, and it is the quality of the people who make the choices and the integrity of the structures within which they work. Above all, it is local, informed knowledge that matters. All these hard-headed scruples are expensive. Yet, when the media fail to scrutinise political decisions, we make mistakes. But if we do not want to retreat into narcissistic, inward-turning news, adjusted just for our own prejudices, then we need the media to go on metabolising our diversity.

Perhaps this is only another stage in a long process, yet it is worth recognising how powerful the relationship is between forms of communication and political realities. Mass politics and political parties were made possible by the mass media. Every technical and social twist in the evolution of the press and broadcasting has influenced the very form of politics, reshaping political parties, the role of members, the role of representatives and the role of leaders—throwing up new opportunities, but repeatedly relocating aspects of power. The authority of legislatures has been perhaps eroded—it has certainly been altered—by the emergence of the media as a competing public space. Local parties emerged to mobilise voters: local parties declined as broadcasting offered new vehicles for leaders to communicate with voters over the heads of members. Successful political rhetoric adapted from the formal requirements of mass meetings to the new informality of broadcasting: now politicians have responded to the avid hunger for the 'unintended performance' (what the sweat on your shirt says about your sincerity) by choreographing their performances in new ways. What is going on now will also have similar effects.

Indeed, a key new problem is the behind-the-scenes moderating of the more easily expressed and plentiful public opinion, and the selection of 'representative' views that are then given prominence. The other vital thing that the media in democracies have done traditionally is to distinguish reality from rumour, and adjudicate between real shifts in public opinion and fomented storms. This has often been done haphazardly and in a 'biased' way but, nevertheless, over time, with some discretion. Thus, learning from the contemporary rushes of audience communication, and yet judging its provenance and authenticity in order to represent it back to audiences as opinion, is one problem. Broadcasters are keen to elicit response and engagement (although dealing with it is something they are less willing to discuss in public), yet consider the difference between an American 'shock-jock' broadcaster, who simply chooses the most outrageous views, and the thought that we expect the BBC to put into selecting and exhibiting 'typical' and 'representative' views for broadcasting, and this back-room work immediately seems a vital democratic task—one we may need to talk about more openly.

More peculiarly, one might observe, there is simply the problem of anyone listening to what anybody else is saying. Mothers know that obeying the imperious child demand 'Look at me'—'Look at what I've done'; 'Look!'—takes up a measurable quantity of parenting time. I have, indeed 'looked' at more Lego constructions and people doing headstands on the bed than I would have thought possible, but the proud performers would not have felt the same without the iota of devoted maternal attention (especially, of course, if they felt some other sibling was getting it). Well, at the moment, I sense an uneasy dissembling in our public institutions: ever keener to elicit views but not, in person, 'looking' at the eager opinionators. Everybody wants to show off, but no one is watching. In this, the media are in the front line, although other institutions have a similar problem. Thus, a BBC news website will get 10,000 messages during an average lunchtime. If a Ronnie Barker dies, this number will increase to 60,000.[10] These messages will only be read, in the main, by increasingly sophisticated software that will sift and sort communications by using word recognition groups. So far, the BBC, for example, has not found it hard to identify huge, but organised, attempts by interest groups to swamp it with opinions that it has felt were, in fact, unrepresentative of wider views. Thus the decision it made about the huge influx of messages objecting to the showing of *Jerry Springer, the Opera* was made easier because such groups tend to copy and paste formulaic messages and so can easily be identified. Yet the worry that particular interest groups will push political and taste agendas by overwhelming broadcasters and institutions with messages is real—as is the anxiety that a genuine and significant shift in opinion will be ignored or dismissed. Nevertheless, this will surely grow as an aspect of political campaigning, and we will still need the discriminating and evaluative intelligence of news organisations to place such campaigns in a democratic context.

Thus, the urge to perform rather than observe will have to be accommodated in the news. Indeed, new commercial models may develop: thus, for example, when the 7 July 2005 London bombings occurred, the BBC was offered several hundred mobile-phone clips within an hour of the events.[11] Witnesses wanted their experiences disseminated by the most authoritative source. But in the future, people may want to sell the images they capture from their own experiences more directly—and the Front Line Agency, for example, is attempting to develop an online model for this.[12] Of course, the news disseminators have to authenticate the material that is beginning to pour in. This is becoming a more onerous task, as so much is available that looks like news, but is fabricated or illegitimate. Paradoxically, in an age of increasing communication, we may become more dependent on the authority and principle of individual reporters, whose 'known' faces and reliable reporting from trustworthy institutions may be the only guarantees that what we see is genuine. In a multi-communicating world, the integrity of the reporter may come to matter even more.

Nevertheless, if politics is in difficulties, and so too is the traditional form of the news—and, up to a point, so are all traditional ways of reaching audiences—what can be done? The gloomy interpretation of all of this, and one pursued ruthlessly by commercial media interests, is that nothing can or ought to be done except let the market have its way. The weary old shibboleth of 'choice' is supposed to answer every public need. But it is—at least in part—ridiculous. Just as parents are rightly not remotely interested in having a 'choice' of schools for their children, but are very interested in the availability of good schools, we ought to be very suspicious when vested interests claim that serving consumers of the media as citizens can just be left to 'choice' and 'competition'. Public goods in the media have always been a product of protective and positive policies, subsidies, interventions and institutions. If you want quality political life, you need carefully nurtured institutions.

The BBC and the mutuality of our institutions

Thus supporting the BBC (whose licence fee may be secure for another decade, but which may, in the fast eddies of the communication revolution, be in real trouble after that) is important, because we can demand that it re-imagine the fractured audiences and engage them in public, as well as private, pleasures. We are lucky to have the Corporation; we are lucky to have other institutions that keep the fragile mutuality of the British unwritten constitution decent. This does not mean that we should not criticise the Corporation, yet in a moment of news, audience, content and political transition we need the public interest pursued actively more than ever—by a big player. The government has backed the BBC so far: despite all the political fracas of the Hutton moment, it seems to have accepted the importance of a large, and ultimately constitutionally sensitive and public-interested organisation in news and programming. Yet, there is still much that could be lost. The BBC works because it is simple to understand, and is accountable to audiences through the licence fee. It also works because what used to be the Board of Governors, and is now the Board of Trustees, is uniquely attuned to its responsibilities. The Ofcom suggestion to muddy the waters with a new body responsible for all public service broadcasting is dangerously seductive and reasonable sounding. It is also very wrong—and a good example of an important battle that needs to be won. It is a classic case of regulatory imperialism, which must be resisted.

Yet, in many ways, the 'old' broadcast model still works: people are not only watching programmes on television but they like local programmes (as well as American ones). While they do not always 'like' the news, they want it there to turn to, as an authoritative source for reliable information during crises and, indeed, at times to show them the world in which they locate themselves. Indeed, what one could call synergies, more complicated relationships between different media outlets, combining all sorts of delivery mechanisms and novel relationships to content and public involvement, are also very effective. Thus the clip most commonly downloaded on to the mobile phones of the nation's youth at the moment is a peculiarly gruesome bit of *The X Factor* (in which a toothless, tuneless, elderly lady sings startlingly badly).[13] The point is that, however dismaying the example may be (you have to see the clip for the whole horror to hit home), what it shows is a new use of conventional programming. The issue is whether it is possible to develop some of these more complex opportunities across media for public purposes. We are used to being dismissive about 'infotainment'—the reduction, as in the terrifying format of the American Fox News, of things that matter to short bursts of opinion-corrupted fun. But what we need is that the whole range of programmes and genres are alive with discussions that take us forward into the technological future. Thus content still matters: the problem is how to make its finances work.

The media create a pseudo-environment that is all most people can know of large areas of public life—the public in contemporary complex communities have many sources of information, but are paradoxically more dependent on media-mediated reality to make sense of them. The quality of news-gathering and dissemination may not matter that much when what it is concerned with is the jolly cut and thrust of humiliating minor publicity vehicles, but sustaining our capacity to survey the world does matter. There is a traditional, rather pious plea for more 'serious', 'responsible' media when, in fact, the issue may be attracting audience attention to what matters in any innovative way you can. Calibrating stories for importance is not trivial; selling is vital.

Of course, all these changes in the media and politics can also lead to new and innovative forms of political understanding and engagement. Moreover, as we are past the easy evangelism of the advocates of the first wave of new communications (which led to a great deal of public money being wasted on new technological applications that were mistakenly seen as solutions to policy problems), we can begin to see audience habits, desires and competences in a more realistic way. This book brings together a range of journalists, academics, administrators and experts to begin to suggest some of the things we could do to make the coverage of political issues and the engagement of audiences more fruitful. It is neither gloomy nor pessimistic: there are many things that can help—there is work to be done.

One aspect is to see where we are, but also to kick-start a conversation that progresses beyond the happy consensus that as long as everyone is blaming someone else across the politics/media divide, then things are all right, really. This is no longer true. The first thing to do is grasp the dimensions of the revolutionary moment in which we find ourselves.

In a reflective essay, Jürgen Krönig, the influential German journalist and commentator, argues how common the problem that we face here is across all mature democracies. This is salutary to a cosy parochialism (although some of the answers are indeed local, and must in our case deal with the chemistry of the media in the UK), but it is also a wake-up call. We need to be more self-conscious about what we need, lest we lose it. Michael Schudson, one of the most perceptive and witty academic commentators and historians from the US, provocatively turns much of the solemn pontificating about the role of the media on its head, and points out that it is the noisy, not the quiet, the brash, not the elegant—what you could call the 'vulgarly responsible'—coverage that has often delivered real gains for its audiences, and that this tradition needs to be re-invented in a more uncertain climate. John Lloyd, who has done so much to encourage debate about the dysfunctional relationship between the media and democratic politics, then casts a passionate and unflinching eye over the condition of the contemporary newspaper, and raises the alarm with a willingness that few commentators have demonstrated. Whatever 'news' and its vital combination of specific, detailed practical knowledge and editorial intelligence will become in new technological and social conditions of the transformation of media use, it is the economic foundations that will call the tune. By frankly acknowledging the tipping moment of a revolution, Lloyd also proposes some novel ways of thinking about the coverage of politics. His essay is followed by an elegant, corrective (and funny) essay on the state of television in the UK by an authoritative insider/outsider, Tim Gardam. A distinguished shaper of our broadcasting culture (and now in a different, academic, branch of the knowledge game), Gardam corrects a narrow interpretation of what matters in broadcasting—and points to the wider culture beyond news rooms that shapes public comprehension and enthusiasm so powerfully. Academic and researcher Steven Barnett confronts more directly the impact of current conventions of political broadcasting, especially the political interview, and explains how accidental the route has been to our current, rather arid predicament. The political interview is still a key touchstone of the capacity of the media to test politics and politicians rationally, but is desperately in need of some attention, as both sides become more rehearsed and confrontational, and less willing to discuss or explore. Barnett proposes some new and innovative ways forward.

Peter Riddell, *The Times* commentator, and wise-eyed observer of the Westminster political scene in the UK, looks at just how invigorating the new 'citizen reporting' may be. In a typically positive and reflective way, Riddell celebrates a transformation that is already under way in how politics is represented and argued about. In a contrasting piece, Martin Woollacott, considers the problems and lessons of foreign reporting from a lifetime of bringing world affairs back to domestic audiences. In particular, he puzzles creatively at how the 'pack-life' of journalists on a story produces a consensus, but also at the ways in which individual journalists, out of experience, legitimacy and knowledge (and perhaps temperament), can decidedly change dominant perceptions of a story—and get it right. This is something that is rarely discussed yet profoundly important, and it is peculiarly important to stress the value of human judgement in our audit-driven times. In a similar way, the researcher and academic Suzanne Franks considers how the reporting of Africa, one faraway place of which we still know little, and which is, perhaps, representative of all the mysterious communities (even in the road around the corner) of which we are ignorant, could be made better. Locally based reporting is the first condition of accurate understanding, and perhaps the new technologies can begin to inform us in more engaged ways of other places.

Meanwhile, Georgina Born, an academic and policy expert, backs these proposals up with a sharp, critical assessment of the very basis of broadcasting regulation, and while exposing the limitations of the current philosophy, proposes a new agenda and a new set of principles. Jean Seaton considers what we have to do with the media to re-engage children with politics, and argues that a continued role for the BBC is vital. Finally, Don Redding argues passionately and persuasively that we desperately need new public campaigns to articulate the public interest in scrupulous well-made media; for without them, the media revolution could dispense, in the interests of commerce and competition—not for quality, but for revenue—with everything that holds the media to the urgent work of reflecting our society as it actually is. Societies that lose touch with the capacity to understand their true condition are endangered. There is, of course, much important territory that the book fails to consider. Thus simply re-inventing the reporting of Westminster would help: reporters and politicians know there is a problem—perhaps we should devote some more energy to solving it. Then why

12

not ask that august body The Audit Commission to investigate how news is financed across the range (not just the BBC)? Getting Ofcom to use more of its powers would also help. There are things that need to be done, things that need to be protected, and things that need to be torn down and rebuilt.

However, there is no doubt that there is a stealthy, swift revolution taking place in the media and that the terms of exchange with politics will inevitably alter again. This collection of essays begins to ask what we can do to make the most of it, and to sustain our capacity to discuss together, in public, in a rational way, things that matter. De Tocqueville observed that, 'People in a democracy are frightened of losing their way in visionary speculation. They mistrust systems; they adhere closely to facts and study facts with their own senses.'[14] We need a conversation to make sure that this continues to be possible—and that it develops to include more of us.

Notes

1 A. de Tocqueville, *Democracy in America*, edited by P. Bradley, New York, Vintage, 1995, vol. 2, ch. 6, p. 141.
2 J. Lloyd, *What the Media Are Doing to Our Politics*, London, Constable, 2004.
3 For one summing-up of this evidence, see M. Russell, *Must Politics Disappoint?*, Fabian Society, London, 2005; see also Electoral Commission, *What's Up With Politics?*, Electoral Commission, London, July 2005; and the BBC Broadcasting Politics review, 2002–2004. The Neil Report on news at the BBC (available at http://www.bbc.co.uk/info/policies/neil_report.shtml) also deals with aspects of this issue and the BBC's response to it.
4 A. Keyssar, *Why Votes Matter: a History of Voting in the USA*, New York, Basic Books, 2004, p. 321.
5 Interview with Jon Plowman, Head of BBC Comedy Entertainment, November 2005.
6 C. Seymour-Ure, 'Are the broadsheets becoming unhinged?', in *Politics and the Media*, J. Seaton, ed., Oxford, Blackwell, 1997, pp. 43–55.
7 A. Tolson, 'Political discourse in TV news: talk, trust and the end of ideology,' unpublished paper, De Montfort University, Leicester, 2005.
8 See J. Seaton, 'Nano-truths and the story', in *Where the Truth Lies: Morality and Trust in PR and Journalism*, ed. J. Hobsbawm, London, Atlantic Books, 2006.
9 Thus none of the newspapers either here or in the US have yet managed to make money from their websites. People read what is free online but are, so far, far less willing to pay for it.
10 BBC News Response Unit, BBC and Social Responsibility Conference, December 2005.
11 Interview with Richard Sambrook, BBC World News, October 2005.
12 Vaughan Smith, Front Line News Agency, 2005.
13 Nick Aldridge, Product Director, MIG Media. The next product in development is 'karaoke' comedy, in which you insert yourself as a part in a television show, and then send the clip to all your friends.
14 De Tocqueville, *Democracy in America*, vol. 2, ch. 5, p. 111.

Hotting It Up

JÜRGEN KRÖNIG

DEMOCRACY seems in crisis. Democratic politics has, in the words of Philip Gould, Tony Blair's strategy guru, become 'a minority sport'. Apathy and cynicism have become the dominant feature of modern democracies. Turnouts at elections have been falling everywhere, in the case of the United Kingdom dramatically; a culture of contempt for politicians is spreading, and political debate is more and more contaminated in our hectic media societies.

What a contrast to the mood of the recent past. Not even ten years ago, there was excited talk about a new golden future lying ahead of us. Technological change and information revolution would lead to an unprecedented supply of information. Knowledge and understanding would increase between individuals and nations. There was talk of an evolving democracy— about new, direct forms of participation. Much was expected from the Internet. Some politicians suggested that we were experiencing the beginning of the end of representative parliamentary democracy: it would be replaced by a more direct, plebiscite-driven model. This was the message conveyed by techno-enthusiasts and many reformers on the left.

Flowing together in this vision of the future of Western liberal democracies were the belief in the inevitability and intrinsic value of technological, scientific progress and the conviction that any extension of democracy would be beneficial for our societies. After all, this is what parties of the left had fought for all along. When Willy Brandt, former German chancellor and for many years leader of the SPD, promised in 1972 to 'dare more democracy', he was expressing a belief in the virtue of an ever-expanding democratic principle.

We are facing a new question, as unexpected as it is awkward: Can there be too much of a good thing? Could it be possible that the extension of democracy in our societies is not just a blessing, a undeniable good, but that it could in fact be creating new problems and challenges? Fareed Zakaria, editor of *Newsweek International* and a political scientist from Harvard, answers this question with a qualified 'Yes' in his recent book *The Future of Freedom—Illiberal Democracies at Home and Abroad*.[1] He reminds us that freedom and democracy do not automatically go together. In many parts of the world, from Russia to Venezuela, we are observing democracies that produce elected autocrats or establish a dictatorship of the majority. Fear about the possible or even inevitable tranformation of democracy into ugly mob rule or populist dictatorship has been expressed before, by philosophers such as Plato, Burke and Kant. It is remarkable that the worry about the spread of illiberal democracy is emerging now, at a time of growing doubts about American democracy.

 Published by Blackwell Publishing Ltd, 9600 Garsington Road, Oxford OX4 2DQ, UK and 350 Main Street, Malden, MA 02148, USA

The democratic age

Democracy has spread around the world with an enormous speed. In 1900 not a single country had what one today would consider a democracy; that is, a government created by an election in which every adult has a vote. Today around 120 states do—62 per cent of the world. Democracy has become the only game in town, the only accepted form of government for humanity. The alternatives, communism and fascism, are totally discredited. Even dictators are trying to create the impression, at the very least, that they follow democratic rules and are organising elections.

Furthermore, democracy, the rule of the people, has been extended in our Western liberal societies. Zakaria calls this development 'democratisation', a process that goes far beyond politics. Hierarchies are breaking down, closed systems are opening up and pressures from the masses of citizens are now the primary force of changes in all walks of life.

In Western societies, which are experiencing historically unprecedented mass prosperity, economic power has been shifting downwards to the consumers, away from the exclusively rich. The tastes and wishes of the many need to be taken into account more than ever before. This extension of power to the masses is the dominant feature in our democratic societies. It has changed the shape of education, not necessarily for the better. It has even helped to to change modern agriculture. Intensive farming, heavily sub-sidised by tax revenue, has given people a chance to eat food, meat for instance, which used to be the privilege of the few. Modern agriculture has not only benefited the agrochemical complex. It is and has been a hidden form of redistribution in favour of the less well off, who have turned into alarmingly overweight 'industrial eaters', addicted to processed and fat food.

Culture too has been shaped by the extension of democracy. 'High culture' is no long at the centre of the cultural life of our societies: it has retreated into niches. Popular music, blockbuster movies and prime time television are the dominant expressions of modern culture. In the past, cultural elites were able to determine what the masses should watch and listen to: 'Inform, educate and entertain' was the guiding principle of the old Reithian BBC. Today, as the most influential cultural medium, modern TV reflects the preferences of mass audiences. The elites have lost the battle for influence.

Central control over distribution has become more difficult, if not impossible—which, of course, is a positive development. This is a result of the information revolution, which has produced hundreds and thou-sands of outlets for news. As Thomas Friedman has remarked about the Internet, 'everyone is connected but no one is in control'. The demo-cratisation of technology means that everyone can get his or her hands on anything, from anti-globalisation, porn and weird conspiracy theories, floating through the World Wide Web, to weapons of mass destruction. In its camps in Afghanistan, Al Qaeda was working on chemical and biological weapons programmes, using information downloaded from the

Internet. The 'democratisation of violence' is the most terrifying feature of today's world.

There seems to be a dark side to democracy, which progressives can't afford to ignore. This doesn't mean to say that democracy is a bad thing. No one wishes to return to a time and an age in which choice, individual freedom and autonomy were in short supply. Instead, we need to examine coolly the consequences of democratisation. We should reflect that liberal democracy is not only based on rule by majorities, formed in elections, but on the rule of law and on many intermediate institutions—the judiciary, central bankers, churches, associations, trades unions and media—which often are not democratically legitimised, but nevertheless play a vital part in securing freedom. We don't elect judges, public officials or editors.

Furthermore, representative democracy was established to function as a filter between the electorate and the executive, 'to tame the beast' of raw emotions and mood swings, to prevent the unfettered rule of the majority, which could all too easily lead to a dictatorship of the majority.

Media and democracy—power without responsibility?

The fourth estate, the media, has also been shaped by the forces of democratisation, even if this isn't reflected in the ownership of media companies. The dream that the new information age would be one of greater enlightenment, of rational discourse and greater participation, has not become true. Governments feel haunted by an aggressive media. The complaint in London is that the media act like some kind of conspiracy, attempting to keep the population 'in a permanent state of self-righteous rage'. In Germany, one day a tabloid such as *Bild* demands tough action against the pensions crisis; when politicians act, it accuses them of 'stealing the pensions'.

To avoid any misunderstanding: a natural tension between politics and the media has always existed, and that is right and necessary. Without a free press there is no public sphere, no informed citizenry and thus no democracy. As de Tocqueville wrote in the nineteenth century, 'It would diminish the importance of newspapers to say they serve to maintain freedom. They maintain civilisation.'[2]

The only problem with this glowing tribute is that one may find it difficult to relate it to today's media, with its vulgar entertainment trends and often irresponsible campaign journalism. Even so—in essence—de Toqueville's observation about the role that the fourth estate has to play is as true today as it was then. But some things have changed dramatically since the nineteenth century.

Media power

The fourth estate is more powerful than ever before. In defining media power, the left has concentrated on media tycoons and conglomerates, worrying about their capacity to suppress the free flow of information—to influence, even manipulate, their audiences. This fear is not unfounded. Governments and parliaments should never forget the danger of too much concentration in the media industry. Italy, where political and media power have been merging in an unprecedented way, should serve as a stark warning.

But there is another side to media power, more often than not overlooked by the left. The mass media have gained their status because they express and reflect the instincts, gut feelings and aspirations of the masses. Otherwise, the *Financial Times* or the *Frankfurter Allgemeine*, and BBC 2 or Arte—not ITV, *The Sun* or *Bild*—would be the media of the majorities. The mass media have to be seen as what they really are: they are tools and instruments of the power of the people. Electorates are more demanding, emotional, erratic and self-interested than ever before. The culture of deference is dead, replaced by an attitude that can be described as 'having your cake and eating it'.

Hyper-commercialisation

The fourth estate is shaped more than ever before by two dominating principles, sensationalism and simplification, which the American sociologist Robert McChesney, in his book *Rich Media, Poor Democracy*,[3] defines as the consequence of hyper-commercialisation. It has fostered ever-fiercer ratings and circulation wars, which inevitably leads to what is called 'dumbing down'. To succeed, the media industry tries to appeal to people's lower instincts.

Of course, it is one thing to pander to lower instincts. But they have to be there in the first place, and so has the willingness to be pandered to. In the end, people have a choice. One has to face an unpalatable reality: a Rupert Murdoch or Silvio Berlusconi, whose media outlets are giving the people what they want—fun, games and entertainment—is more 'democratic' than the cultural elites, who tried to impose their values and standards on the masses.

Entertainment

The appeal to the lowest common denominator is shaping the content of TV and popular culture more than ever before. The result is dumbed down entertainment, the triumph of banality. TV has turned into an endless attempt to lure and titillate the audiences with ever-stronger attractions. For TV programmes to be successful, they have to promise to be ever more out-rageous—explicit sex, exhibitionism, violence and voyeurism have become their vital ingredients. Highly successful reality TV formats such as *Big Brother*, *Island of Seduction*, *Superstar* or *I'm a Celebrity, Get Me Out of Here* (the 'jungle show') are tellingly equipped with an element of direct democracy. Audiences are asked to vote; it does not matter if they are using their right to vote just once or dozens of times. Most of these programmes belong to the category of what I call 'sado-maso TV'—the participants must accept being humiliated; they have to satisfy lower human instincts such as gloating and voyeurism; to gain their moment of TV fame, they must be prepared to do ghastly things, such as eating worms or beetles, diving into a snake-infested swamp or literally wading through shit.

News and political coverage

In the 'democratic age', news and information have been transformed. The way in which politics is covered has changed radically. Papers don't 'report' news; they quite often present it according to their preferences and prejudices. The growth of columnists has led to the birth of a 'Commentariat'. It includes a few excellent and analytical minds, but—all too often—reasonable, balanced voices are drowned out by journalists who seem untroubled by facts or deeper knowledge, but who gleefully present their own prejudices.

A lot of modern political journalism ignores context and complexities, and presenting everything in black and white, while—for most of the time—the nature of politics is a balancing act between contradictory interests and demands. It is no surprise, then, that politicians are losing control over the political agenda. The much maligned spin doctor was an attempt to win back the initiative. It failed a long time ago, but the myth of the spin doctor is being kept alive by the media, which presents itself as a heroic knight in shining armour, battling against the dragon of spin. The loss of control over the political agenda would not necessarily be such a bad thing, had significant elements of the press not eliminated the opportunity for thoughtful debate between people and politicians.

Electronic media

For a while, the last trusted bridge between politics and the public seemed to be TV and radio. But here too, as Richard Tait, former Editor of ITN, has noticed, commercial pressures and audience research are 'pushing editors away from political coverage'. News has become more superficial and sensational. The need for images and pictures is greater than ever before. News is all too often degenerating into 'disastertainment'. Public broadcasting is not immune from this trend. Ofcom, the new regulator for the electronic media in the UK, has registered a decline of up to 25 per cent in PSB political content over the past decade. But more has changed than just the extent of the coverage.

A survey by the British Film Institute, published in 1999,[4] revealed a worrying trend. The overwhelming majority of TV programme makers believed that ethical standards had collapsed. Among those working in news and documentaries, 52 per cent said that they had been pressured to distort the truth and/or misrepresent the views of contributors to create an 'exciting, controversial or entertaining programme'. The BFI report stated that 'some respondents felt that bowing to pressure had almost become habitual within factual programming'. It may only be distortion by oversimplification, or by altering or concealing facts. However, it is often 'serious falsification by omitting inconvenient evidence, misrepresenting contributions and some-times knowingly restating untruths'. That was five years ago. The situation has hardly improved since then. And it is by no means a problem specific to British TV. Reporters from German TV stations tell me that this kind of pressure is all too well known. Political reports that are considered to be too boring will be worked over, to make them more exciting. The method is called 'hotting up'.

The breakdown of trust

Sensationalism and oversimplification are affecting the output of all media outlets. There is less room for a balanced approach, for analysis instead of going for the crass headline or extraordinary story. The merciless hunt for weaknesses and inconsistencies of politicians and other figures from public life has become a prevalent feature.

Furthermore, the rhythm of politics and the media is drifting apart. Since the end of the great ideological divide, politics is more often than not undramatic, complex, not easy to understand and therefore more difficult and boring to report. Quite often, the results of political decisions, in education or welfare, can only be judged years after their implementation. This is exactly the opposite of what the modern media needs and demands. The media has a twenty-four hour mind-set, shaped by the demand for ever-shorter soundbites. It is impatient and short-termist; it wants results here and now.

Media language has changed too. What we are observing is an adjectival degradation. Every report that contains some form of criticism, whether it comes from inside government or from an outside institution, is described as 'damning', 'devastating' or 'scathing'. Warnings, which for most of the time are not heeded anyway, are 'stark'; differences of opinion between politicians of the same party are 'dramatic splits'; developments are 'alarming'—the media consumer is confronted with a permanent linguistic overkill. Official language is evolving in the opposite direction; it is becoming more sanitised, cautious, bureaucratic and politically correct.

All of this has contributed to changing democratic politics for the worse. The electorate has become hostile and distrustful of the media and politicians alike. Trust has broken down threefold: between people and politicians, and between media and people, while journalists and politicians observe each other with deep distrust and mutual antipathy. A vicious circle has established itself. Journalists claim that the political culture is not appealing to the public; driven by commercial considerations and market pressures, the media are therefore reducing their political coverage even further. The chances of the public participating in the rituals of democracy are not improving. The Phyllis Committee, set up in the UK to look at the relations between media and politics, has confirmed this bleak outlook. Politicians have given up trying to get their message across via newspapers, which they regard as hopelessly partisan and biased; and newspapers no longer believe much of what the government is saying—which leaves public broadcasters in an even more important and responsible position. If public broadcasting, torn between commercial pressures and public duty, also surrenders even more than it has done already to the culture of contempt, there will be only a few niche outlets left in the fourth estate that are willing to promote and practise a fair journalistic approach to politics. Sections of the BBC are operating on the basis of a strong anti-political bias, like many of their colleagues in the press, regarding all politicians at the end of the day as 'lying bastards', who can never be trusted.

Self-criticism is not popular among the media. Sometimes it seems that the only taboo for the media is the media itself. Some journalists and broadcasters are aware of the danger—not least John Lloyd, author of *What the Media Are Doing to Our Politics*,[5] an analysis of the effects of 'anti-political journalism'. Andrew Gowers, editor of the *Financial Times*, wrote at the beginning of 2004, after Lord Hutton had delivered his judgement, 'while the crisis at the BBC is deep seated, it is merely part of a broader malaise; . . . journalists' reflexive mistrust of every government action is corroding democracy'.[6] And Martin Kettle remarked in *The Guardian*, a paper that was deeply critical of the decision to go to war in Iraq, that 'the episode [the Kelly and Gilligan affair, triggered by the controversy over the British government's weapons dossier] illuminates a wider crisis in British journalism than just the turmoil at the BBC'.[7] Kettle remains deeply sceptical about the willingness of the fourth estate to address this crisis.

Democracy and civil society need informed citizens; otherwise, they will find it difficult to survive. Without media aware of their own power and responsibility, an informed citizenship cannot be sustained. What our democracies have got today, to a considerable extent, is an electorate that is highly informed about entertainment, consumer goods and celebrities, while being disinterested and/or deeply cynical about politics—one equipped with a short attention span and a growing tendency to demand 'instant gratification'. Politics in Western democracies is mutating into a strange kind of hybrid, a semi-plebiscitarian system, in which the mass media represent the new *demos*.

If this trend cannot be reversed, the stadium of democracy might become even emptier than it is now. It might only be filled again if seductive populism calls. When democracy is running out of control, it is the politicians who suffer first. Once the *demos* in ancient Athens and during the French Revolution had developed a taste for more power, they sought out and disposed of their victims with the same ease as authoritarian tyrannies.

But nothing stays the same. No trend will continue endlessly. Movements spring up to counter these trends and to turn things round. Amidst noisy sensationalism and hyper-emotionalised media output are signs of change—tentative and not representative, but clearly recognisable. Take the BBC. Britain's public broadcaster has decided to leave the populist path, along which Greg Dyke had walked energetically. His successor has promised a return to more serious journalism and less dross. Judging two recent products of the Corporation's Current Affairs department, 'the New Al Qaeda' series by Peter Taylor and the *Panorama* programme 'A Question of Leadership', which looked at the most important Muslim organisations in the UK, one can detect signs that the 'old BBC', which was known and respected all over the world for its cool, detached journalism, is trying to reassert itself.

Equally interesting is the output of new formats of reality TV. Of course, there are and will be more examples of 'sado-maso TV', such as *Island of Seduction*, *Big Brother* or the 'jungle show', that combine voyeurism and exhibitionism and appeal to lower human instincts. But there is a new type of reality TV—*Supernanny*, for example, or *Honey, We're Killing Our Kids*, along with *Tiny Tearaways* and *Transformation*—that uses this popular format to help to teach hopeless parents and their neglected, overweight and aggressive offspring how to cope with life and with each other. Of course, the TV industry needed a new stimulant: new, innovative formats were required, and the success of one example of this new 'educational' format inevitably triggers a dozen imitators. But these are eternal laws of the TV jungle. This does not diminish their important contribution to an urgent Western problem. There are many hopelessly dysfunctional families around. It seems that in quite a number of cases only the presence of a TV camera can motivate the children and adolescents of the XBox and video generation, who have grown up in the light of constantly flickering TV screens, to abandon the self-destructive cycle of aggressive behaviour, junk food intake and passivity. *Jamie Oliver's School Dinners* was rightly applauded as a helpful contribution, which might even have a long-term effect. So, not all is lost. But even these positive signs of greater responsibility won't re-establish the dominance of the cultural elites. In the battle between the elites and the masses, the elites are the losers.

Notes

1 F. Zakaria, *The Future of Freedom—Illiberal Democracies at Home and Abroad*, New York, W. W. Norton, 2003.
2 A. de Tocqueville, *Democracy in America*, Ware, Wordsworth Editions, 1998.

3 R. McChesney, *Rich Media, Poor Democracy*, Urbana, University of Illinois Press, 1999.
4 British Film Institute, *Television Industry Tracking Study*, London, BFI, May 1999.
5 J. Lloyd, *What the Media Are Doing to Our Politics*, London, Constable, 2004.
6 A. Gowers, 'The BBC's failings are a warning to all journalists', *Financial Times*, 31 January 2004.
7 M. Kettle, 'The threat to the media is real. It comes from within', *The Guardian*, 3 February 2004.

The Virtues of an Unlovable Press

MICHAEL SCHUDSON

Introduction

ALEXIS DE TOCQUEVILLE, widely cited for his view that the American press is a necessary and vital institution for American democracy, did not actually have much affection for it. He objected to its violence and vulgarity. He saw it as a virtue of the American system that newspapers were widely dispersed around the country rather than concentrated in a capital city, because this limited the harm they caused. He confessed, 'I admit that I do not feel toward freedom of the press that complete and instantaneous love which one accords to things by their nature supremely good. I love it more from considering the evils it prevents than on account of the good it does.'

It may well be, taking a leaf from de Tocqueville, that today's efforts to make journalism more serious, more responsible and, generally speaking, nicer are misplaced. I want to suggest the possibility that we—we critics of journalism, in and outside journalism itself—have attacked just those features of the press that, for all their defects, best protect robust public discussion and best promote democracy. The focus of the news media on events, rather than trends and structures; the fixation of the press on conflict whenever and wherever it erupts; the cynicism of journalists about politics and politicians; and the alienation of journalists from the communities they cover make the media hard for people to love. But these are just the features that make journalism indispensable. These are the features that most regularly enable the press to exercise a capacity for subverting established power.

This is not to suggest that there is anything wrong with in-depth reporting of the sort that Pulitzer juries and media critics applaud and I greatly admire. Nor do I mean to suggest that the public dialogue of democracy should jettison editorial writers, op-ed columnists, investigative reporters and analysts who can produce gems of explanatory reporting. That would be absurd. But I do mean to suggest that the power of the press to afflict the comfortable derives more often than not from the journalistic equivalent of ambulance chasing. Just as the ambulance-chasing trial lawyer sees another person's tragedy as a million-dollar opportunity, the newshound reporter sees it as an attention-grabbing, career-advancing, front-page sensation. I want to explore here the ways in which the most narrow and unlovable features of news may make the most vital of contributions to democracy.

Media criticism, to paint in very broad strokes, tries to make journalism more responsible, analytical, sophisticated, long form, and engaging, but calm and reasoned. Media critics speak in a populist voice in one sense—they

Reprinted by permission of Louisiana State University Press from *Freeing the Presses: The First Amendment in Action,* edited by Timothy E. Cook. Copyright © 2005 by Louisiana State University Press.
Published by Blackwell Publishing Ltd, 9600 Garsington Road, Oxford OX4 2DQ, UK and 350 Main Street, Malden, MA 02148, USA

typically ask journalists to engage citizens more effectively with the real issues before the city, state or nation. But at the same time they advocate a kind of Madisonian 'cooling' therapy, practices that are wary of emotions, wary of stories or approaches to stories that will be too appealing to irritable and angry citizens.

Do the premises of media criticism deserve our assent, or is there value for democracy in news media that are conflict-oriented, scandal-ridden, melo-dramatic, histrionic and unconstrained by the long view or deep under-standing?

The press as an establishment institution

The press is presumably the bastion of free expression in a democracy, but too often it has been one of the institutions that has limited the range of expression, especially expression that is critical of leading centres of power in society. Almost all social scientific study of news shows that journalists themselves, of their own volition, limit the range of opinion present in the news. There are at least three significant ways this happens. First, there is source-dependence. Reporters rely on and reproduce the views of their primary sources and these tend to be high government officials. Second, reporters and editors operate according to a set of professional norms that are constraints on expression in themselves. Third, journalists operate within conventional bounds of opinion, opinions common among a largely secular, college-educated upper middle class. All of this has been abundantly documented, but let me take a moment to remind you of this argument before I go on to suggest that it has been overdrawn.

Dependence on official sources

Media scholars have consistently found that official sources dominate the news. This is invariably presented as a criticism of the media. If the media were to fulfil their democratic role, they would offer a wide variety of opinions and perspectives and would encourage citizens to choose among them in considering public policies. If the media allow politicians to set the public agenda, they narrow public discussion and diminish democracy. This is the argument made, for instance, by W. Lance Bennett in his account of the 'indexing' function of the press. For Bennett, the media 'tend to "index" the range of voices and viewpoints in both news and editorials according to the range of views expressed in mainstream government debate about a given topic'. Bennett argues that this helps perpetuate a 'world in which govern-ments are able to define their own publics and where "democracy" becomes whatever the government ends up doing'.[1]

The constraints of professional culture

Journalists favour high government officials—but why? The answer is that their professional culture holds that a journalist's obligation is to report government affairs to serve the informational functions that make democracy work. But why should that general function lead to such a strong emphasis on government officials? The answer seems to me that newspapers, once divorced from direct service to political parties (the leading nineteenth-century model) and once aspiring to neutral or objective professionalism, developed occupational routines and a professional culture that reinforce what media scholar Janet Steele calls an 'operational bias' in news reporting. That is, in the work of political reporting, journalists emphasise 'players, policies, and predictions of what will happen next'. So even when the press goes to outside experts rather than inside government officials, they seek people with experience in government, access to and knowledge of the chief players in government, and a ready willingness to speak in the terms of government officials, interpreting and predicting unfolding events. In television reporting and to a large degree in the print media, too, historians or area experts on the Middle East, for instance, are very unlikely to be asked to comment on developments there to set contemporary events in a broader historical and cultural context. It is rare almost to the vanishing point for the press to seek out people even further from the policy community to comment on daily political affairs—for instance, religious leaders.[2] Why? No publisher dictates that religious opinion is irrelevant. There is no force anywhere dictating anything about this except the well-learned habits and patterns of journalists.

The constraints of conventional wisdom

Journalists seem to be paragons of conventional wisdom. They are wrapped up in daily events, and it would be disconcerting for them and for their readers if they took a long view. It might also be disconcerting for them to take a comparative (non-American) view. It would certainly be disconcerting for them to spend too much time with academics or others removed from the daily fray of political life. Individual journalists may take issue with convention. Some journalists who work for publications with non-conventional audiences may write with unconventional assumptions and unusual points of departure. But the mainstream journalist writing for a standard news institution is likely to be ignorant of or dismissive of opinions outside the fold.

Some factors limit the range of opinion in the American media, although they lie outside the news media as such. For instance, the American political system generally offers a narrower political spectrum, and one less accommodating of minorities, than most other democratic systems. Ralph Nader complained bitterly after the 2000 election that he had not been well covered in the press. Why, he asked, when he had been raising real issues, did he get no coverage, while Al Gore and George W. Bush, the Tweedledum and Tweedledee of American politics, got coverage every time they blew their noses? The answer seemed pretty straightforward: Ralph Nader was not going to be elected president of the United States in 2000. Either Al Gore or George W. Bush would. The press—part of its conventional wisdom—believed its job was to follow what the American political system had tossed up for it. It was not the job of the press to offer the public a wide range of issues, but to cover, analyse and discuss the issues the two viable candidates were presenting. Imagine, however, if Ralph Nader had been running for president in Germany. Would the German press have shown greater interest in his ideas? Yes, but not because the German press is better or more democratic, but because Germany has a parliamentary political system with proportional representation. If Ralph Nader received 5 per cent of the vote in Germany, his party would receive 5 per cent of the seats in Parliament and would be a force in forming a government.

So there are many reasons why the media discourse in the US is more restricted than in an ideal of robust and wide-open discussion. All this said, journalism as it functions today is still a practice that offends powerful groups, speaks truth to power and provides access for a diversity of opinion. How and why does this happen despite all that constrains it? The standard sociological analysis of news places it in so airless a box that exceptional journalistic forays are not readily explained. They are the exceptions that prove the rule. But these exceptions happen frequently, every year, every month and at some level every day. How can we explain this?

Strategic opportunities for free expression

Eventfulness

There is a fundamental truth about journalism that all journalists, but almost no social scientists, recognise: things happen.[3] Not only do things happen but, as the bumper sticker says, shit happens. That is what provides a supply of occurrences for journalists to work with. Shit even happens to the rich and powerful and it makes for a great story when it does.

Because shit happens, journalists gain some freedom from official opinion, professional routines and conventional wisdom. Journalism is an event-centred discourse, more responsive to accidents and explosions in the external world than to fashions in ideas among cultural elites. The journalists' sense of themselves as street-smart, nose-to-the-ground adventurers in places where people don't want them has an element of truth to it and it is very much linked to event-centredness.

News, like bread or sausage, is something people make. Scholars emphasise the manufacturing process. Journalists emphasise the raw material their work brings them to; they insist that their jobs recurrently place them before novel, unprecedented and unanticipated events. Whereas sociologists observe how this world of surprises is tamed, journalists typically emphasise that the effort at domestication falls short.[4]

The journalists have a point. Sometimes something happens that is not accounted for in any sociology or media studies. Take President Bill Clinton's efforts to create a system of national service. This was part of his 1992 campaign and he mentioned it as one of the priorities of his administration the day after his election. He appointed a friend, Eli Segal, to run a new Office of National Service and Segal set to work to get appropriate legislation through the Congress. The administration's efforts led to passage of the National and Community Service Trust Act that Clinton signed into law in September 1993. One year later, 'AmeriCorps' would be officially launched. Segal took charge of orchestrating a major public relations event, which would feature President Clinton swearing in 9,000 AmeriCorps volunteers at sixteen sites around the country by satellite hook-up. Every detail was checked; every contingency plan was rehearsed. Segal looked forward to a triumphant day on the South Lawn of the White House, followed by extensive, favourable news coverage. At 4:30 a.m. on the morning of the ceremony, Segal's phone rang. The event as planned would have to be scrapped. Why? Because at that hour a deranged pilot had crashed his Cessna aircraft into the back of the White House, precisely on the spot where the ceremony was to be staged. The news media predictably went gaga over this bizarre and unprecedented event, and could scarcely be bothered by the launching of AmeriCorps. *The New York Times* ran the plane crash on page one and AmeriCorps on page seventeen.

If you read the academic literature on the news media, it is all about how most news is produced by Eli Segals, not deranged pilots. And this is correct; the vast majority of daily news items on television or in print come from planned, intentional events, press releases, press conferences and scheduled interviews. Even so, journalists find their joy and their identity in the adrenalin rush that comes only from deranged pilots, hurricanes, upset victories in baseball or politics, triumphs against all odds, tragedy or scandal in the lap of luxury, and other unplanned and unanticipated accidents, mishaps, gaffes, embarrassments and wonders. The scholars delight in revealing how much of news is produced by the best-laid plans of government officials who manoeuvre news to their own purposes; the journalists enjoy being first to the scene when the best-laid plans go astray.

The archetypal news story, the kind that makes a career, the sort every reporter longs for, is one that is unroutinised and unrehearsed. It gives journalism its recurrent anarchic potential. And it is built into the very bloodstream of news organisations; it is the circulatory system that keeps the enterprise oxygenated.

Conflict

Almost all journalists relish conflict. Almost all media criticism attacks journalists for emphasising conflict. But conflict, like events, provides a recurrent resource for embarrassing the powerful.

Consider a story by Randal C. Archibold, with the headline 'Nuclear plant disaster plan is inadequate, report says,' that appeared in *The New York Times* on 11 January 2003. To summarise, New York Governor George Pataki had commissioned a report on safety at the Indian Point nuclear power plant just thirty-five miles away from midtown Manhattan. The report was produced by a consulting group the governor hired, Witt Associates. James Lee Witt, its chief executive, was formerly the director of the Federal Emergency Management Agency. So journalists knew the report was being written, knew its chief author was a high-ranking former federal official and knew roughly when it would appear. This sounds like the kind of government-centred 'official' news story critics complain about.

But is it? In this case, Governor Pataki commissioned the report after the September 11 terrorist attack had made more urgent the concerns that citizens and citizens' groups had already expressed about the safety of the Indian Point Nuclear Reactor. The plant's safety had become a major local political issue in 2000, when a small leak forced the plant to shut down for nearly a year. So an event—a leak at the plant—spawned political mobilisation; lively political mobilisation plus September 11, another event, made it necessary for the governor to at least make a show of doing something. September 11 further mobilised opposition to the plant, particularly because one of the hijacked jets flew very close to the plant *en route* to the World Trade Center. The Witt Report, whose conclusion could not have been fully anticipated by the governor or anyone else if it was to have legitimacy, declared that the disaster preparedness plan was inadequate for protecting people from unacceptable levels of radiation in case of a release at the plant.

The elected executive of Westchester County, Andrew J. Spano, commented, '. . . the bottom line is the plant shouldn't be here'. The reporter made it clear that the report's view of the emergency plans for the plant 'largely reflected complaints voiced for years by opponents of Indian Point'.

The Witt Report became news not because the governor's office generated it, but because continuing public conflict made the story news and made the news story interesting.[5]

What is the result of the story? The report obviously gives legitimacy to the environmentalists and others who have been urging that Indian Point be shut down. The news story helps keep opponents of government policy alert, encouraged and legitimated.

Cynicism

Political reporters in the past generation have increasingly made it a point not only to report the statements and actions of leading public officials, but to report on the motives behind the actions. They report not only the show and the dazzle that the politician wants foregrounded, but the efforts that go into the show and the calculations behind them. They may not specifically intend to undercut the politicians, but they do intend not to be manipulated. The result is a portrait of politicians as self-interested, cynically manipulative and contemptuous of the general public.

Take, for instance, *The New York Times'* front-page story on the proposed Bush tax cut on 16 April 2003, 'In a concession, Bush lowers goal of tax cut plan'. The story begins by curtly observing that President Bush lowered his target for a tax cut in a tacit admission that his original package was 'dead'. Then reporter Elisabeth Bumiller cites White House advisers who said 'that they were now on a war footing with Capitol Hill' to pass the biggest tax cut they could. They, along with other Republican strategists, said 'it was imperative for Mr. Bush to be seen as fighting hard for the economy to avoid the fate of his father, who lost the White House after his victory in the 1991 Persian Gulf war in large part because voters viewed him as disengaged from domestic concerns'. The orientation of the story was to the timing and style of the president's speech on the economy, not to its substance. The background is the foreground. This kind of a story, once exceptional, has become standard.[6]

To cite another example: at the end of September, Laura Bush went to Paris as part of ceremonies signalling the American re-entry to Unesco after a boycott of nearly two decades. The First Lady's trip was, of course, a well-planned public relations gesture. Would anyone have suspected otherwise? But Elaine Sciolino, the *Times'* veteran foreign correspondent and chief Paris correspondent, made a point of it, noting that Mrs Bush did not face the American flag as the American national anthem was sung: 'Instead, she stood perpendicular to it, enabling photographers to capture her in profile, with the flag and the Eiffel Tower behind. The scene was carefully planned for days by a White House advance team, much to the amusement of long-time Unesco employees'.[7]

Reporting of this sort—showing the president, or in this case his wife and her aides, to be buffoons—is a sign of a free press. The most dramatic example in the past year is the decision of *Time Magazine* to run as a cover story the photo of President Bush on the aircraft carrier with the 'Mission Accomplished' banner behind him, underscored with the emphatic headline 'MISSION NOT ACCOMPLISHED'. This may not be a sign of a press that motivates or mobilises, or turns people into good citizens. It may do more to reinforce political apathy than to refurbish political will. But it may be just what we require of the press.

Outsider news

Why is Trent Lott no longer majority leader of the US Senate? The answer is that on 5 December 2002, he made remarks at Senator Strom Thurmond's 100th birthday party that suggested we would all be better off if Senator Thurmond, running on a segregationist platform for the presidency in 1948, had won the election. The room was apparently full of politicians and journalists, none of whom immediately caught the significance of the remark. It was all part of the general celebration of the extraordinary event of a 100th birthday party for the man who had served in the Senate longer than any other person in American history. No one objected to or even noticed the over-the-top encomium that could at best have been interpreted as thoughtless but, if it was judged to have any real content at all, would have to have been viewed as racist.

But if no one noticed, how did it become news and force Lott's resignation from his leadership post?

The first part of the answer is that several practitioners of the still novel 'blogs', or personal websites of a kind of highly individualised public diary, took note of Lott's remarks. These included several prominent and widely read bloggers, amongst them Joshua Marshall (at talkingpointsmemo.com), Timothy Noah (at slate.com) and Andrew Sullivan (at AndrewSullivan.com) —all three of whom are journalists once employed by opinion magazines. Although mainstream press outlets, both print and broadcast, noted the remarks (and C-SPAN had aired them), the bloggers pressed the fact that Thurmond ran as a segregationist and that Lott had taken many conservative stands through the years, including speaking before white supremacist groups and voting against the Civil Rights Act of 1990. Matt Drudge, in his online report, even found that Senator Lott had made an almost identical statement in praise of Thurmond in 1980.

Thanks to the 'blogosphere', the party that Senator Lott and nearly everyone else present regarded as an insider event was available for outsider news. Moreover, the bloggers succeeded in getting the 'dump Lott' bandwagon moving not simply by pointing out an indiscreet remark, but by documenting Senator Lott's long and consistent history of association with organisations and policies offensive to African Americans. This persuaded mainstream journalists that Lott's remarks were not casual and thoughtless, but representative of a racism that Lott had repeatedly expressed and acted upon.[8]

Cyber-pamphleteers today can attract broad attention, including the attention of the old media. They do so, I might point out, by name-calling sensationalism. The most prominent and most consequential cases are that of Matt Drudge breaking the Monica Lewinsky story—'The president is an adulterer', and the bloggers who cried 'The senator is a racist'. An unlovable press, indeed, but perhaps just what democracy requires.

Outsiders are always troublemakers. The news media are supposed to be institutionalised outsiders even though they have in fact become institutionalised insiders. There is much more that might be done to keep journalists at arm's length from their sources. This is something that journalism education could orient itself to more conscientiously, for instance, insisting that journalism students take a course in comparative politics or a course on the politics and culture of some society besides the US. A serious US history course would also help. The idea would be to disorient rather than orient the prospective journalist. Disorientation—and ultimately alienation of journalists—helps the press to be free.

Social scientists regularly observe how much reporters have become insiders, socialising with their sources, flattered by their intimacy with the rich and powerful, dependent on intimacy for the leaks and leads officialdom can provide. All of this is true, but it is all the more reason to observe carefully and nurture those ways in which journalists remain outsiders. Bloggers, in the Trent Lott case, were outsiders to professional journalism altogether. But even standard issue journalists are outsiders to the conventional opinions of government officials in several respects. For one, they want to be noticed; they are eager to advance the journalistic agenda of setting tongues a-flutter across a million living rooms, breakfast tables, bars, lunch rooms and lines at Starbucks. I have said enough about this already. Second, journalists have access to and professional interest in non-official sources of news. The most important of these non-official sources is public opinion, as measured by polls or by informal journalistic 'taking of the pulse'. The American press in particular has a populist streak that inclines it towards a sampling of civilian views. This is another feature of journalism that media scholars regularly criticise—too much reporting of polls. I think it is terribly important for journalism to report on public opinion, even if there are ways, as there certainly are, to do it better.

Conclusion

I have been defending, somewhat to my surprise, the worst features of the American press—a preoccupation with events, a morbid sports-minded fascination with gladiatorial combat, a deep anti-political cynicism and a strong alienation of journalists from the communities they cover.

I hasten to add that the journalists I most admire get behind and beneath events, illuminate trends and structures and moods and not just conflicts, believe in the virtues and values of political life and the hopes it inspires, and feel connected and committed to their communities—global, national or local. The journalists of greatest imagination find the non-events that conceal their drama so well and know there is a story in the conflict that never arose because of strong leadership or a stroke of luck, or the conflict that was resolved peacefully over a painstakingly long time without sparking a front-page 'event'. I have enormous admiration for the journalists who can produce work of this sort. Even so, some of the greatest service the media provide for democracy lies in characteristics that few people regard as very nice or

31

ennobling about the press. These features of journalism—these features more than others—make news a valuable force in a democratic society. This means that—if all goes well—we are saddled with a necessary institution we are not likely ever to love.

Notes

1 W. L. Bennett, 'Toward a theory of press–state relations in the United States', *Journal of Communication*, vol. 40, Spring 1990, pp. 103–25; at pp. 106 and 125.
2 J. Steele, 'Experts and the operational bias of television news: the case of the Persian Gulf War', *Journalism and Mass Communication Quarterly*, vol. 72, 1995, pp. 799–812.
3 The most notable exceptions are H. Molotch and M. Lester, 'Accidents, scandals, and routines: resources for insurgent methodology', *Insurgent Sociologist*, vol. 3, 1973, pp. 1–11; and R. Lawrence, *The Politics of Force*, Berkeley, University of California Press, 2000. And I would like to add, however belatedly, me—see *The Sociology of News*, New York, W. W. Norton, 2003, pp. 1–8, from which I borrow in this chapter.
4 Scholars have not ignored the question of journalistic autonomy. They have provided important explanations for this autonomy. Daniel Hallin sees autonomy provided structurally by divisions among elites. See D. C. Hallin, *'The Uncensored War': the Media and Vietnam*, New York, Oxford University Press, 1986. Journalistic independence is also enhanced by laws that make it tough to sue for libel. These explanations direct attention to structural opportunities for aggressive reporting, but they do not show what provides journalists with a motive to pursue challenge and critique.
5 The story stayed in the news as the conflict widened—see R. C. Archibold, 'Indian Point is safe, N.R.C. official says', *The New York Times*, 22 February 2003, p. A18; and the op-ed column by H. Specter, 'Nuclear risk and reality', *The New York Times*, 20 May 2003, p. A31.
6 This is not to mention background stories that are exclusively focused on stagecraft. See, for instance, E. Bumiller, 'Keepers of Bush image lift stagecraft to new heights', *The New York Times*, 16 May 2003, p. 1.
7 E. Sciolino, 'Paris journal: a photo op: I say, can you see the Eiffel Tower', *The New York Times*, 30 September 2003, p. A4.
8 H. E. Gorgura, 'Lott gets a blogging: did the amateur journalists of the blogosphere bring down Trent Lott?', unpublished paper, University of Washington.

The Epiphany of Joe Trippi

JOHN LLOYD

Introduction

I asked Joe Trippi about the future of newspapers recently. He gave me the Ghandian answer—the one the Indian nationalist leader gave when asked about Western civilisation: 'It would be nice'. He doesn't think they have one.

Joe Trippi is regarded as an authority on future movements in the media and communications, because he was the man who organised and developed Howard Dean's presidential campaign. He says that when he was first persuaded to become Dean's campaign manager in January 2003, the Vermont governor had no money, little visibility in US national politics and 432 known supporters. A year later, they had nearly one million supporters, and the campaign had raised tens of millions of dollars, largely through Internet pledges.

Though Trippi had been a political professional, working on Democratic presidential bids since the late 1970s, his moment of epiphany came in the early 1990s, when he had given up politics for a career as a consultant on the Internet, working for companies who wanted to explore what was then still a new medium. One of the companies for which he worked, called THQ, made the games that children would play on a Game Boy. An Internet bulletin board had been started about its games, which attracted a virtual community of people who commented on the games, on the company stock and on gaming generally.

One day, a new messager, called Dave Haines, appeared on the board. Haines immediately established himself as a bright, interesting and attractive messager: 'when you went on the board, you would immediately look to see what messages Dave Haines had posted, because he was such fun'. He took to giving out personal details about himself in his regular daily posts. One week, he disappeared for five days, and the board was full of anxious queries as to his whereabouts. He returned to say that his wife had given birth to their first child, a son named Christian—and that the latest THQ game sucked. A year later, a daughter was born.

A few months after that, another absence, longer than the previous ones. This time, it wasn't a birth, but a death: his own—by heart attack, announced by a friend who knew of his popularity with the games messagers. Instantly, a message went out—that Haines was young, with a family of two, could not have had large savings, and thus that a collection should be held for his family. Trippi subscribed $200: the messagers raised thousands of dollars for his widow and children.

Published by Blackwell Publishing Ltd, 9600 Garsington Road, Oxford OX4 2DQ, UK and 350 Main Street, Malden, MA 02148, USA

'So this was my thought,' says Trippi. 'If people can do this for someone they've never met, but got to know and like through the net—then look at the power of it. And look what it could do for something of larger importance.' The thought stayed with him, unused, for years—until he joined up with Dean, and put it into practice—reaching out through the Internet to the online liberally inclined masses, who were fed up with George W. Bush, the Iraq war, the state of America, and who had a feeling of being neglected by the parties. He had an enormous success (a success much greater for him than the campaign was for Dean, since the governor lost, having been seen to blow it on television after an over-emotional speech at a rally, following the loss of a state he had expected to win). He had succeeded, as he would say himself, in creating a new electoral paradigm.

He thinks it means more than that. He believes that the Internet—with its attendant offshoots, e-mail, blogging and Google—have up-ended the order of the world, and that its effects will, bit by bit, change that world. He thinks it will do it in politics—and that it means the death of the political party. And he thinks it will do it in journalism—and that it will mean the death of the newspaper.

Trippi's epiphany is a vision of the end of established hierarchies. He also sees a new beginning: of an era of new communities, replacing the old. 'Those communities which were formed by people living together in one place, or even working together or worshipping together, are declining in importance. The Internet didn't do that: the process was happening in any case. My view is that the Internet came along at the nick of time, to save society from further disintegration by creating new communities of people—to be sure, not living next to each other, maybe not even ever meeting—but brought together by common interests . . . Communities of this kind aren't going to respond to top down organisations. They are taking power into their own hands. They need to get involved. So the newspaper model is under real threat. People in the newspaper business need to understand that the feeling out there is increasingly—*we should do this (whatever) together!* It's the us vs. them thing which is causing the problem.'

Dying at the peak

Trippi's view of newspapers is a more coherent version of what many people now vaguely think. The common wisdom about newspapers—in the Internet community, and thence into the business world—is that they're yesterday's news, even when they're today's editions. This, it seems, is the central dilemma, and the largest fear: that newspapers may be slowly dying out while nothing of equal worth has been developed, or is in sight of being developed, that will do what they do and have done.

What do they do, and what have they done? In free societies they have functioned in many ways: as a source of information; as a means of amusement; as a centre for disseminating opinion and counterposing contrasting opinions; as a medium through which to achieve influence for the individuals and corporations that control them; as profit centres (and also as loss leaders); as political weapons; and as campaigners for reform, or against reform. They typically combine many of these functions—so that, for example, *The Guardian* (probably the paper of choice of the larger part of PQ readers) will give news, be amusing, disseminate opinions and have them clash, seek influence, make a profit sometimes and a loss at other times, and campaign constantly for reform. The mix of these functions is what gives newspapers their character: *The Sun* does all of the things listed above, but in quite different proportions and in a wholly different manner.

Indeed, in their (possible) twilight, newspapers are fulfilling some of these functions with unprecedented vigour. Spurred by competition that grows fiercer as loyalty to newspapers decreases and circulations fall, papers in the UK—and elsewhere—are striving to please their readers ever more mightily, with extra sections, more star writers and more tempting giveaways. It's probable, however, that there is less straight news: foreign reporting is less full than it was, parliamentary coverage has decreased dramatically and national, especially regional, reporting is highly selective—concentrating on personalities, scandals and shocks in the tabloids and even, to a greater degree than before, in the upmarket newspapers. The trend has been, for two decades, towards more amusement and consumption, since that attracts advertising—and that trend remains strong, if not everywhere decisive. The complementary trend—towards much more comment, and 'opinionated reporting', also remains strong, and affects all newspapers. Nevertheless, in 'value for money' terms, present-day British newspapers do not offer a worse deal than their predecessors, except to those who want a great deal of straight reporting: that has probably shrunk, more or less everywhere.

Is the same happening elsewhere, outside the United Kingdom? Yes, in differing ways. Most newspapers are taking on more consumer sections to attract both extra readers and advertising. In the more austere—such as *Le Monde*, *Corriere della Sera* and the *Frankfurter Allgemeine Zeitung*—this is relatively marginal: others, as for example the Swedish upmarket papers, *Svenska Dagbladet* and *Dagens Nyheter*, which were hit first and hard by free newspapers (*Metro* was invented in Sweden), have cut back to tabloid shape, expanded their consumer and entertainment sections, and reduced foreign bureaux and hard news. US newspapers have also cut, especially on foreign news: and, in the most 'communicating' country in the world, saw themselves harder pressed by new media—of all kinds. The 2005 'State of the American Media', published each year by the Project for Excellence in Journalism, described the situation thus (in a description that held much truth for the news media throughout the advanced world):

A year ago, we saw in the larger trends something of a vicious cycle partly of the press's own making. As audiences declined, because of technological and cultural changes, news organisations felt pressure on revenues and stock performance. In response, they cut back on their newsrooms, squeezed in more advertising and cut back on the percentage of space devoted to news. They tried to respond to changing tastes, too, by lightening their content. Audiences appeared to gravitate to lighter topics, and these topics were cheaper to cover. Those changes, in turn, deepened the sense that the news media were motivated by economics and less focused on professionalism and the public interest.

In 2005, the sense that the press's role in relation to the public is changing seems ever clearer. A generation ago, the press was effectively a lone institution communicating between the citizenry and the newsmakers, whether corporations selling goods or politicians selling agendas, who wanted to shape public opinion for their own purposes. Today, a host of new forms of communication offer a way for newsmakers to reach the public. There are talk show hosts, cable interview shows, corporate websites, government websites, websites that purport to be citizens' blogs but are really something else, and more. Journalism is a shrinking part of a growing world of media. And since journalists are trained to be sceptics and, in the famous phrase, speak truth to power, journalism is the one source those who want to manipulate the public are most prone to denounce.

The reaction of newspaper corporations—to ever more desperately woo their audiences with more supplements, more celebrities and more giveaways—is prompted by a feeling of panic. The International Newspaper Marketing Association (INMA) reported in its 'Newspaper Outlook 2005' that in 2002–3—the last two years for which full international and comparative figures have been produced—'circulation performance in mature western democracies was the worst in any two years in which INMA has tracked data going back nearly two decades'. In every year of the past ten since 2003, daily newspaper circulation has declined in North America, western Europe, the South Pacific and Japan. In western Europe, the aggregate decline over the decade has been 10 per cent; in the South Pacific, 9 per cent; in North America, 8 per cent; in Japan, 2 per cent. Europe appears the hardest hit: in the six years between 1997 and 2003, Denmark's daily circulation fell 15 per cent, Greece's 13 per cent, that of the Netherlands 12 per cent, Germany's 11 per cent and France's 10 per cent: there are few signs of an upturn, though individual newspapers, usually through format change, do experience rises. This doesn't mean that newspapers have everywhere become unprofitable; indeed, in the US, their return on capital has gone up, to an average of well over 20 per cent. But that's been achieved by trimming staff—first on the administrative side, but increasingly in newsrooms.

The oracle speaks

Newspaper journalism is suffering badly. A profession that has existed for four centuries and that, for most of the past two hundred years could lay some claim to providing ever fuller accounts of local, national and global events, is now deeply unsure of itself—most of all in the lands where it was born and grew to what maturity it attained. In the rich world, where journalism is well funded, independent and accorded an honoured place in the democratic pantheon, it now doubts its utility and worse, its popularity. It even doubts—at least in some forms—its very survival. The countries of newspaper decline are very different, with different media cultures, different balances between elite, popular and regional papers and different histories. Only the rate of the decline unites them. Philip Meyer, who has studied newspapers' decline, says that on these falling trends, 'the last newspaper reader will recycle his final paper copy in April 2040'—well within many readers' (or non-readers') expected lifetimes, and within the working lifetimes of the many graduates of journalism schools who clamour for (unpaid) work at newspapers like mine, just to get a toehold in an industry that may be dying.

The issue has been dramatised by the man whose influence on the news business has been greater than that of any other—and who has consistently claimed his success to be built on discovering what the mass of people wanted, and giving it to them. Rupert Murdoch told the American Society of Newspaper Editors, at their gathering in April 2005, that 'we need to realise that the next generation of people accessing news and information, whether from newspapers or any other source, have a different set of expectations about the kind of news they will get, including when and how they will get it, where they will get it from, and who they will get it from'. These expectations, he said, were based on impatience with the once-a-day, we-tell-you-what's-important-and-how-to-think-about-it attitude of the newspapers: but were also, more importantly, based on the proactive engagement with news and opinion that interactive technologies made possible for the Internet—'they [the young] want their news on demand, when it works for them. They want control over their media, instead of being controlled by it. They want to question, to probe, to offer a different angle'.

The study on which Murdoch largely based his views was done by a consultant called Merrill Brown, for the Carnegie Corporation. Brown had reported on Wall Street for *The Washington Post*, helped found both Court TV and the business channel MSNBC, and had been a vice president of Real Networks. He knew the business in most of its manifestations—newspapers, television and the Internet. Brown was at once more definite and more monitory about the future of newspapers, and of national TV news, than most other researchers: he called his study 'Abandoning the News' because he thought that's what the rising generation is doing—abandoning it, that is, in the form in which it had been presented for many decades.

One graph at the end of Brown's report summed up the reasons for his pessimism about conventional news. It showed the intended use of news sources by 18–34 year olds in the next three years: the Internet led with just under 40 per cent; then local news, on 14 per cent—little more than a third of the Internet; cable news on 10 per cent; newspapers on 8 per cent; and national network news on only 5 per cent. Newspapers, still seen by older people as the most important (because most prestigious) elements in the news-and-opinion sector, are now squeezed in a series of vices about which, it seems, they can do little—since everything they do to arrest decline serves to accelerate it. Earl J. Wilkinson, one of the industry gurus, wrote the INMA report for 2005, in which he pointed out that much of what newspapers did was self-defeating. They were, he wrote: 'expanding the number of pages: a "more is more" philosophy – when people have less time; adding colour capacity: [thus] drawing attention to a richer medium, television; extending their content to a broader audience – [thus] making their content more generic at a time when consumers want more specificity; offering more content for free, in real time – [thus] giving away the company's most valuable resource'.

As newspapers, geographical products first and last, strain to make their 'community' (national, regional or local) more loyal to them, so communities— as Trippi warns—become increasingly more interest-based than geographic- ally based. A 25-year-old executive in Sydney today has more in common with a 25-year-old executive in New York than with his or her 50-year-old counterpart in Sydney. As newspapers have sought to make themselves the resort for everything a reader may want, so the choice on television has expanded hugely—from around twenty channels on average in the mid-1980s to around 100 in the mid-2000s. In fact, in some cases, more has meant worse, for the newspaper: in 2004 the Paris daily *Libération* added a thirty-six page supplement to its seventy-two page newspaper—and had circulation fall 30 per cent to 140,000 copies: 'On conducting research, editors discovered that the newspaper continued to have high brand affinity, but readers felt guilty they could no longer consume the product in one sitting. The editors dropped the supplement and circulation returned to its previous level.'[1]

Like other forms of media, newspapers are being urged, continually, to be more 'niche'; that is, to get away from addressing mass audiences (no one wants to be part of a mass any longer) and address groups, even individuals. Tom Glocer, the chief executive of Reuters, says he's shaping his company to provide to individual subscribers the kind of news they want every day— through building up a profile of the customer, scouring the news sources for the news that they want or must have, and delivering it to them daily or hourly through a handset, or a desk or home screen. 'You must know your audience,' says Glocer: 'Otherwise personalisation doesn't work. Our target group is a mobile business community. We think we can address this audience at a global level and deliver news to them—and that they will pay for it. They want fast news, serious analysis, lowbrow as well as highbrow material and they want to be shown what "people like me" are doing or looking at. Pictures and videos are critical to this personalised news delivery, and in this environment, quality journalism still matters.'[2] Glocer, becoming visionary, saw a time when he would be able to deliver to his clients personalised advertisements: knowing that the client might be looking for a new high-powered car, the system would choose to show him BMW advertisements. Knowing that he liked skiing, it would show him a BMW driving through snowy mountains—to a backdrop of his favourite music.

'Personalisation', said Glocer, 'will be the dominant theme of the media for the next 100 years.'

When they listen to—or work for—executives like Glocer, journalists realise that their world has changed, is changing and will change utterly. Glocer would say—did say—that 'in this changing environment, quality journalism is crucial'. He believes it, but believes it because his target audience want 'quality journalism' as part of the mix of news, analysis, entertainment, what's on, shopping tips and travel guides that will be delivered to them. The place of news as a pillar of democracy may be valued, but can be taken for granted: news in its role as an investigator of power and uncoverer of wrongdoing is one part of the offering, which must be and should be tailored to fit in with the rest. That doesn't necessarily mean that the individual who receives the news, in whatever form it may come, will be less concerned about wrong-doings, less devoted to democratic habits, or less engaged in civic pursuits: he or she may be more so, than in the past—and may use personalised news services to serve these concerns. The huge, and unnerving, change is that an individual getting a personal service is in a wholly different relationship to the service provided than if he or she were one individual in a mass: at once more critical of its shortcomings and more functional in how it's used. Anthony Smith wrote of Joseph Pulitzer—the Hungarian immigrant to the US who built up *The New York World* into the biggest-selling paper of the late nineteenth century and then left a fortune to found Columbia University journalism school, and the awards that bear his name—that he offered his public 'a ringside seat as a great display, rather than a conscientious enlargement of their citizenship'.[3] Now, both of these missions of the news-paper—ringside seats and citizenship enlargement—are more vividly and more conscientiously done (or not done) by other media: and however they are done, the customer will choose, individually, what mix of the ringside or citizenship he or she wants at any given hour.

Newspapers haven't done 'niche' well, and it's difficult to see how they can. Indeed, the one niche they have done—and that too well—is, like other wheezes, self-destructive. In the mid-1990s, beginning is Sweden, free news-papers aimed at a young urban reader began to be distributed: they are now present in most Western countries, and in some—as in Spain and Italy—they account for as much as one third of the newspaper readership. Criticised as being bland, they aren't necessarily so: in the US, the New York free papers *Metro* and *AM* have, respectively, a lot of local content and at least one scoop a day: Dallas' *Quick* is a repackaging of *The Dallas Morning News* (like the London *Evening Standard*'s *Metro*)—but Chicago's *RedEye* is a snappy tabloid aimed steadily at a twenty-something market, written largely by twenty-something journalists. Sometimes the success of these papers coexists with still-rising circulations for paid-for papers: more often, it doesn't—and they certainly leach away advertisements. They also, in the main, defy news values that stress originality, investigation and analysis: much of their material is from wire copy or public relations sources. Though in many cases, the publishers of the free sheets are also the publishers of the paid-for news-papers—better to make profits from one's own competition than have some-one else make these profits—the signs that the two can coexist in harmony and mutual profit are slight.

Libération, subordination

As this happens—and in part because it is happening—the normal crises and problems in newspapers coalesce into a general unease and lack of confid-ence. They do so in the citadels of the most confident media cultures in the world — the United Kingdom, France, the United States. In France—where the national papers have prestige, rather than strong readerships—the prin-cipal newspapers are in a bad way. They are paying the price that newspapers usually, sooner or later, must pay for long-term unprofitability: loss of independence. And in this case, their tradition doesn't help.

Le Figaro, launched in the 1860s to give a voice to the gathering forces of the right, found a new proprietor in 2004 in the shape of Serge Dassault, head of the defence and media group that bears his name. Dassault has the lack of illusions that must go with the job of selling weapons, and wants his paper to have none either. He told his senior editors last August (according to a report in the rival *Le Monde*) that 'you sometimes have to take a lot of care with the news. Some of it does more harm than good—the risk being to put the industrial or commercial interests of our country at hazard'. Agence France Presse later reported that an article on the sales of the Dassault Rafale jet fighter was banned, as was an interview with the businessman Andrew Wang, implicated in a scandal over the sale of French frigates to Taiwan.

Le Monde was launched by Hubert Beuve Mery towards the end of the Second World War, prompted by General de Gaulle, with the explicit aim of erasing the stain of the collaborationist press. Early in 2005, another media and defence group, Lagardere, took a 17 per cent stake in it—a decision made necessary by its deteriorating financial situation. Arnaud Lagardere, the defence group's chief executive, said that he would put up to €35 million into it and swore not to interfere in its editorial line.

The third French institution, and the newest, to seek capitalist assistance is *Libération*, founded on a wave of support for the far left in 1968. Its most famous co-founder was Jean Paul Sartre, the philosopher and supporter of most things leftist (including some of what proved to be hideous regimes). In January 2005, *Libération*'s staff accepted a plan for financier Eduard de Rothschild to take a 37 per cent stake in the paper—by far the largest single holding—in return for a €20 million investment. Unlike Dassault but like Lagardere, he pledged non-interference—and went further, promising to allow the staff to retain their veto over senior appointments. In each case, the staffs were in turmoil, but were constrained to accept the changes more or less in the forms in which they were proposed. The editors of *Le Figaro*, who were put in the worst position, issued a statement in December 2004 saying they wouldn't be influenced by commercial pressures: it seems unlikely that they can hold on to that line, and their jobs, if and when push comes to shove.

The French press is ideologically diverse, and its writing is often of a high calibre. But it's not well equipped to face a tightening market, and the commercial and political pressures that go with it. The French national press has been produced for political elites—conservative, Catholic, leftist, Marxist—with a combined circulation of the national dailies of about 2.2 million in 2004. There is no mass popular press—though the regional daily and evening press is often better supported than the national: *Ouest France*, for example, sells about 800,000 copies daily, double the circulation of *Le Monde*. Paul Starr, who published a lucid history of the Western media in 2004, writes that US and to a lesser extent British eighteenth-century newspaper publishers had 'more freedom to create new publications and sought wider markets by making the content of their publications more varied and practical. French periodical publishers, by contrast, sought monopoly privileges and cultivated a more limited, aristocratic readership'. Starr also observes that, throughout the nineteenth and into the twentieth centuries, 'the cultural framework of the public sphere was radically different in the two countries [the US and France]. Journalistic authority belonged to information in America and to literary distinction in France.' The present can never wholly escape the past.[4]

All three of the national dailies struggling with the issue of ownership and independence have shown themselves capable of hard, courageous reporting, especially abroad. Georges Malbrunot, one of the two French correspondents held for four months in 2004 by an Islamist group in Iraq, was a *Figaro* correspondent: in January 2005, Florence Aubenas of *Libération* went missing with her translator in Baghdad (and survived unharmed). But the papers remain above all *journaux d'opinion*—in which capacity they receive a state subsidy, a sign of the ambiguous relationship between state and media, one pitched somewhere between obeisance and rejection, dependence and scorn. Restrictive union agreements hamper their commercial development, and their efforts to become more investigative and factual have attracted criticism—from the left even more than from the right. *Le Monde* had, under the leadership of Jean-Marie Colombani and Edwy Plenel, exposed areas and incidents in French public life that those commanding it had always kept hidden—including the important revelation that the French secret services bombed a Greenpeace boat in Auckland in 1985, killing a passenger. But in a slashing, book-length attack on the paper, Pierre Péan and Philippe Cohen accused it of trading its power for cash, using distorted evidence in its exposes and forcing a minister—the socialist Finance Minister, Dominique Strauss-Kahn—out of office on suspicion of a fraud from which he was cleared.[5] Though much of the book reflected an ideological, even a personal, hostility rather than a well-grounded argument, the attack—which was enormously popular—dispirited a paper that was then running into financial problems, and Edwy Plenel resigned in early 2005.

The editor of *Le Monde Diplomatique*, Ignacio Ramonet, reflected that all papers, including his own—a leftist foreign affairs weekly more or less independent of its parent, *Le Monde*—were now in decline: 'We are seeing the triumph of the journalism of speculation and spectacle, to the detriment of factual reporting. Presentation is winning out over the proving of facts.' In spite of his own paper's formidable record of a reportage that makes no attempt at objectivity, Ramonet set himself the task of improving his own content—relying more on reporting, less on opinion: 'nothing', he wrote in January 2005, 'is more important than not to betray the confidence of the readers'. But past practice has weakened the roots of a strong reportorial culture: and the new owners of the most prestigious French newspapers may not be overly keen on strengthening them now.

False fame

The most obvious phenomenon has, however, been the massive loss of confidence of newspapers in the US. The great moments in this have been the scandals—at *The New York Times*, at *USA Today*, the *New Republic* and more distantly at *The Washington Post*, the *Los Angeles Times* and *The Boston Globe*. Each case—and many others, in less prestigious journals—involved, essentially, the same event: a reporter inventing quotes, or people or events . . . or all of these. The first of these to become a large scandal, and for a time the unique instance (in modern times: fabricated stories were and are common in all ages, and in all press cultures—almost certainly much more common than now, and still more common in other media outside the US), was that of Janet Cooke, a young *Post* reporter who wrote stories in 1981 about an eight-year-old heroin addict called Jimmy. The first (front-page) story contained this vivid scene, which describes how Jimmy's stepfather injected the boy: 'he grabs Jimmy's left arm just above the elbow, his massive hand tightly encircling the child's small limb. The needle slides into the boy's soft skin like a straw pushed into the centre of a freshly baked cake. Liquid ebbs out of the syringe, replaced by bright red blood. The blood is then re-injected into the child.' Cooke was caught not because the paper believed the many people who queried the story, but because it discovered that the curriculum vitae on which she had gained the job was fake, and thus the editors were inclined to take more seriously the allegations of fabrication, against which they had for months closed ranks, while Cooke won a Pulitzer in April 1981.

The same pattern then re-emerged in the early years of the present century—with Stephen Glass at the *New Republic*, Jason Blair at *The New York Times* and Jack Kelley at *USA Today*. All fabricated, on a large scale—none larger than the ultra-bright Stephen Glass at the *New Republic*, who, in two and a half years at that weekly Washington magazine, was found to have fabricated all or part of twenty-seven of the forty-two stories he had published, being discovered only when a computer magazine, furious (with itself) that it had missed a story on a raucous hackers' conference that Glass had 'attended', investigated and found that the personalities in the story, the events and the conference itself didn't exist. Jason Blair at *The New York Times*, in tune with his predecessors, larded his stories—some of which were based on facts—with vivid, novelettish descriptions of grief, joy and pride on the part of the participants, most of whom he had never met in person, and at least one description of whom he had lifted from another newspaper, the *San Antonio Express-News*.

The deceptions at *USA Today* and at *The New York Times* claimed victims—the top editors. In the twenty-plus years since Janet Cooke's unmasking, however, the burden of blame has shifted. Though all of the perpetrators were fired, at least two—Stephen Glass and Jayson Blair—landed big book contracts: Glass' case was the subject of a film (*Shattered Glass*) and a film about the Blair events was planned. Janet Cooke, by contrast, had—according to a profile in *GQ* magazine twenty years after her disgrace—spent much of the intervening years as a saleswoman in a department store, at six dollars an hour.

None of this—neither the revelations, nor the elevation of the villains into cult heroes with six-figure book and film contracts—has done much for the self-image of serious American journalism. Worse—because more serious in content—was the criticism levelled at American journalism over its failure to be more probing in reporting the run-up to, and the aftermath of, the Iraq invasion—especially on the evidence of the existence of Iraqi weapons of mass destruction (WMD). In an influential piece for *The New York Review of Books*, the media scholar Michael Massing charged that America's most authoritative and reportorially strong newspapers—above all *The New York Times*, which had seen itself, with some justice, as the best newspaper with the highest journalistic standards in the world—had failed to print, or if printed, to adequately display, stories that reflected doubts they knew were held by officials and military people on the grounds for going to war. In a further piece, also for the *Review*, Massing lashed the *Times* for what he said was the 'leisureliness' of its reporting on the postwar insurgency—cruelly adding that this was 'especially apparent when compared to [the *Post*'s] sharp and insightful reporting, in both Washington and Baghdad . . . when it comes to Iraq, the rivalry between the *Times* and the *Post* has become a "tale of two papers," the one late and lethargic, the other astute and aggressive.' The *Times* did—after the first of these pieces, and probably in at least partial response to it—publish a *mea culpa* blaming 'editors at several levels [who] should have been challenging reporters and pressing for more scepticism'. Massing welcomed this grudgingly, saying it was too easy an apology—for it could lay the blame on the previous editorial regime, that of Howell Raines, who had resigned because of the Jason Blair scandal.

Raines' resignation from the *Times* because of the Blair scandal had over-tones of the tragic, certainly as he saw it. He had single-mindedly lusted for the job for many years, since his appointment as Washington bureau chief signalled that he was on the inside ring for the top. He had chafed during the editorship of Joe Lelyveld, the editor whom he succeeded in 2001, believing that Lelyveld ignored most of the trends (and thus marketing opportunities) of the time. Raines had heard many predictions that the newspaper would soon die—the futurologist Herman Kahn had been making that prediction at his Hudson Institute conference, which Raines attended, for years; the Viacom President Mel Karamzin, asked at an annual meeting of the *Times* business and editorial staff what he would do if he owned the *Times*, said 'sell it'—because, as he explained, it was a brand at the peak of its value and was unlikely to be able to buck the anti-newspaper trends all around it. Raines' response was to do the same thing the *Times* had long done, only (in his view) much better: to widen its appeal to its national audience; to cover popular culture better in order to attract the 20–40 year olds, who were drifting away from the paper; above all, to do better, fuller, longer and sharper hard news. In an essay after his resignation,[6] Raines wrote that he had believed that 'the *Times'* image as a bastion of quality had become even more important as tabloid television, Britain's declining newspaper values and the unsourced ranting of the internet bloggers polluted the journalistic mainstream of the United States'. This, an accurate summary of some of the contemporary trends in journalism, impelled Raines to go back to—or create—the fundamentals of hard graft, full-as-possible journalism. That he was forced to go because of the fictions of one of his trusted and rapidly promoted reporters was very cruel indeed; and it sent a symbolic, as well as a practical, message that high-intensity newspaper journalism was a doomed profession. The man charged with stabilising the paper after Raines went, Bill Keller, then ran into his own nemesis in the shape of Judith Miller, whose reporting on Iraqi WMD came under suspicion for over-reliance on sources to whom she was too close, and whose choice of jail rather than betraying a source came to be seen as quixotic, even mendacious, rather than brave.

Conclusion

Joe Trippi's epiphany—his insight into the *Zeitgeist*—worked, up to a point, for an obscure Vermont governor. Can it work for newspapers? It may work, if they can learn to overcome what Trippi called the 'the us vs. them problem'. A much quoted straw in that wind is the Greensboro *News-Record*, a North Carolina daily that has created 'an online community, or public square', in the words of its editor, John Robinson. It seeks to harness what is described by Jay Rosen, the New York University professor—whose blog, Pressthink ('the ghost of democracy in the media machine'), charts the most salient trends in the industry—as an unusually lively blogging culture in the city, one which seeks to re-create community through the Internet in the way Trippi describes. Rosen reports that, at a blog conference in the city, the prominent bloggers demanded that a raft of officials produce blogs on their work, in order to make them more accountable. The *News-Record* piggybacked on this, developing a culture in which all possible stories give links—including to other newspapers, unheard of in the profession; reporters and editors, including Robinson, develop blogs that give the background to their stories and their activities; and, above all, readers come back at the reporters and columnists with their comments, complaints and alternative analyses. It is a living example of a newspaper destroying its own myth of omniscience, powered by a view that it is the only way to survive.

Yet it still seems probable that the Ghandian answer is the right one: a future for newspapers would be nice, but it won't be for the products we know in the present. In the next decade, more titles will die and many more will be cut back. The trend is likely to continue to be that newspapers that cannot establish themselves securely in a 'virtual community' of people prepared to pay, by historical standards highly, for their daily read, together with advertisers who believe that text and design on paper still commands attention from prospective buyers, will go out of business. Those that remain may become more like magazines, with analysis, essays and reportage at length—ceding the ground of spot news to the screen, which is increasingly likely to be hand held. In the end, the desire to learn and the delight in reading—assuming that these urges remain—may save something of the newspaper culture. The Internet may, if a business model can be found, preserve something of newspapers in digital form. What we, including we who work in newspapers, do not know is how the best of the culture—long-haul investigation, serious analysis, hard-won news stories, informed and experienced commentary—will support itself. But so much of that has been debauched and lost already that it may not be much missed.

Notes

1 INMA Report, 2005, New York, p. 9.
2 T. Glocer, speech to FT Media and Broadcasting Conference, London, 7 March 2005.
3 A. Smith, *The Newspaper*, London, Thames and Hudson, 1979, p. 160.
4 P. Starr, *The Creation of the Media*, New York, Basic Books, 2004, pp. 18 and 42.
5 P. Péan and Ph. Cohen, *La Face Cachée du Monde: du Contre-pouvoir aux Abus de Pouvoir*, Mille et Une Nuits, 2003.
6 H. Raines, 'My Times', *The Atlantic Monthly*, vol. 293, no. 4, May 2004.

What's Good on Television?

TIM GARDAM

RATHER like a heroine with a high fever in a Victorian novel, British television periodically reaches a moment of crisis, at which point the narrator suggests that recovery may be beyond hope, only for the temperature to abate, the sun to shine in through the window and recuperation to begin. Even so, it remains a truth near universally acknowledged by those who write about television (if not so much by those who most watch it) that the quality and challenge of its discourse and ideas have progressively diminished as its prevalence has increased. Though there are moments of remission, it is the frequently held view of opinion formers and newspaper commentators—what passes for an intellectual class in this country—that what was once a vibrant medium of imaginative and intellectual daring has largely stultified. The infection is invariably traced to a virus within the BBC—and the infection hits fever pitch at that moment when the BBC's Charter is about to be renewed.

The renewal of the BBC Charter in 2005 follows close on the far-reaching Communications Act of 2003. For the past four years, these two institutional measures have defined the nature of the argument about the qualities and purposes of British television in the digital age. Yet there has been little serious consideration in this debate of what we mean in television by 'good'. Indeed, there is marked reluctance by those involved in broadcasting decision-making to venture too deep into the terrain of cultural criticism and qualitative discrimination: What makes a good programme, and do these criteria change over time? Invariably, the argument reduces to anecdote; cultural pessimists identify a few programmes that exemplify the triumph of vice over virtue—invariably reality programmes—and the broadcasting institutions reel off a list of names of programmes that sit comfortably within the cultural canon. Opinion polls are then commissioned to gauge how satisfied viewers are with what they get. All this is has its own validity, but there is an increasing lack of connection between the arguments of the broadcasting industry, which focus on organisational structures and the balance between market mechanisms and public intervention, and critical analysis of the imaginative range and depth of insight that television as a medium attempts.

Digital television

There is perhaps a good reason for this. The broadcasting industry is seeking to come to terms with a digital world in which television is ambient, and in which the technological revolution in distribution systems changes

Published by Blackwell Publishing Ltd, 9600 Garsington Road, Oxford OX4 2DQ, UK and 350 Main Street, Malden, MA 02148, USA

definitions of content. Amidst such a volume of material, it is more difficult to argue from the particular programme to the whole system. In one sense, this is the logical consequence of television attaining the ubiquity of print. On the other hand, it calls into question whether television still 'matters', in terms of cultural importance, in the way it once did. This chapter will first consider the terms in which the arguments over the Communications Act and BBC Charter have been couched. It will then look at television through a different prism, and consider whether one can reach with any confidence critical judgements about the merit of programmes and programme genres that have relevance to the debate about our broadcasting market and institutions.

The Communications Act recognised the fundamental changes that digital technology is making to the nature of broadcast communications, and the redundancy of most of the suppositions, both economic and cultural, on which British television has been based since the beginning of competition in the 1950s. In short, the relationship between broadcaster, producer and viewer, and the basis of the transactions between them, has changed beyond recognition. In the digital world, for which the Communications Act prepared, there is no limit on the distribution of broadcast content, and that content will be increasingly accessed by the user across television, radio and online in such a variety of ways that the manner in which it is selected, appreciated and paid for will fundamentally change.

However, though the Communications Act has recognised this revolution, and in setting up the new regulator, Ofcom, has sought a consistency of approach in monitoring it, the issues regarding programme quality are inevitably more intractable. The problem is simple: a plethora of choice in the number of digital channel options available does not necessarily translate into increased satisfaction in any single option once chosen.

Ofcom's Public Service Television Review

In 2004, Ofcom set about assembling for the first time a consistent set of data (which, extraordinarily, had not existed before) in order to establish an evidential base from which to reach conclusions about the output of public service broadcasters.[1] The evidence was in many ways revealing. It showed, in quantified terms, that the proportion of hours and spend on differing types of programme and subject on British television over the past five years had changed, in some cases significantly. In broad terms, the appetite for entertainment had pushed out the imperative for information. There was markedly less current affairs, arts and religious programming in peak time (though audiences valued the arts and religion noticeably less than other factual genres). Factual entertainment had significantly increased as a proportion of factual programming. It was true that in news the volume and spending had increased. The public, perhaps with an element of self-congratulation, also felt that television was extremely good at keeping it well informed. Most significantly, Ofcom concluded that there was a growing deficit in investment in traditional public services genres of programming that over five years would amount to some £400 million.[2]

Defining itself as primarily an economic regulator, Ofcom sought to cut through disputes about the merit of television as a cultural medium by defining it in market terms. Ofcom invented a Dr Doolittle hybrid creature, the 'citizen–consumer'. Like the Pushmepullyou, this modern viewer was happy to be tugged in two directions at once; the role of the regulator was simply to ensure that the citizen–consumer had sufficient room to move about. Ofcom's regulatory approach has had real strengths. It undoubtedly shed clear light on the previously blurred arguments about programming trends and the balance of television genres. It surveyed the range of programming on offer; it costed it and offered a financial analysis of the public service contribution to the overall market. As a result of its analysis, Ofcom also advocated an imaginative intervention in the market through the creation of a Public Service Publisher, a new body, with the aim of having, in the broadband digital age, the same catalytic effect on the creativity of the British market of the 2000s as Channel 4's invention had on the old three-channel world of the 1980s. The unspoken implications of Ofcom's proposal are, first, that the market in future will fail to provide the competition for quality that was a feature of the old system of public service licences, and, second, that the money for this independently run public venture should come from the future monies that might be allocated to the BBC licence fee.[3]

What Ofcom did not do was to interrogate possible definitions of 'good' television. This is perhaps sensible, because such a debate cannot easily be measured in terms of 'outcomes', the currency of regulators. Nonetheless, revealing as its exercise had been, Ofcom has fallen into the inevitable trap of trying to measure quality: it has the inconvenient habit of coming out as quantity. In the end, the debate about the health of British television cannot be answered by numbers. It lies in less precise judgements about how far a society can share common perceptions of qualitative value. British television is unusual in so far as it is, more than anywhere else on earth, a creature of public purposes and democratic will, enshrined in its dominant player, the BBC. In such a system, the evidence of statistics may influence perception, but—as with economic indicators in an election campaign—numbers do not settle the argument. The quality of British television is, in the end, not a matter of statistical analysis but of public argument, its health determined by the conduct of the debate itself.

The Review of the BBC Charter

The Ofcom Public Service Broadcasting Review, far from settling the matter of the quality of British television, became merely a backdrop for the subsequent argument that dominated 2004 and 2005: the role and purpose of the BBC in the digital landscape that Ofcom had surveyed. The subsequent debate about the BBC took on a very different form. If the Ofcom approach had been that of a data aggregator, the debate on the BBC was a visceral argument over motives, ambitions and behaviour.[4] The ethos of the BBC was put on trial by its competitors, and by the myriad of stakeholders with whom the BBC interacted. The scope and virulence of the debate reflected the expansive commercial ambitions of the BBC, assiduously pursued during the ten years of its previous Charter. The BBC's critics included not simply rival radio and television broadcasters and politicians—the usual suspects—but magazine publishers who had come up against BBC magazines that had no relationship to any BBC programme; commercial entertainment websites competing with better funded BBC equivalents; and educational publishers whose global competitiveness was being eroded by the weight of publicly funded competition as the BBC further expanded its brief.

The government encouraged this debate as it prepared a Green Paper on the Charter. The BBC's role was argued over, primarily in terms of its impact on the market. In seeking to prime the pump of digital technology in the UK, the government, in 1999, had increased the BBC's income with a 'digital' component in a generous licence fee settlement. At the same time, the BBC had been urged to become more entrepreneurial. The consequence was a rampantly expansionist BBC, colonising the commanding heights of the UK digital broadcasting landscape just at a time, in 2001–2, when the commercial sector had faced a rapid and disconcerting (though in the event short-lived) advertising downturn. The BBC, driven by the most swashbuckling, commercially competitive Director General in its history, Greg Dyke, had positioned itself as a threat to the rest of the UK's creative industries.

As a result, the debate surrounding the BBC took a somewhat different course to the debate initiated by Ofcom. Ofcom had sought measurable formulae to define the additional public service benefit across the entire terrain of British broadcasting. The debate about the BBC, the greatest land mass in that terrain, was being conducted in terms of the competitive impact of the BBC on the commercial market. The central question surrounding the BBC became the manner in which it should properly be regulated or governed. This was clearly a pressing issue, and one where government could provide, in legislation, a structural solution. But it meant that once again a considered critical discussion of the relative merits of television programmes—whether television is getting better or worse—slipped though the legislative debate.

The Green Paper on the BBC was published in February 2005; the government's intentions towards the governance structures of the BBC are now clear; Ofcom has also now completed its own analysis of the future shape of the market in commercial television. The most significant consequence of more than four years of debate about the future of British television is that government and regulatory authorities alike have abandoned the last vestiges of a belief that they have a role in ruling on the quality of programming in anything more than market terminology. The BBC's performance will be judged by measuring its distinctiveness from the market. Ofcom will assess the range of programming on offer to the citizen–consumer in terms of what the market does or does not provide. Whether these 'public service' programmes are any good, whether they are intellectually shallower or conversely intellectually self-indulgent and boring, is not a question that a wise regulator will want to confront. It is therefore all the more important that there is a lively and noisy conversation that does not confine arguments about television simply to institutional tussles. It is more necessary than ever to explore the imaginative and intellectual strengths and weaknesses of current television, and ask whether one can judge if it is better or worse than it was. In large part, this debate will concentrate on factual programmes, because it has been in the blurring of lines between information and entertainment, and in arguments about instant gratification squeezing out programmes that demand concentration, that the debate has been most intense.

Television as event

Television used to be special—in itself. When, even ten years ago, you asked 'What's on television tonight?', you expected that someone could tell you. TV content had a clear definition, as it was still possible to hold all of it in view. As a generation, we still use the term as an inclusive noun. Television describes the set, the programmes, the culture. How meaningful a word will it continue to be in a world in which programmes are receivable on devices ranging from mobile phone to laptop to home cinema system, with programmes available on demand, and from a library of near universally accessible content?

Despite the fact that television is now available everywhere in near limitless quantities, certain television events continue to have the power to exert a hold not dissimilar to that of a generation ago. A generation now in their twenties will look back to *The Office* as the defining satire of its youth in the same way as those in their fifties might look back at Alf Garnett and *Till Death Us Do Part*, and those in their forties at *To the Manor Born*. The drama series *Shameless*, in 2005, comically romanticises working-class subculture with similar impact to *The Darling Buds of May* fifteen years before. A twenty year old in 2005 will have experienced Live8 with the same intensity that, in the year in which they were born, their parents' generation experienced Live Aid in 1985. Definitive programmes stand out as individual artefacts. They have a personal impact on individual lives, and act as a frame for collective memory.

News

Nowhere is this more resonant than in news. In a very simple sense, television is the medium that allows the sharing of the history of the times we all live through. Changes in technology, which allow for video on demand on broadband, or twenty-four-hour news channels, merely enhance provision for a continuing appetite and need. In so far as news is a record of the memorable public events that shape our lives, there is little doubt that news programming has got better. Over the past twenty-five years, it has first become more sophisticated and intelligent, and more recently, more available and immediate. Yet its proliferation has not undermined its quality.

In 1980, *Newsnight* was launched to break down the barriers between news and current affairs. It transformed the relationship between reportage, debate and comment, and in so doing emancipated intelligent television. For the first time, television offered daily journalism as up to date and as in depth as that of daily newspapers. In 1982, *Channel 4 News* was launched as the first one-hour news bulletin and brought a range of agendas, international and cultural, that broadened the role of the news in contemporary life. Twenty-five years on, both programmes now are arguably anachronisms in the world of instant access news, twenty-four-hour news channels, online and on demand, yet both remain definitive programmes of record and set the terms for the interrogative accountability necessary in a modern media literate democracy. Both flourish alongside the, at least, five free to air twenty-four-hour news channels now available to the majority of people on their television sets.

The ownership of news has in one sense fragmented. Technology increasingly permits the signature of the professional journalist to be added to by the people caught up in the story. Digital cameras, and cameras on mobile phones, have allowed for a far wider perspective of the world due to the availability of pictures and eyewitness reporting from across the globe; online news, with its sites for blogs and conversation, has expanded news coverage from one-way traffic from reporter to viewer to a conversation between journalist and user. The digitisation of cameras has allowed for an intimacy of personal reporting that did not exist before. The devastation of the 2004 South Asian tsunami was recorded on family video recorders. The most graphic images of the bombings in London of 7 July 2005 were recorded by participants on their mobile telephone cameras. The expansion of international news on television is in marked contrast to its shrinkage in printed media. Yet the technological breaking of barriers to news reporting, has not, as might have been expected, destroyed the salience of the authoritative journalism. In a world of unrestricted information, the premium on reliable understanding increases.

Remarkably, the expansion of news outlets has defied expectations that, in a world of increased competition for ratings and programme investment, the established news broadcasters would no longer be able to afford to invest. More money is spent on television news than a generation ago. The increased investment in the BBC, on screen and online, the expansion of *Channel 4 News* and the advent of Five, not to mention the invention of twenty-four-hour news by Sky, more than offsets the crumbling of a commitment to news by ITV, in its wanton destruction of the ITN brand. Add to that the availability of a plethora of worldwide news channels on digital television, from the United States, South America, the Middle East, India and the Far East, and it is safe to argue that television news in the United Kingdom offers a more textured and complete picture of the world than ever before. In short, news on British television is good.

Authority

In a digital world of hundreds of channels, one might expect the impact of the individual signature of presenter or producer to decline. In fact, the profile of the famous has intensified (and individual producers have become far more widely known than in the past). Though this lust for fame is frequently seen as proof of television 's decadence—the evanescent glorification of the know-nothing reality show exhibitionist—there are as many cases of television fame being based on personal authority and knowledge. Interestingly, in news, the presenter is today often respected by the modern public for his authoritative voice precisely because it seems to distance itself from authority. Andrew Marr, the BBC's Political Editor, Jeremy Paxman and Jon Snow, of *Newsnight* and *Channel 4 News,* all exercise, in different ways, the tribune's role as the viewer's champion every bit as effectively as their predecessors, Robin Day, John Cole and Alistair Burnett, who performed in a far more hierarchical and politicised culture. The tone of voice, however, has changed. In the corporate state television of the 1970s, the authority of the broadcaster came from the sense of their being part of the pool in which the politicians swam. A clubland familiarity invested them with the status to talk head to head with the politician. Today, the interviewer asserts his or her right to interrogate by emphasising distance. Even the archetypal insider idiom of the BBC Political Editor has been interpreted by Marr in a more ironic, almost anthropological perspective on his subject. The broadcaster's authority today lies in proving sceptical distance.

However, in other forms of factual programming, especially history, science and documentary, the location of authority is far more problematic. At the end of the 1990s there was a flourishing of the academic voice; David Starkey, Simon Sharma and Robert Winston appearing, as if begat by Kenneth Clark, Jacob Bronowsky and Jonathan Miller. However, the cult of celebrity, though it undoubtedly made them stars, somehow calcified their capacity to grow their authority further. In subsequent series, they became caricatures of themselves and, more significantly, their appeal declined. The historians, in particular, found themselves consumed by the verdict of celebrity that they had courted. They became yesterday's stars and, regardless of the qualities of their subsequent programmes, the audiences for their series fell away. In the past three years, there has not emerged a fresh generation of history and science presenters who have the same resonance. By contrast, the archaeology programme, *Time Team,* has kept its freshness, perhaps because its authority lies in the format of the programme itself; its presenter, Tony Robinson, portraying himself not as the voice of knowledge but as the viewers' friend, his enthusiasm for understanding based on his relative lack of expertise.

Narrative

Digital television has led to an unprecedented expansion in history and science programming, but with somewhat perverse consequences. The growth of specialist digital channels, for the most part driven by the need to feed the American market, has vastly increased the numbers of hours of programming made but has done little to expand their editorial range. Rather, history and science have become commoditised, as the same subject areas are trawled again and again. Though science programmes that public service broadcasters can afford fully to fund themselves have attempted theoretical physics and quantum theory with great imagination, in most cases, particularly where the science programming is co-produced with an American digital broadcaster, contemporary science seeks to attract attention not through the on-screen authority of the scientist, but in the extremity of the stories uncovered. Science on television has, at its worst, retreated to the freak show of the Victorian fairground. But even programmes that are more discerning tend to seek out the pathological and 'unnatural', the better to grab the viewer's interest in the world of nature. Significantly, in such programmes, which use science to concentrate on the pathos of the human, authority is invested in the anonymous narrator.

Innovation

In all genres of factual television, the pressures of distraction in a market of 500 channels are having a marked effect not only on choice of subject but on narrative form. Modern viewers, tyrannised by choice, are nagged by the temptation that maybe there is something more worth watching elsewhere than the programme they have selected. Impatience with slowly unfolding narrative is an incentive to look elsewhere. Hence, the objective of the producer is constantly to coerce the viewer to stay put. This has had two effects: a reluctance to try out unfamiliar subject matter and a determination to find more diverting ways of telling the familiar. The most significant change in factual television in the digital age is that exploration and innovation are defined almost entirely in terms of form and not of content. Viewer and programme maker have entered into a Faustian pact. The viewer will not be asked to risk watching unfamiliar subject matter in which they may not be interested but, in return, the producer will reformat familiar stories in intriguing and surprising ways.

These invariably invoke a vicarious sense of shared experience: modern youths become Spitfire pilots; suburban families recreate life in eighteenth-century America or nineteenth-century Britain. In the very different genre of lifestyle programming, there seems no limit to programmes on house purchasing, each one exploiting a different fantasy. The television of promise of perfection in the home has spread to the promise of bodily perfection too. Plastic surgery has become the perfect metaphor for both the ambitions of television and the society it portrays. In bawdier mood, programmes, dressed up as educational, delight in uncovering the obese in order to slim them down, and root out the filthy in order to scrub them down. Yet, as the ingenuity of creating a confection of experience gets ever greater, so the range of experience encountered on television diminishes.

Reality programmes

This change in the narrative idiom of factual programmes is, in part, the result of the invention of the reality genre. Digital technology has allowed the raw material of filmed experience, which was once the clay of the director–sculptor, to be on display for all to see. (It also is the perfect cheap material with which to fill hours of digital television.) However, in the five years since its inception, reality television has changed its nature. The enormous success of *Big Brother* came initially from the fact that it broke all rules of editorial control. The producer initially used the technology deliberately to withdraw from the action; the behaviour of the cast was defined by their lack of awareness of their impact on the audience in the world beyond the Big Brother House. Inevitably, as the programme has grown year by year, so those principles have been inverted. Increasingly, the cast have defined their actions by playing on their awareness, as past viewers, of the impact of their performance on the viewer; consequently, the producers' intrusion into the action and manipulation of its narrative, in order to counteract the cast's self-consciousness, has become more and more marked. A genre that took its name from its sense of freedom from artifice has become the most contrived television genre of all.

Interestingly, while other factual programme genres have succeeded in cloning each other to feed the appetite of the digital market, most reality programmes have failed. The notoriety of *Big Brother* and *I'm a Celebrity, Get Me Out of Here* had led to accusations of 'wall-to-wall' reality. In fact, there are very few reality programmes that have grabbed the viewers' imagination. A myriad of titles, most now forgotten, from *Touch the Truck* to *Jailbreak* to *Celebrity Love Island*, reflect the difficulty of persuading viewers to invest loyalty in such programmes. Most reality programmes have retreated to more conventional tricks, relying on B- and C-list celebrities to gain them notice. What remains so interesting about *Big Brother* is that the authority of the format still persuades the viewer to invest time in people hitherto unknown. As other reality shows are entertainment formats, *Big Brother's* significance lies in the ways it has changed the narrative idiom of documentary.

Documentary

This impact has not necessarily made television worse. A very successful and well-watched series such as *The Monastery*, which charted the spiritual journey of characters who retreated into the disciplines of a religious order, clearly owed its inspiration, in part, to *Big Brother*. But reality programmes have changed the portrayal of individual experience on television. Narrative 'observational' documentary, in the sense that the documentary maker sets out on an exploration with a subject and records an unfolding narrative as it is observed, has almost ceased to exist. Documentary has stolen the clothes of *Big Brother* and is now formatted into some sort of medieval morality play, with the individuals who take part shaped into emblematic caricatures. The defining programmes of this genre, *Wife Swap* and *Faking It* (now cloned by their makers into a coarser version for ITV—*Ladette to Lady* and similar formats) were constructed according to dramatic disciplines as rigorous as Aristotelian drama. Points of hubris, catharsis, nemesis and reconciliation are openly plotted into the narrative to coincide with the commercial breaks. Interestingly, many of these programmes rely on openly fomenting class conflict between families, a provocatively successful approach in a contemporary society that likes to boast that it is no longer class conscious.

Such programmes can have great emotional power and uncover moral truths. The most successful has been *Brat Camp*, where British problem children are transported to the merciless regime of an American camp of correction. This format does not bowdlerise the participants' emotional experience; rather, it is a narrative framework that allows the moral growth of the key participants to unfold before the camera over the weeks.

Such programmes are also often extremely good. Some, such as Jamie Oliver's campaign to improve school dinners, have had an electrifying social and political impact. But they are crowding out a less rhetorical narrative wherein once lay the strengths of British documentary. In 1999, the last moment before the digital revolution took hold, a series called *Death* was commissioned. It charted the dying of a number of people and the effects of their deaths on the lives of those they knew and loved. It was a series that took far longer to come to the screen than anticipated, not least because the act of taking part in the programme gave the participants the energy to continue living far longer than had been expected. When it was transmitted, over five weeks, its cumulative power attracted surprisingly large, though relatively small, audiences. It is difficult to see how such a series, both in subject matter and idiom, would readily be commissioned today.

One reason for this change derives from one of the provisions of the Communications Act. This legislated for a shift in the ownership of intellectual property rights in programmes from broadcasters to independent producers. The government believed that this was essential if British production companies were to achieve sufficient assets and the scale to be competitive in the globalised world of digital communications. In one sense, the policy has been extremely successful. The shift in rights ownership has encouraged third-party finance to invest in the television production sector and rapid consolidation has taken place. But this has had a marked editorial impact. Production companies, now answering to investors, are as keen to maximise return as commercial broadcasters. The television formats they develop have to be saleable in the international marketplace; they need to be easily replicable. There is little to be earned in international markets from a series on death; a great deal from manipulating family life and exploiting people's vanity.

Conclusion

The common cause of all the editorial trends identified above is the impact of digital television. It is not only the technological effects of digital television that are changing editorial priorities; there are the economic effects as well. Digital has for the first time created a real market in television and, in so doing, is changing fundamentally not only the way programmes are viewed but the way they are made. Markets drive out cross subsidy. When rights are owned by producers, not broadcasters, cross subsidy of one genre of 'public service' programme by a more commercial one is as unappealing to the modern producer as to the shareholder-driven broadcaster. The terms for television success are changing, but that does not mean that programmes cannot be good.

In the world of limited channels, what mattered was distribution. In a world in which distribution is effectively open to all, what matters is the battle for attention. Such a world can still provide a healthy climate for 'good' television, but it will only do so if the makers of programmes, broadcasters and producers alike, acclimatise to it. In the vast digital sea of anonymous product, where float the flotsam of countless, anonymous commodity programmes, the individual signatured programme will have the greater value for those who find it. Programmes that break through the white noise of digital distraction will attract the greater notice. This is by no means impossible. For the first time in history, online technology allows television programmes the longevity of print, as on-demand libraries make television content as accessible as Amazon's stock of books. Those programmes that signal their difference of creative intention will have more time and space in which to be found. As the time they have to pay back their investment becomes longer, so the incentives to invest in them may become greater.

This, however, is not a certainty. The greatest threat to the continuance of 'good' television, as we have known it in the past, is that those who want to make it will not adapt to the terms on which it can be made in the fundamentally changed world in which it must seek to flourish. The temptation is to scuttle for the easy, quick fix, imitating the new exemplar genres of the first wave of digital television, just as those ideas are beginning to run dry. However, the smart producer and broadcaster might realise that the new economics of television offer new opportunities for audiences to discover the 'good'. In the digital future, television will still allow for programmes that will shape our common imagination, interrogate our sense of our moral selves and define our collective memory of the times we live through. But the technology, economics and structures of television have now changed more fundamentally than ever before and the programmes that are made will inevitably change as a result.

Notes

1 Public service broadcasters are defined as those whose licence to broadcast carries with it statutory obligations to deliver certain genres of programmes in certain proportions. The PSBs are the BBC, ITV, Channel 4 and Five. In 2004, they amounted for 72 per cent of total television viewing.
2 This is slightly more than the total annual budget for BBC2 (£375 million in 2005).
3 Vehement objections from the BBC, and scepticism from government, seem to have buried this idea.
4 A poll commissioned on the BBC by the DCMS to launch the public consultation on the BBC Charter showed an overall 75 per cent satisfaction rating for the BBC, but an overall perception that its standards had declined.

Can the BBC Invigorate our Political Culture?

STEVEN BARNETT

Introduction

DURING the course of October 2005, a fascinating saga unfolded in the British press, which offered an interesting—if somewhat perplexing—insight into the fraying relationship between media and politics. The events themselves were, and remain, somewhat hazy, but they illuminate some of the problems we face if we are to resuscitate a healthy political culture. The saga also casts light on the role and importance of the BBC.

It started with an after-dinner speech by the BBC *Today* programme's John Humphrys to the Communication Directors' Forum on 8 June, a fairly routine knockabout affair in which Humphrys made some indiscreet, although scarcely earth-shattering, comments about senior cabinet ministers. Unbeknownst to him, the speech was videotaped by the PR company for which he had agreed to speak, Richmond Events, and a copy found its way to *The Times*. The newspaper felt the story significant enough to splash with the juicy headline 'Radio's king of rude launches another salvo at Labour "liars"'.[1]

According to *The Times*, Humphrys described Chancellor Gordon Brown as 'easily the most boring political interviewee I have ever had in my whole bloody life'. And it reported some unflattering comments about Deputy Prime Minister John Prescott's tendency to mangle the Queen's English: 'I'm sure he makes a great deal of sense but it's just that you can't understand a bloody word he says.' Moving from the specific to the general, Humphrys then observed that there were essentially three types of politician: 'There are those who do not lie at all ever and they don't get in to government . . . The second lot are those who will lie but really don't like it. And the third lot couldn't give a bugger whether they lie or not. And there are some of those.'

Given the continuing debate within broadcasting and political circles about the degradation of political discourse and the potential impact on political engagement, this may have been a story worth pursuing. What most exercised *The Times*, however, was Humphrys' remarks about Andrew Gilligan's report for the *Today* programme on the existence in Iraq of weapons of mass destruction. While accepting that complaints from Alastair Campbell, the former head of communications at Downing Street, might have been better handled, Humphrys declared, 'The fact is that we got it right. If we were not prepared to take on a very, very powerful government, there would be no point in the BBC existing—that is ultimately what the BBC is for.'

 Published by Blackwell Publishing Ltd, 9600 Garsington Road, Oxford OX4 2DQ, UK and 350 Main Street, Malden, MA 02148, USA

How these comments, expressed at a private dinner, actually found their way to *The Times* is as relevant as the story itself. Alastair Campbell's former deputy, Tim Allan, had set up his own public affairs consultancy after leaving Number 10. He had asked for and obtained a video of the Humphrys speech and was, according to Richmond Events, the only possible source of *The Times'* story.[2] *The Times'* article was written by Tom Baldwin, widely seen as being close to the Labour Party and particularly Alastair Campbell. The fact that it was splashed across two pages and deliberately exaggerated some of the more unguarded comments all gave credence to allegations of a manu-factured smear campaign. Speaking six days later to the Institute of Directors, Humphrys himself described the article as a 'piece of mischievous journalism . . . Inaccurate, misleading and clearly designed to give the impression that I have nothing but contempt for Labour ministers. That is simply not true'.[3]

He also went on to make more general observations about the role of the BBC, on which I want to elaborate. The first was, quite simply, that by virtue of its public funding the BBC was 'a big, juicy target'. The second had to do with what the BBC represented in the world of broadcast journalism: 'If anyone draws . . . the conclusion that the independence of people like me has been restricted, they are wrong. Independent journalism is too ingrained in the BBC. It is our lifeblood. It is the main reason for the BBC's existence. It is by a mile the most important thing we do.' Those that make comedy, drama, children's, nature or arts programming for the BBC may beg to differ, but certainly in terms of the BBC's integral role at the heart of our democratic culture—and in terms of the BBC's role in a fragmenting, proliferating, more mobile and market-driven broadcasting environment—Humphrys has a point. Stripped of the personalities and malicious gossip, this little episode tells us something quite profound about the revered and unique position of the BBC, about the repercussions of the Gilligan affair and the Hutton Report, and about the feverishly partisan nature of the British press.

The BBC, political journalism and civic engagement

First, the authority of the BBC matters: the reaction to Humphrys' comments, both by *The Times* and subsequently by the BBC itself, would have at worst been wry amusement and at best complete indifference if the BBC was not felt to have real influence within the political sphere. It matters partly because of the institutional legacy—or in modern parlance the 'brand image'—born of resources, professional ethos, a hard-earned and visible independence from government, and individual journalists who have themselves developed reputations as independent, cerebral and well-informed tribunes of the people. Its journalists and news presenters are imbued with a believability for listeners and viewers simply by appearing on and being part of the BBC.

And it matters partly because the broadcast medium itself has historically been subject to both traditions and statutory obligations of impartiality that have never been applied to the print media. Despite periodic and somewhat hysterical accusations of right-wing bias during much of the 1960s and 1970s, and equally hysterical cries of left-wing bias during much of the 1980s and 1990s, the BBC's approach to politics has been viewed by the vast majority of the voting public as fair, accurate and non-partisan. This bond of trust with the British citizenry—which extends to other broadcast journalism such as ITN and Sky, but is not as institutionally defined elsewhere—allows the BBC enormous latitude in its attempts to seek out different methods of engaging with politics in ways that are meaningful and accessible to an electorate that has become disillusioned with professionalised forms of political communication. Over the past five years in particular, the BBC has immersed itself in internal discussion and enquiries on how its programming strategies might overcome the widespread 'politics is boring' mantra and use the power of its reach and reputation to re-engage audiences.

This debate has been qualitatively different to that initiated by—some would say imposed by—John Birt when he arrived at the BBC in 1987 as deputy Director General and declared that News and Current Affairs was the cornerstone of the BBC. In the wake of Birt's arrival, money was diverted from virtually every other programme-making department of the BBC to underscore this new institutional priority. Recently, the new DG, Mark Thompson, reflected about that era, 'There was a new seriousness and conviction about what BBC journalism should stand for and how it could play a distinct and valuable role in the building what we would now call democratic value.'[4] But I would argue that there is a very different emphasis: that today's debates inside and outside the BBC are less about investment of resources and beefing up output, and more about the role that a publicly funded, publicly accountable broadcasting institution can play in fostering that democratic value.

In 2002, in the wake of concern about falling voter turnout in the 2001 General Election, the BBC commissioned research into public disillusion with politics amongst 16–44 year olds. Introducing the research report, the BBC's Head of New Politics Initiative (itself an interesting title) said, 'The point of the research and the current BBC initiative on politics is not to focus on individual programmes. Rather, the emphasis is on understanding how a large section of younger people today relate to politics, and therefore how we can better engage them through our programming.'[5] More recently, in partnership with the The Work Foundation, the BBC produced a report on social capital and public service broadcasting that explicitly tackled the interrelated issues of citizenship, community and technology in the context of analysing the BBC's role within a proliferation of private-sector broadcasting opportunities.[6] In November 2005, the BBC organised a major one-day event to promote discussion of new BBC initiatives that might help to 'sustain citizenship' by inspiring audiences—through BBC programmes and online support—to involve themselves in reporting, in debating, in engaging in some kind of collecting activity, or in donating time or money to civic causes.

These initiatives are predicated on definitions of political engagement and civic participation that go well beyond concern for fair, accurate and independent reporting. Devoting energy and resources to this kind of priority within broadcasting requires four conditions to be met: a trusted institution; a mission to take politics and political engagement seriously, regardless of audience size or impact on profits; access to large audiences; and money. In the intensely competitive and increasingly multichannel world of modern broadcasting, it has become almost impossible for commercial broadcasters to maintain a sustained approach to political broadcasting. The public service Channel 4 is still a notable exception in the United Kingdom, but does not have the same resources or mass appeal across a number of different platforms. It will also, as audiences fragment, face funding problems that will impose more pressure on less popular programming.

The BBC, independence and political neutrality

The second lesson to be taken from the Humphrys episode is the enduring sense of resentment against the BBC, and specifically the *Today* programme, which still simmers just below the surface within some parts of the Labour Government. We should perhaps remember that, in the immediate aftermath of Lord Hutton publishing his report, which completely vindicated the government, Alastair Campbell made a rather ungracious victory speech from the staircase of the hotel where he was staying. He effectively called for the resignation of four key BBC people: the Chairman, the Director General, the journalist Andrew Gilligan, and the man who interviewed him on the *Today* programme to kick-start the whole affair—John Humphrys. Of the four, only Humphrys survived.

Although Campbell had by then already stepped down from his post as Director of Communications, he continued—and some believe continues even now—to wield enormous influence. Both he and his former deputy Tim Allan are believed to retain close links to the Blair administration. The suggestion from Humphrys that the BBC had the right story all along—given far more credence by subsequent evidence from Iraqi, American and British intelligence sources—would only rub salt in the wounds of government advisers who felt that the Hutton Report and the BBC's grovelling apology that followed was the satisfactory closure they had sought.

In the immediate aftermath of Hutton, there was grave concern that BBC journalism might suffer from excessive caution as senior management imposed burdensome standards of journalistic restraint on any story that might embarrass the government. Although the short-term impact involved a little more caution—which might be interpreted as self-censorship—there was little evidence over the longer term of any lasting journalistic damage. Ironically, more long-term damage was probably sustained by the government than by the BBC, as opinion polls in the wake of Hutton consistently showed that voters trusted the BBC a great deal more than the government.

The systematic leaking of the Humphrys' speech, and the underhand means of obtaining it, suggested a government coterie still seething about the way in which apparent vindication was turned on its head.

The third lesson from this episode is the stark contrast between the neutrality of broadcast journalism and the blatant one-sidedness of the press. It is of course part of the attraction of a vibrant print culture—and, in the modern media market, a vital selling tool as well—that newspapers should be passionate and opinionated in their editorial stance. The tub-thumping columnist or the impassioned leader has always been a hallmark of a healthy, readable newspaper. Increasingly, though, the political agendas that inform the op-ed pages are seeping through to the news pages, and indeed the news values, of newspaper reporters. Either at the instigation of the editor—who in turn may be passing on the proprietor's prejudices—or through editorial osmosis, news stories are frequently prompted by or written according to the political slant of that newspaper or that journalist. Accuracy, fairness, balance and integrity can all suffer as a result.

In the case of this particular story, there was therefore no surprise that *The Times*—which, like the rest of the News International stable, had vigorously supported Tony Blair in his pursuit of the Iraq war and in the government's spat with the BBC over Andrew Gilligan's report—should have carried the Humphrys story. Given the actual speech by Humphrys, which was more moderate and more considered than the rather dramatic interpretation placed on it by *The Times*, there was little obvious justification for a two-page news spread leading with the statement that Humphrys had 'ridiculed senior Labour politicians and implied that all ministers are liars'.

The ambivalent nature of even *The Times'* editorial staff was demonstrated in the paper's editorial of the following Monday in which—given the prominence of the story and the severity of the charge—it might have been expected to plead for the whole weight of the BBC's complaints machinery to be brought down on the miscreant presenter. Instead, *The Times* suggested that Humphrys' views were 'not . . . a suitable subject for an exhaustive internal BBC inquiry. Michael Grade, the corporation's Chairman, is said to have requested a full transcript of [Humphrys'] speech. He should read it, chuckle and move on'. Even then, however, *The Times* could not resist indulging in its (and its proprietor's) long-standing complaint that there was a rather more fundamental 'problem' with the BBC: '[Grade] has the more serious issue of institutional bias to confront, and on this score the BBC's frontline presenters are far from blameless.'

Being accused by *The Times* of institutional bias may be akin to facing a charge of clinical negligence from Harold Shipman, but it does remind us that the BBC has very few friends within the British press. This arguably places a greater burden of responsibility on those who represent the public face of the BBC—and in particular the public face of its interaction with politicians—to exercise some care in their public statements about the parties, issues or individuals with whom they interact on a daily basis. Those at the coal-face of the BBC's political journalism do not have a duty to exercise self-restraint in their public utterances because they are public figures, or because they are paid for out of public funds via the licence fee. They need to do so because in their hands lies the burden of fulfilling all the BBC's expectations and traditions of sustaining a vibrant political discourse. In a world in which politics is easily trivialised and politicians even more easily ridiculed, an institutional commitment to believing that politics and politicians matter—and an institution which is *perceived* to believe that—is vital, and is easily undermined by the contorting prism of press misinterpretation. The BBC must be the modern Caesar's wife—particularly at a time when its funding, its structure and possibly its survival as a major British institution are under threat.

The problem with this argument is that it very easily metamorphoses into accusations of undue deference, institutional self-censorship or blatant surrender to pressure from political masters—which is precisely what the Humphrys story became. The lead article in the *New Statesman* of 6 October was promoted on the front cover with a picture of the white flag of surrender hanging from a TV and the catchline 'Broken, Beaten, Cowed – How Auntie lost her nerve'. It was written by the *Statesman*'s editor, John Kampfner—a well-connected and long-standing political reporter, who had himself worked at the BBC. Kampfner reported that 'According to a number of people involved, Michael Grade, the BBC's chairman, phoned several executives that weekend demanding that [Humphrys] be sacked.' He went on to allege that Director General Mark Thompson had been minded to agree until he saw the 'furious reaction to the government's antics' in the rest of the media. Kampfner concluded that, in the run-up to Charter review and negotiations about increasing the licence fee, here was irrefutable evidence of the BBC 'muzzling journalism and deliberately avoiding giving offence to the Government and the Establishment'.

The BBC's denials were unequivocal. Grade acknowledged that he had phoned his Director General to establish what exactly had happened (and would have been roundly condemned for irresponsible indifference had he done nothing), but the most vigorous public defence came from the DG. Talking to presenter Nick Clarke on BBC Radio 4's *World at One* three days after its publication, Thompson called the story 'untrue, preposterous—wholly without foundation'. His subsequent remark was an interesting reflection on journalistic values within the BBC: 'I passionately believe in the BBC's independence. Supposing I rang you up and said there was a tricky licence fee negotiation coming up and asked you to go soft on the Government, how long do you think *that* would stay quiet?'

This is fundamental. Thompson was essentially saying that, in an organisation as extensive as the BBC, with an institutional DNA that is hard-wired to believe that independence matters, any compromise of those institutional ideals inevitably creates a backlash amongst those charged with leading and practising the BBC's political journalism. Not only does it employ individuals who are independently minded, but it imbues them with a *modus operandi* that will not accept any attempt at formal restraint. There are enough awkward, thinking, self-motivated individuals who work there to make life impossible for any DG or chairman who tries to compromise that journalistic ethos.

Can the BBC's role be sustained? Proposals for the future

These, then, are the two cornerstones of the BBC's relationship to politics: an internal culture that jealously guards its reputation for independence from political manipulation—to the point sometimes of over-compensating in the treatment of individual politicians—and a more recently articulated commitment not just to covering politics, but to playing an integral part in generating an engaged and dynamic democratic culture.

These institutional values may be embedded but, whatever their history and deep-rooted tradition, they are not invulnerable. Today's values have their roots in a structure and funding which, partly by accident and partly by design, produced an organisation that embodies democratic values and understands its value in promoting a vibrant, informed political culture. Radical changes, perhaps even tinkering at the edges, can over time erode that ethos. So what exactly is being proposed for the BBC's future, and what might those proposals mean for the BBC's capacity for 'doing politics' and sustaining democracy in the twenty-first century? Current plans for the future of the BBC—for its structure, funding and governance—will all have implications for the continued strength of the institution and its approach to politics.

Since the BBC derives its authority from a Royal Charter that is generally reviewed every ten years, the period leading up to renewal has always provided scope for a major examination of the Corporation's structure and funding. The current Charter expires at the end of 2006, and with a plethora of new commercial and technological initiatives in broadcasting, the review process has been the most wide-ranging and thorough in the Corporation's history. After an extended period of open consultation, seminars and reviews during 2004—including the establishment and reporting of an independent panel headed by Lord Burns, which reported in January 2005—the government published its draft proposals in a Green Paper on 2 March 2005. Following consultation on that document during the summer and autumn, a White Paper will emerge early in 2006. The process will be complete by the middle of 2006.

Two crucial points have been broadly agreed and are not up for negotiation. First, the Charter will be renewed for a further ten years; second, the BBC will continue to be funded entirely by the licence fee. This follows a firm commitment by the government, even in the face of growing competitive hostility to the BBC, that the BBC should remain a well-resourced, mass-audience broadcaster, at the heart of British cultural and democratic life.

This broad political endorsement does, however, come with caveats. The funding issue is not closed, and there is some support for the notion of 'contestable funding' that would allow other broadcasters to bid for a proportion of the licence fee revenue to fund their own 'public service' programmes. Channel 4 in particular is concerned about a funding gap in its own revenues by 2012 and has been keen to kick-start a debate about whether the BBC should continue to have a monopoly over the licence fee. Any top-slicing initiative would inevitably have severe consequences for the BBC, which would be required to cut back its own programming by whatever proportion of its public funding was diverted elsewhere. Since it would not be acceptable to cut back on its more serious programme commitments, there would be fewer popular programmes, which in turn would make the BBC less attractive to audiences. The spiral of decline that would follow would undoubtedly have consequences for the popularity of all its output, including political programmes.

That, however, is a longer-term debate (and one that is at least twenty years old). In the short term, there are two issues that have been thoroughly aired in the Charter review process and will have a bearing on the BBC's role at the centre of the UK's political culture. The first concerns the precise service remits and public service framework within which the BBC will be required to work in return for continuation of its public funding. And the second concerns the whole structure of accountability that will determine how BBC performance is monitored, how it is regulated, and how it remains account-able to Parliament for the fulfilment of its obligations, while at the same time remaining wholly independent from government influence.

The first of these is the more interesting, because it demonstrates how, for the first time, a public service philosophy is being spelt out for the BBC in much more precise terms than the long-standing duty simply to educate, inform and entertain. Partly because of pressure by some intense lobbying by commercial channels, and partly because in the modern political climate the levying of taxes requires more justification and transparent 'outcomes' than simply assuring licence-payers that the BBC is a jolly good thing, the government Green Paper sets out the new rationale:[7]

'Inform, educate and entertain' will remain the BBC's mission statement. But a large number of other broadcasters also fulfil some part of that mission – it does not explain what is meant to be distinctive about the BBC in an age of ever increasing choice. We will sharpen up the BBC's remit. We will introduce five distinctive purposes that all BBC services should aim to fulfil:

- sustaining citizenship band civil society
- promoting education band blearning
- stimulating creativity and cultural excellence
- representing the UK, its Nations, regions and communities
- bringing the UK to the world and the world to the UK

For the first time, then, the BBC's democratic role will be defined more precisely in terms of 'sustaining citizenship and civil society'. Some within the BBC would argue that this is precisely what its news and current affairs output has been striving to do for eighty years, but it has never been articulated as an ambition that goes beyond impartial reporting. Such an explicit commitment allows for greater discussion both inside and outside the BBC about how these aspirations might be fulfilled beyond a simple quota for broadcasting news and current affairs in peak time. The Green Paper itself elaborates on this theme by saying that 'The BBC has a particular respons-ibility to help people understand Parliament and the UK political system . . . so that they can be informed, media literate participants in our democratic system.' More importantly, it is prepared to recognise and encourage the BBC's democratic role by arguing that it should be able to contribute to democratic debate by 'organising seminars and e-discussion forums, distri-buting information and working on campaigns with partners in the public and voluntary sector'.

In its own response to the government Green Paper, the BBC warms to this theme. It draws on the report prepared for its Board of Governors in 2004 by Ronald Neil, which was the BBC's internal response to the Gilligan story and subsequent events that culminated in the Hutton Report. As a direct result of the Neil Report, the BBC established a Journalism Board with a brief extending across all BBC journalism, whether local, national or global. Its aims are 'to strengthen the practice and reputation of BBC journalism at all levels' as well as examining the audience reach of relevant BBC programmes and, crucially, developing a system of measuring 'the extent to which BBC journalism helps members of the public to become better informed citizens'.[8]

What matters here is that, in a commercialised, commodified broadcasting world, where the most important measurement criteria are audience size, audience demographics and the number of paying subscribers, here is a huge journalistic operation that is attempting not just to understand but to improve its role in British citizens' democratic life. However journalistically profes-sional the operations of ITN or Sky News, or however well intentioned the mandated current affairs programmes of ITV or the serious documentaries of Channel 4 or Five, they cannot provide that kind of institutional commitment at the very heart of their organisational life. Through its resources, through its non-commercial status, through its access to mass audiences via a number of freely accessible platforms, the BBC can both aspire to and fulfil the rather lofty ambition of 'sustaining citizenship'.

What it does and how it does it are matters both for its senior managers and those to whom they are accountable—at the moment, the Board of Governors. This, however, brings us to the second area of proposed change within the Green Paper.

There was much concern in the aftermath of the Gilligan Report and following the way government complaints were handled by the BBC Board of Governors that the governors had two potentially conflicting roles: on the one hand acting both as cheerleaders for the institution and protecting it from government interference, while on the other regulating and holding manage-ment to account. The Green Paper describes this approach as 'increasingly out of step with best corporate governance practice' and states that 'the two functions need to be more clearly separated in future'. To this end, it proposes replacing the Board of Governors with a new body called the BBC Trust, which will be ultimately responsible for the licence fee and for holding the BBC to its public purposes. In tandem, it proposes to establish a new Executive Board, which will be responsible for the delivery of the BBC's services within the framework set by the Trust.

This proposal is widely seen as a compromise (or by government and BBC critics as a 'fudge') between the status quo and handing the BBC's regulation over entirely to an external regulator such as Ofcom, or to an entirely new public service regulator. The external regulator option—frequently canvassed as offering a 'level playing field'—has found particular favour amongst the BBC's commercial competitors, on the grounds that a regulatory body detached from the BBC may be more inclined to restrain or even terminate some of the BBC's activities. Where exactly the additional constraints might operate usually depends on the interests of those promoting the idea, but the general thrust is that the BBC is 'too big' or is allowed 'too much flexibility' in its operations and therefore needs a more stringent regulatory body to rein it in.

Though resisted by the government, this option unfortunately seems to have found favour with Ofcom. While not—at this stage—suggesting that it should take over regulating the BBC itself, Ofcom's response to the Green Paper was distinctly cool about the BBC Trust idea and was clearly intent on moving the debate towards greater external scrutiny of the BBC. It asked the government to consider whether the 'BBC Trust' should actually be called 'The Trust', on the grounds that it would be 'less possessive'. It also called on the government to consider 'how the Trust might evolve into an external, independent body in the future'.[9]

There is little justification offered for this view, and apparently little understanding of the potential damage that might be done by turning the BBC over to another set of (government-appointed) regulators, who would have no stake in nor understanding of the institutional uniqueness of the BBC. The BBC Trust, as currently envisioned, will formalise a structure of regulation for the BBC's newly articulated public purposes. While, so long as government sets the licence fee and appoints the chairman, there will always be heated debate over the real ability of the BBC to be fearlessly and uncompromisingly independent of government, that conundrum is integral to a publicly funded institution that has somehow to remain democratically accountable. There is no reason to fear that the new structure will make life any more or less difficult for a government intent on interference, and the clearer statement of its aims for enhancing citizenship should make it easier for members of the BBC Trust to monitor performance and criticise where the BBC falls short.

This, however, can be done within the framework not of 'public service broadcasting' in general, which has no DNA nor organisational philosophy, nor institutional history, but within the framework of understanding and appreciating both what the BBC stands for and what it is capable of achieving. However imperfect the system of governors, the fact is that the system has survived eighty years of often turbulent political relations, and has still produced an institution that is acknowledged throughout the world as a bastion of democratic freedom and political neutrality. For an 'imperfect' constitutional system, that is a hell of an achievement. We—and the government—should pay careful heed to the words of Patricia Hodgson, in her last speech as Chief Executive of the Independent Television Commission before it became absorbed into the all-encompassing Ofcom:

> When under pressure, politicians of all parties may be tempted to lose faith in the BBC and yearn for more control. It's tempting then to turn to a body which they can appoint, and which doesn't have the independent power of the BBC that comes from programme making . . . But the strength of the current Charter settlement is that Governors *can* be independent, are required to be so and *are* reinforced by 80 years of precedent. That independence is, in the long term, a vital support for an independent and impartial national service of television news. It is more important to democracy than any rows about an individual issue. We dismantle it at our peril.[10]

In all her public utterances about the future of the BBC, Culture Secretary Tessa Jowell has been at pains to emphasise the government's commitment to a 'strong, well-funded BBC independent of government'. This is partly no doubt to reassure a sceptical public that the government has no wish to pursue a post-Hutton vendetta, nor in any way to stand in the way of a healthy BBC. But I believe it is also born of a genuine sympathy for the institutional values of the BBC within the current government, and a determination to reinforce the structure and public funding that will protect those values—even in the face of the growing band of commercial and ideological foes who would prefer to see a much diminished and less omnipresent institution. For this reason, it is unlikely (though not impossible) that the government will at this late stage concede the argument about governance. It will, however, be an argument that will arise again over the next ten years, and one that will inevitably have repercussions for how effectively the BBC can continue at the heart of the UK's democratic and political life.

The BBC derives its strength from its sheer size as well as its internalised values. We should not forget that its ability to invigorate our political culture is not just born of an institution committed to thinking about politics in terms of engagement and democracy, rather than worrying about 'bums on seats'. It is also born of its ability to attract large audiences, to be popular as well as serious, to deal in comedy as well as documentaries, and to have a significant presence outside the formal political sphere. The very fact that we can talk about our public broadcaster's potential for influencing the nation's political culture is an astonishing tribute to the enduring power of a public institution in a commodified world. It still provokes envy when compared to the marginalised influence of sister institutions such as PBS in America, ABC in Australia or CBC in Canada. There will no doubt be more controversies around high-profile presenters like John Humphrys, fuelled by a self-interested press, and there will certainly be further allegations of both journalistic hubris and journalistic cowardice. In the meantime, the structures now being put in place should allow the BBC, if it so wishes, to play a major part in invigorating democratic life in the UK.

Notes

1 'Radio's king of rude launches another salvo at Labour 'liars', *The Times*, 3 September 2005, pp. 28–9.
2 According to *The Daily Telegraph*, the director of Richmond Events, Mark Rayner, was 'very annoyed about the way the information was obtained from us and subsequently used'. See *The Daily Telegraph*, 6 September 2005, p. 6.
3 Extracts from his speech were published in *The Guardian*, 9 September 2005, p. 23.
4 'Defining public value', speech to the Edinburgh International Television Festival, 29 August 2004.
5 BBC, *'Beyond the Soundbite': BBC Research into Public Disillusion with Politics*, BBC Publications, 2002.
6 M. Brookes, *Watching Alone: Social Capital and Public Service Broadcasting*, The Work Foundation/BBC Publications, 2004.
7 *Review of the BBC's Royal Charter: a Strong BBC, Independent of Government*, Department for Culture, Media and Sport, 2005, p. 5.
8 *Review of the BBC's Royal Charter: BBC response to A strong BBC independent of government* [the Government Green Paper], BBC Publications, May 2005, pp. 15–18.
9 Ofcom, *Review of the BBC's Royal Charter: Ofcom Response to the Green Paper*, Ofcom, June 2005, p. 26.
10 P. Hodgson, 'Broadcasting and democracy', The Ninth Eleanor Macdonald Lecture for Women in Management, November 2003 (emphasis in the original).

The Rise of the Ranters: Saving Political Journalism

PETER RIDDELL

Introduction

POLITICAL journalism can be saved, and deserves to be saved. At present, it is easier to see what is wrong with reporting about politics in the United Kingdom than to find grounds for hope and evidence of improvement. But there is no reason to despair. The solution lies in the very competitive and technological trends that so threaten the traditional broadsheets, what used to be called the serious press. (In this chapter, I limit myself mainly to written journalism, rather than to television or radio. This is partly because I am more familiar with newspapers, but also because, while some of their current flaws are similar, differences in technology and patterns of regulation and ownership mean there are also significant contrasts.)

The Internet, the BlackBerry and the text message, now the main means of information and exchange for younger people, are also increasingly the ways in which political journalism could be communicated—if media groups adapt. This is already starting to happen, but not nearly rapidly enough. According to research commissioned by the Carnegie Corporation of New York among 18–34 year olds, the Internet beats newspapers by most image measures—by 49 to 9 per cent in providing news only 'when I want it', by 20 to 9 per cent on offering news 'I can use', and by 29 to 4 per cent on being up to date. Only on trustworthiness is there a virtual tie, at 10 to 9 per cent.

Adapting to the Internet

At present, newspapers are struggling to escape from two centuries of conventional thinking that their message has to be communicated via pages of newsprint, distributed in a cumbersome fashion around the country. All newspapers now have online sites, but most are not yet central to the ethos and operations of the paper. A common view among many, especially older journalists is 'Oh, yes, I will dash something off for the website'. For many, the online version does not yet have equal standing with the pages of newsprint. Most newspaper journalists still look askance at online journalism, let alone at Vodaphone's provision on mobile phones of video news directly from broadcasters such as ITN.

That is not just tradition, and the continuing influence of post-Renaissance culture, with its emphasis on printing and the written word. It also reflects a failure to think out what journalism is really about, to confuse the medium

© 2006 The Author. Editorial organisation © 2006 The Political Quarterly Publishing Co. Ltd.
Published by Blackwell Publishing Ltd, 9600 Garsington Road, Oxford OX4 2DQ, UK and 350 Main Street, Malden, MA 02148, USA

and the message. Journalism is essentially a collective activity carried out by individualists. That distinguishes it from blogging, which, with its freshness and vitality, is personal and individual, unconstrained and immediate. Blogging is an increasingly important complement to conventional journalism, not a replacement for it. Political bloggers have become a widely noticed, and in some ways more democratic, alternative voice challenging mainstream opinion. But the very unchecked spontaneity of blogging is also its major weakness. Blogging can easily descend into the spreading of unreliable and untested allegations. There is no intermediary to ask: Is this right? By contrast, newspapers consist of groups of reporters and news executives who gather and analyse information. Contrary to popular impressions, journalism is a disciplined activity, which should require checking and testing of stories. The group aspect is crucial, as shown, for example, by the coverage of the terrorist attacks in London in July 2005. The best work was carried out by journalists working together. The bloggers provided immediate on-the-spot reports, but they did not, and could not, provide a rounded picture of what happened. Newspapers also determine what to cover and how. A wide variety of different approaches are on offer for the reader to choose amongst. Yet what the reader is buying is that collective product, under the brand name of the title. The means of communication is separate. It does not really matter whether this is through pages of newsprint shoved through a letter-box or on an online site shown on a computer screen. The main, still under-appreciated difference is that an online site suffers from none of the constraints and limitations of space and length that the printed product does.

What is wrong now

But before discussing how the Internet and other electronic means of communication offer hope for political journalism, let us look at what is wrong. The diagnosis is not as obvious as it seems. The fashionable view that the press/media have grown powerful, too powerful, at the expense of elected politicians is hardly new. Back in 1854, Anthony Trollope wrote in *The Warden*, the first of his Barchester novels, about Tom Towers, a thinly disguised portrait/caricature of the editor of *The Times* of the day. Towers loved 'to listen to the loud chattering of politicians, and to think how they were all in his power—how he could smite the loudest of them, were it worth his while to raise his pen for such a purpose. He loved to watch the great men of whom he daily wrote and flatter himself that he was greater than any of them.'[1] How some of the big media egos of today would agree.

Paul Dacre and Alastair Campbell are often depicted as the twin demons. They regard each other in these terms: one denouncing the other as evil and corrupt: the one, partisan, strident and degrading public life by distorting the news and pursuing unfair campaigns against the personal lives of politicians disliked by the *Daily Mail*; and the other, manipulative, devious and degrading public life by arrogant disregard of the normal standards of truth and spinning the most favourable interpretation of events. In the middle, according to this popular viewpoint, are idle, supine political journalists, willing to take the line of their owners or the government (a revealing contradiction, since it cannot be both). Or, as Jeremy Tunstall, that most astute observer of the journalistic scene, wrote in the late 1960s, lobby correspondents—a now largely defunct term—act as a 'tame lapdog, alert watchdog and fierce fighting dog', often on the same day. It all seems so easy: denounce the *Daily Mail* and spin, and insist on all sources being named, and all will be well. Some critics would add Rupert Murdoch to the demonology, though the widely advertised faults of political journalism did not originate in News International's stable of papers, nor are at their worst there. Far from it. *The Sun*, for instance, treats politics far more seriously, and at greater depth, than any paper in Richard Desmond's ownership. These are all easy targets. Some of the attacks are justified, but they usually exaggerate and miss the point.

The real problems of political journalism are more complicated. Excessive partisanship is part of the story. It poisons our political culture by turning healthy scepticism about politicians' claims into corrosive cynicism about everything they say or do, as John Lloyd[2] and Geoff Mulgan[3] have argued. There is ample polling evidence that journalists, particularly on tabloids, and MPs came far, far lower than business leaders and trade union officials, let alone the police, teachers and doctors, on any measure of trustworthiness. Much journalism is lazy and some dishonest. But this is only part of the story.

The underlying difficulty is commercial. Newspapers in their conventional printed form are having to compete hard to maintain sales, particularly among young people. Just look at the monthly circulation figures for the main national papers. No matter how massaged the numbers are, sales overall are broadly flat. Most papers are fighting to maintain market share, with only the new compact/tabloids/'Berliner' format papers such as *The Times*, *The Guardian*, *The Observer*, and *The Independent* and *Independent on Sunday* able to buck the trend and increase their sales. Sales figures are much worse in the United States, even though there is often no real competition from other newspapers in an area. Readers are shifting from newspapers to local television and, overwhelmingly, to the Internet.

Market forces have been by far the most significant influence on the form and content of political journalism in the past decade. Editors have tried all kinds of devices to win and retain new readers, as their traditional readers go elsewhere or die off. That has put the emphasis on the marginal reader. The assumption has been that he or she wants to be excited and entertained. Political news seldom fits that definition; or, rather, the traditional reporting of what is said and done is seen by newspaper executives as boring. So not only has the space devoted to political news been cut, but, equally importantly, its treatment has altered. The emphasis has increasingly been on personalities, not policies—certainly not on process; and splits rather than substance. Hence the fascination with marginal, narcissistic figures such as Ann Widdecombe or Boris Johnson.

Direct reporting has suffered, as has any sense of sequence or perspective. A row—it is always a row—is reported on day one as if it is of seismic consequence, but is then completely forgotten a day or two later. The reader is left puzzled. What happened? What is the follow up? In most cases, however, activities at Westminster are not reported at all. Major bills may be discussed when they are introduced—as often by a specialist correspondent as by a political reporter. Then, they are forgotten unless there is a rebellion, which is reported largely in terms of its impact on the standing of the Prime Minister or the government, not on the merits of the issue concerned. Then the bill is ignored, and there is seldom, if any, analysis of its implementation: Parliament is also at fault in the lack of post-legislative scrutiny. Similarly, constitutional issues are regarded as boring. The UK has been through a series of far-reaching constitutional changes since 1997—devolution to Scotland and Wales, the London Mayor, the Human Rights Act, Freedom of Information, and a radically new system for regulating the conduct of elections—but you would hardly know from the pages of most papers.

The days of the 'paper of record', always a rather pompous and misleading concept, are long gone. Few would pretend that what appears in any newspaper any more than touches the surface of what is happening in the political world. This is not to indulge the ultimate sin of 'golden ageism'. Much political reporting thirty or forty years ago was both badly written and boring. The old-style parliamentary pages (known as gallery coverage), which reported what was said on the floor of the Commons, were very dull, filling space with turgid speeches. They had outlived their usefulness when they disappeared in the late 1980s. Similarly, much lobby, or broader political, coverage was sloppy and hid as much, or even more, behind unnamed sources as nowadays. Nor did spin and unattributable sources begin in 1997 with Alastair Campbell, or in 1979 with Sir Bernard Ingham, his predecessor as Downing Street press secretary during the Thatcher years. Despite their mutual animosity, they were remarkably alike in their rumbustious style and loyalty to their leader.

Moreover, Parliament has ceased to be as central to political debate as it was half a century ago. Up to the mid-1950s, there were formal rules banning discussion on the BBC, then a monopoly, of any item expected to come before Parliament over the next fortnight, or any interview with an MP or peer about any bill between its introduction and its final passage, or abandonment. Since then, the *Today* programme and *Newsnight*, let alone twenty-four-hour news, have all become central to political debate. The courts have become more active, as have various semi-independent regulators and the European Union.

Changing coverage

So there was a strong case for a change in political coverage, away from just a focus on events on the floor of the Commons. However, the shift has not been towards more coverage of these other centres of power: select committees, or the day-to-day workings of the regulators or the European Commission. The Bank of England's Monetary Policy Committee is properly reported, but that is largely because City/business pages have preserved their independence and space. You will not find much about regulators or select committees on the political pages, or about developments in the Civil Service and implementation of public service reform.

Readers of newspapers looking for reports on politics will often find good coverage of the big events of the day—a budget, the general election or the 7 July 2005 terrorist attacks. This is often now much richer and more thoughtful than in the past. What readers do not, however, see these days is the secondary story; about, say, a new government initiative, a report by a select committee, events in smaller political parties, or the new ideas of a think tank. This is paralleled in foreign coverage, where a cutback in full-time correspondents overseas has meant a focus on the crisis of the day, which often springs on the reader who has not seen stories about the gradual build-up to the drama. What readers get now is the tip of the iceberg. The rest, largely hidden below the water, may be reported by assiduous political journalists, but their stories only rarely appear, and if they do, they are often truncated.

The decline in consistent coverage has been linked to two other developments. First, there is the belief that reporting must be personality driven. Hard cases, or scandals, make good stories, not analysis or a sense of perspective and proportion. Policy and analysis are seen as boring. Again, this is not new. John Brewer, the historian, has written of the late eighteenth century press in London in his book *A Sentimental Murder*: 'There were tales of political corruption and moral depravity in high places. The culture of scandal, propagated by the press, thrived on supposition, rumour and speculation. It took the facts and wove them into a variety of seamless narratives that opened up all sorts of possible interpretations. Such stories were designed to sell newspapers and magazines, attack the government, traduce and shame individuals, and settle personal scores.'[4]

Second, the move away from broadsheets to a tabloid or compact format has accentuated these trends. That is partly for the simple reason that, with twice as many pages, there are twice as many page leads. This has produced a preference for the eye-catching. Front pages that used to have three, or even four, stories on them now have just one, plus a summary of single paragraphs on the other main news. Not surprisingly, the one story is presented more vividly and sharply. Other, often important, stories get relegated to later in the paper. The tabloid format has advantages in presentation, notably in spreads on big stories, but the secondary story suffers. There is a trend in some papers towards a more populist type of front page, dominated by stories about health or consumer interest scandals. This has fuelled claims that papers have moved 'down market'. The reality is more complicated since newspapers are a combination of junk food and haute cuisine. But the changes have squeezed both the breadth and depth of political coverage.

74

Why political journalism matters

Does this matter? If the public is less interested in politics, then newspapers—and, even more, broadcasters—are only responding: giving the market what it wants. But political journalism does matter: indeed, is essential to the health of a democracy. If voters don't know what is going on, then they are likely to be further alienated from the political process and even less likely to vote. In that sense, readers are ill served by the patronising and often glib assumption of news executives that they do not want to know about government and what politicians are doing. There is widespread disillusionment with the yah–boo style of adversarial politics, particularly at Prime Minister's questions every Wednesday. That leads into the trap, particularly beloved of broadcasting executives, of moving away from Westminster coverage. Of course, politics is much more than what happens within the Palace of Westminster. But by 'moving away from Westminster', these broadcasters do not mean examining the work of regulators and quangos, and certainly not the EU. What they mean are personalised stories. Showing a crowded accident and emergency department can itself only tell part of what is happening. Striking human-interest stories can obscure, not illuminate, the arguments about, say, the allocation of health resources. Reporting about how political decisions affect 'real' people is fine, but it can also be an excuse not to report on how those decisions are taken. I have never seen a broadcaster, and only a tiny number of newspaper journalists, try to explain the work of the Downing Street Delivery Unit in ensuring that targets on waiting lines are met.

Political journalism is worth saving for the simple reason that what Parliament and government does still matters to the mass of voters: what is going to happen to their pensions, to their local schools or to the choice of treatment in local hospitals. These are big issues that should be fully reported, but they are only covered intermittently at present. The debates between the Treasury and the spending departments are central to people's lives. Reporting these issues requires a more imaginative approach than in the past, less narrowly centred on the floor of the Commons or on the day-to-day party battles, and more on what political scientists like to describe as policy networks, the interaction of ministers, civil servants, providers of services, interest groups and even, occasionally, MPs.

How to improve coverage

How is this going to happen? Pious lectures to newspapers about their civic responsibilities are beside the point. No paper is suddenly going to increase the space it devotes to politics. But what they can do, relatively easily, is to ensure that the work already produced by their political staffs just does not disappear on to the spike. The Internet is a real alternative. If the printed version focuses on big stories, or just includes one- or two-paragraph snippets of other reports, why not run the latter in full on the Internet, with short cross-references from the printed version? This sounds rather a mechanistic solution. But doing this would vastly broaden the range of political news that readers—of online sites, as well as printed pages—could choose between each day. So if you are really interested in following, say, the Liberal Democrats, most of the time, outside leadership elections, you would probably find the report on the online site, rather than in the printed paper. This does not have big staffing implications, since many journalists at present find that only a part, and often only a small part, of their daily output appears. This increasingly happens on, for example, *The Times*, with reporters filing for *Times Online*, which also increasingly carries its own specially commissioned stories, columns and regular blogs. The same happens on other papers. But this dual function of journalists could be greatly expanded, and made more integral to the work of newspapers. Journalists would also feel more motivated, seeing a seamless link in their work between the morning paper and the online site. Variations could include brief stories, or news alerts, sent via e-mail or text messages to subscribers.

The potential for regarding an online site as complementary to the printed paper, rather than as a poor relation, is shown by the number of visitors each day to *Guardian Unlimited*. This is now between 700,000 and one million, or as many as read the printed paper. In many ways, the most successful British newspaper, in the sense of communicating via the written, though not the printed, word is the BBC website.

Another advantage of the Internet is that readers—I still prefer that perhaps archaic term—can find information directly. Even ignoring television and radio, the traditional monopoly of newspapers in reporting news no longer exists. There is a cheap, near costless alternative. If I want to find out what has happened in Parliament, I don't have to scan the newspapers for a rare, brief report, or buy the expensive printed version of Hansard. I can merely log on, go to the Parliamentary website, and read both Hansard and select committee hearings and reports. Parliament and most other public bodies still, however, lag well behind in the design and accessibility of their websites. It is often hard and laborious to find out information on a particular topic. The search engines are primitive, as was pointed out by the report on *Parliament in the Public Eye*, produced by a committee chaired by Lord Puttnam for the Hansard Society in May 2005.[5] This was one of the report's key recommendations for improving communications. Commons officials are keen to change, but have been constrained by the traditional conservatism of Westminster. However, improvements are now beginning to happen with a recognition that Parliament has to communicate directly with voters, rather than just via the traditional media.

Traditional journalism will always have an advantage over official websites. By definition, journalists select, highlight and summarise what they think is significant. That is obviously a fallible process. But it is a necessary step for busy readers. Similarly, journalists can analyse, contrast and compare in a way that no official organisation can. Of course, that opens the way for organisations specialising in a particular area to offer a more in-depth service—as, for example, the ePolitix website, part of the broader Dod's publishing group, does for events in Westminster and Whitehall. But, like many of the old-style political newsletters, such websites generally lack journalists with the authority and experience of most newspapers. This underlines the collective advantage that the latter still enjoy.

So, I am optimistic that a diverse and rich political journalism can not only survive but also prosper. This will be based on traditional newspapers, but will increasingly be communicated via websites and other electronic methods. The journalist's ability to find out, analyse and report still remains essential.

Prejudice and partisanship

That is only part of the story. Much of the debate over the current state of political journalism focuses less on the depth and breadth of coverage than on its biases, the increasingly partisan and partial nature of much reporting. There is again a danger here of 'golden ageism'. Reporting and comment have often been blurred. It is only a century ago that many papers received subsidies from political parties. Beaverbrook and Rothermere hardly ran detached papers in the 1930s. Nor was the record of *The Times* in covering the fascist dictators and appeasement a model of straight reporting. Yet partisanship has got worse. Reporting with attitude has become common-place. Commercial pressures have encouraged political reporters to become more strident, and less nuanced, simply in order to get their stories into the paper at all. There is also the paradox that as the electorate as a whole has become less partisan—with fewer and fewer saying they identify with one of the major parties—so newspapers have become more partisan. That is partly associated with long periods of one party being in government, which has encouraged parts of the press, notably the *Daily Mail*, and some big-name broadcasters such as John Humphrys, very much a *Mail* person, to assume the mantle of the opposition parties in challenging ministers and the government of the day.

Moreover, on the comment pages, there has been the rise of the ranters, the columnists with little knowledge but strong opinions. They have tended to eclipse the more considered analytical columnist, who based their opinions on insider information and insights. The leading examples in the past thirty or so years were David Watt, Peter Jenkins and Hugo Young, all of whom died in their prime. They all had a distinctive viewpoint, all three around the liberal centre to the centre-left, but they saw their prime role as informing rather than haranguing. Instead, we have had the rise of the absolutist moralists, denouncing all and sundry. This has been linked to the importation of the American phenomenon of the committed columnist, which originated on the highly partisan, not to say biased, editorial pages of *The Wall Street Journal*. One of the results of the polarisation of US politics from the Clinton era onwards has been the rise of the ideologically committed op-ed writer. In the 1990s, American papers were full of conservative columnists who could find nothing good to say about President Clinton; just as, now, many have sought to justify everything that President George W. Bush does or says, and defend the twists and turns of his Iraq policy. This highly partisan, 'for or against', style of writing is not only predictable but is also not really journalism. It seeks to argue on behalf of particular interests rather than explain on behalf of the general reader.

There are two linked problems. First, the lines between journalism and politics have become more blurred. More columnists are not only strongly partisan, but they also seek to be players in politics themselves—whether in the explicit way of seeking to become MPs or being involved in party debates. That necessarily constrains their independence. The party line is the enemy of vigorous, independent journalism. Second, papers seek big names to boost sales, with the rise of celebrity columnists, who see themselves as bigger than those they are covering. David Broder of *The Washington Post*, that most fastidious and fair-minded of political journalists, wrote, with regret, during the 2004 presidential campaign, about how news organisations began 'offering their most prestigious and visible jobs not to people deeply imbued with the culture and values of newsrooms, but to stars imported from the political worlds. Journalists learn to be sceptical—of sources and of their own biases as well . . . The way to the top of journalism was no longer to test yourself on police beats and city hall assignments, under the sceptical gaze of editors who demanded precision in writing and careful weighing of evidence. It was to make a reputation as a clear wordsmith, a feisty advocate, a belligerent or beguiling political personality, and then market yourself to the media.'

There is no easy solution. External regulation would be unworkable, and wrong on free speech grounds. As long as we have many papers—and the Internet allows the expression of an enormously wide range of views—the market offers the best answer. However, distortion of news coverage can have a big cumulative effect: for instance, scare stories about the number of immigrants and asylum seekers, as propagated in, for example, the *Daily Express*, can become self-reinforcing unless corrected.

Self- and mutual criticism

The answer lies in self-criticism and mutual criticism. Every paper ought to have an independent ombudsman or reader's editor, someone on a fixed contract with no further ambitions or relationship with a paper. They should deal with readers' complaints and write weekly about how the paper has dealt with the issues of the day. These have a more extensive role than the readers' editors that most newspapers now have. The ombudsmen of *The Washington Post* and *The New York Times* write often very lively columns each weekend along these lines, which occasionally make uncomfortable reading for news executives. That takes courage on the part of the papers concerned, as well as humility. Newspapers should be much more cautious about claiming to speak on behalf of their readers. Letters and e-mails from readers are an imperfect measure of their opinions, as bogus phone-in surveys or polls show. They reflect the strength of feeling, not measure the opinions of a representative sample. More humble, less boastful, papers might also be more successful ones. A willingness openly to analyse your own faults should be linked with the exposure of the faults of others. 'Dog does not eat dog' has always been one of the most misleading phrases about newspapers. They eat each other every day in trying to do down their opponents, as their gossip columns show. What is needed, rather, is a willingness to analyse and expose faults in coverage. If misleading claims are being made about 'floods' of new workers coming in from central and eastern Europe, or about the working of the EU, they should be exposed. Of course, there is no such thing as objectivity, but there are important differences between outright lies and differences of nuance. A 'name and shame' policy would go with the grain of more vigorous competition.

The test is, of course, whether readers are better served. Are they able to find out more about what is happening in politics? Even now, big developments are covered well, often much better than in the past. Yet depth, breadth, consistency, fair-mindedness and balance are suffering. None of this need happen. Technology is both a threat to traditional newspapers and a lifeline. At present, we are in a difficult transitional period. Political journalism can—though will not necessarily—come out stronger.

Notes

1 See, for example, A. Trollope, *The Barchester Chronicles*, Oxford, Oxford University Press, 1982.
2 J. Lloyd, *What the Media Are Doing to Our Politics*, London, Constable, 2004.
3 G. Mulgan, 'Lessons of power', *Prospect*, issue 100, May 2005.
4 J. Brewer, *A Sentimental Murder: Love and Madness in the Eighteenth Century*, London, HarperCollins, 2004.
5 D. Puttnam, *Members Only? Parliament in the Public Eye: the Report of the Hansard Society Commission on the Communication of Parliamentary Democracy*, London, Hansard Society, 2005.

Morally Engaged: Reporters in Crises[1]

MARTIN WOOLLACOTT

I have a friend and colleague who had his mother send out to him in Iraqi Kurdistan the Sooty Bear glove puppet he had been given as a child. He had found that the armed 14 and 15 year olds who man road blocks could often be charmed into cooperation by the judicious production of a toy. 'We are journalists,' Sooty would proclaim in squeaky Kurdish and English, 'We are here to help you.' But are we?

In *The Journalist and the Murderer*,[2] Janet Malcolm writes of the way in which journalists sometimes betray their subjects—the way in which they are almost forced to betray them by the nature of their trade. Malcolm wrote of the special case in which reporters attach themselves to the accused in a legal trial, but what she says has relevance to all the situations in which a reporter gains the confidence, takes the time and enjoys the trust of other people. It has particular relevance, I believe, for the foreign reporter in those crisis situations of war, revolution, famine and disaster that make headlines in safer countries. Trust and confidence, but in return for what? At home in safe countries, the journalists' subjects may want something as trivial as momentary publicity, but in the war or disaster zone what is wanted may be as much as redress for terrible wrongs or rescue from the threat of death.

The ambivalence of reporters in these crisis situations is well known. On the one hand, they react as human beings to the suffering they encounter; and, on the other, they react to the story, sometimes finding themselves for purely competitive reasons searching out more suffering, or resenting the fact they have missed it—a truth illuminated in the old joke about the correspondent who 'watched in horror as his colleagues saw atrocities'.

The tension between professional need and human feeling may ease itself in a phenomenon that some correspondents experience—as do aid workers, doctors and soldiers—which is that hours, days, weeks and sometimes years after watching, dry-eyed, what would make others weep, they find unexpected tears flowing down their cheeks. My argument is not simply that correspondents are feeling human beings—obviously they are, with the contradictions noted—but that correspondents are, when they turn to the structural causes of the troubles they cover, instinctive moralisers. That is because the first question before the journalist in these situations is how to respond to the needs that stare him or her in the face.

Such journalists are therefore morally concerned almost before they are anything else. The way in which they try to redress the suffering or injustice or end the violence they witness is by assigning to it causes and by calling, at least by implication, for those causes to be addressed. Journalists argue out their morality with one another in late-night disputation and drink, in the

 Published by Blackwell Publishing Ltd, 9600 Garsington Road, Oxford OX4 2DQ, UK and 350 Main Street, Malden, MA 02148, USA

back of moving cars, and in all the places where they get stuck—waiting for spokesmen to turn up, for roads to be opened, for planes to arrive or leave. On big stories that attract a large press corps from many nations and from many different kinds of news organisations, they may come to constitute a kind of moral corporation.

Andrew Marr writes in his recent book[3] that, since the 1930s, the foreign correspondents of the democracies have been 'bringers of warnings' and of 'moral messages for the folks at home'. This is not, of course, a particularly controversial definition of their role. But when the study of the media is coloured so much by approaches that emphasise the manipulation of journalists by the powerful on the one hand, and the marketisation and trivialisation of news on the other, it is worth re-emphasising.

There are four planks to the argument about the correspondent as moraliser. First, journalists in these crises are instinctive moralisers, for the reasons suggested above. Second, their morality has a strong collective aspect. Third, they are—almost to a man, although somewhat less so to a woman—activists and interventionists. And, fourth, their moral approach has a long duration—both in that reporters take their moral capital from one crisis to another over the years, and in that some of them continue to reflect and tussle with the questions raised by particular crises long after the event.

Reporters as moralisers

Let me define the relevant situations a bit more carefully. It is a crisis story, often a war, but sometimes a more or less violence-free revolution, or a famine or other natural disaster. Crisis, I suppose, is merely to say that it is defined as such and therefore reporters are speeded to the spot, and stay there or keep going back for some time, perhaps for years, as was the case in Vietnam, and as may turn out to be the case in Iraq. I am talking about reporters in the field in crisis situations—not about commentators at home, or specialist writers, not about the home office of the news organisation or its editorial hierarchy. Nor am I talking about the foreign correspondents who plough a lonely furrow in parts of the world whose crises are rarely recognised as of the first rank and so do not attract a large press corps—nor about the more sedentary correspondents who report from stable Western countries to other stable Western countries. These are all moral fields, and they interact with international crisis journalism, but they are tangential to this subject.

As a matter of practical observation over the years, I conclude that the first thing journalists want to know in a new crisis, or one that is new to them, is what are the rights and wrongs of it. They want a briefing on the physical facts—the names, places and numbers, some history and geography—but the moral grid is primary. They get a pretty simple white hats and black hats picture to begin with. If they stuck with this as a given, they would be poor creatures, and sometimes that does happen on stories of brief prominence and short duration. But on the bigger stories the moral view is debated, it deepens, it incorporates the insights of a growing body of reporting, and it moves away from attitudinising. It evolves and changes, and it is distinctly autonomous, insulated to some extent from the pressures of home office and government.

In Denise Leith's book on war correspondents,[4] she quotes David Rieff on Bosnia: 'For me, Bosnia wasn't just a story: it was a cause. I really thought this war marked the revival of fascism in Europe . . . this is where the West really should be making a stand to fight this new kind of fascism: the revival of the ethnic state.' Rieff is exceptionally forthright and passionate, but I think it can be pretty clearly established that the press corps has taken a persistently moral position in most of the major stories of the past forty years.

That is a period that represents a journalistic generation, as veterans of Vietnam in 1965 mingle today with young reporters in Iraq, something that will only be true for a little while longer. I mean by 'moral' that their coverage was and is informed by a sense of right and wrong, that they assigned causes to the wrongs they saw, and identified agents they believed to be responsible. They wrote against the Vietnam war—that is a careful formulation, which covers the minority who were wholly against the war as well as the majority who at first called for a war fought in a different and better way and, later, because by that time they deemed the war unwinnable, also deemed it a crime to continue it.

They were almost universally against the war in Cambodia, and then, after a period of denial, against the Khmer Rouge in power, for the Vietnamese invasion, and against the American and British alliance with the Khmer Rouge rump, and the United Nation's failure of nerve in Cambodia in 1993. They were for Bangladesh and against Pakistan, and for the Indian intervention in 1971. They were against the Indian emergency a few years later. They were demanding about famine from Ethiopia onwards. They were increasingly sympathetic to the Palestinians and harder on Israel from the early 1970s up to the present day. They were sympathetic to the revolution in Iran in 1978, or, at least, unsympathetic toward the Shah. They were, of course, for the most part sympathetic to the African National Congress in South Africa throughout these years. Of course they were in favour of change in the Soviet Union, and they were advocates of more aid to the successor states.

They were indignant about Rwanda, although that was mainly after the fact. They were in favour of more forceful intervention in Bosnia in the 1990s. Finally, without dodging the issue of so-called 'patriotic journalism' after 9/11, if the American media, as opposed to most of the rest of the world's media, went into Iraq in an uncritical state of mind, they did not keep to that position for very long, Fox always excluded. Indeed they, and the media of other nations, may have gone too far in the opposite direction, although that is a shift that involves commentators at home more than reporters on the ground.

In this broad characterisation, I mean to include media of both right and left, of all the different types and different news organisations, and of many nations. The difference between foreign crisis reporting in *The Daily Telegraph* and that in *The Guardian*, for instance, is not that great—so much so that Conrad Black, the former *Telegraph* proprietor, was on one memorable occasion reduced to writing a letter of protest to his own newspaper. Some would say these were easy positions to take up and, with the exception of the Israeli–Palestinian issue, you would not be fighting any big battles with most of your readers, listeners or viewers if you did take them up.

However, in almost every crisis on this incomplete list, reporters on the ground were not where the big governments wanted them to be, and not always where their editors wanted them to be. By that I do not mean they were in outright opposition, although sometimes they were, but that coverage reflected scepticism about government policy in principle and practice, as well as about the probity of spokesmen and politicians. Above all, it reflected the feeling that the facts on the ground as they were experiencing them did not fit the claims and assertions of those responsible for policy. Of course, morality is not the same as opposition to government policy, and the right path may sometimes lie in grasping that the policy is right, or more right than wrong, and in coverage that sustains that view. But in most of the cases mentioned we can see clearly enough now, if we did not do so at the time, that policy was at least flawed and often reprehensible.

Some academic work on reporters in the field shows them as less moral and less independent than my argument suggests. One fine study, Mark Pedelty's *War Stories*,[5] concerned with coverage of El Salvador, argues that, in spite of some outstanding reporting, the media on the spot gave Americans a misleading picture, and one tailored to the interests of those in power at the time in the United States. But Pedelty's subject was a small press corps, mainly American, mainly stringers, in a crisis that never reached the first rank. His conclusions do not necessarily generalise to other situations.

A moral corporation?

In some ways, on big stories the international press acts as a single body, and not just in complaining about access, censorship and other such professional matters. It develops a collective view of the story, and that collective view is moral. On the title page of his memoir of the Vietnam war, *The Cat from Hué*,[6] the American television journalist John Laurence quotes Aeschylus:

> I have a sense of right and wrong, what's more,
> Heaven's proudest gift

His book is both about 'I' and 'we', the 'we' being the press corps as a whole, the group who talk and risk and report together. It is full of stories of what reporters did and thought as a group, accounts of arguments and debates. It shows how this collectivity, after some time on a story, says—and usually says forcefully—that a war is right or wrong, a famine avoidable, that a massacre could have been prevented, or a disaster could have been alleviated. It calls for change in the policy of governments, although the formula of 'objective journalism', particularly for Americans, means that the moral message often has to be delivered in an oblique way.

The language used here may suggest an abandonment of reporting for advocacy, and there is certainly a relatively recent muddling of reporting and comment in the press and broadcasting, which is a very debatable phenomenon. But during most of the period being discussed, from Vietnam on, the journalists concerned, for all their strongly held moral views, believed equally strongly that reporting was primary. You don't say what is going wrong—you report what is going wrong. If the South Vietnamese army is losing most of its battles, you report that. If they win some, you report that too. They would agree with Walter Lippmann that the work of reporters should not be 'confused with the work of preachers, revivalists, prophets, and agitators'.[7]

The debate about what is going on internationally is carried on everywhere—in governments, foreign offices, political parties, universities, think tanks, churches and so on. But the on-the-spot journalistic debate has the advantage of being conducted in visceral contact with events. Like that within some non-governmental organisations, but more openly, it can trump debate far from the scene, or reinforce one side of it, with its suit of authenticity, its 'thereness'. It is not just, for instance, that journalists alerted the world to the Balkan troubles, but that they also weighed on the spot the arguments about the dangers of full-scale intervention, and found them wanting.

They did so to a considerable extent collectively. This collective learns as it works and as a crisis develops. Reporters pool their experience and even their emotions. Here is David Halberstam on the early days in Vietnam, where the press corps was initially small: 'One of the best things about a press corps like the one in Saigon is that good reporters make each other better, that they push each other and that the independence of one and the courage of another become contagious.'[8] John Laurence records the shift of the Vietnam press corps from the time when 'Almost everyone wanted the American troops to win,' and 'We took it for granted . . . that the cause was honourable' to the time when they saw those same troops as 'assaulting the countryside and its people with destruction and terror'.[9]

The collective is influenced by its stars and experts—not always the same people—and by its helpers. Reporters with long experience, knowledge of local languages and proven judgement mould debate and give it a ballast of expertise. The same can be said of the interpreters, fixers and local journalists on hand, but usually unacknowledged, in a crisis situation. The most able of them—and they can be very able indeed—are sought after and wooed in the most extraordinary way, and they play a key part in the debate. The collective is also influenced by its alliances, a word that is sometimes interchangeable with sources. In the Bosnian case, an alliance of journalists, NGO people, the best UN people, some diplomats and some army officers emerged, with roughly similar views on what should be done and a common interest in getting them into the media.

The collective is also influenced by its international nature. American reporters in the Middle East, for example, bowed down for years before two commanding figures—Eric Rouleau of *Le Monde* and David Hirst of *The Guardian*. Rouleau's and Hirst's reporting—they are not of the same mind on everything, incidentally—deeply influenced all Middle East reporting, just as John Burn's reporting for *The New York Times* from Iraq influenced reporters of all nationalities—he himself is originally from Zimbabwe—in Iraq. What the international press corps produces is, in other words, international, and proofed, to some extent, from purely national assumptions and frameworks.

When the Dutch half of Papua New Guinea was effectively handed over to the Indonesians in 1962, the correspondents covering the story were so exercised, and some of them so indignant, that they debated far into the night, night after night. Bruce Grant, who was one of the dozen or so Australian, American, British, Dutch, Russian and other journalists there, recalls that 'There was such an argument that eventually we had to have a chairman and bring in a five minute rule to limit the time of the speakers'.[10] Another example of formal debate, this time on the specific issue of how to report war crimes, can be found in the meetings convened by Roy Gutman of *Newsday* during the war in Bosnia in the 1990s.

Journalistic debate does not usually take such a parliamentary guise. More often, it is of the nature referred to by Tony Clifton of *Newsweek* in *God Cried*,[11] his book on the war in Lebanon and the Israeli invasion of that country. He writes of 'going to the Lamb House'—a well known restaurant—'for shish kebab and salad and arak and talk, sitting there half the afternoon picking at garlicky chicken, filling and re-filling the arak glasses, solving the Lebanon war'. Clifton also refers to the debates at the Commodore Hotel, the main journalistic hostelry in Beirut, over Israeli bombing.

The journalistic debate can be a mere trading of received ideas, and can lead to conformity to what others have decided, or to an approach into which the whole group lazily falls simply because they need a structure into which they can put what they see. Then there is what the French sociologist Pierre Bourdieu calls the journalist's 'spectacles', the eyeglasses through which journalists recognise what are stories and what are not. There obviously is 'group think' among journalists, as in other professions. As for Bourdieu, his is a deeper point, but for the moment it is enough to say that men and women can still 'see' through spectacles—'see' something, if not everything.

But what I am talking about is a more creative, reactive process—one that involves, as I said, much argument, work, emotion, changes of mind and refinement, and may continue, long after the reporter has left the field, in the form of the books, like Lawrence's, that some journalists later produce.

The interventionist impulse

The morality of crisis reporters involves policy—policy for which reporters feel some responsibility, even if it does not specifically involve their own country. Because the West has been, and to an extent remains, one entity, a reporter from Denmark could feel responsibility for American policy in the subcontinent at the time of Bangladesh's travail, just as a reporter from Britain or Australia, allies of the United States, or Spain, an ex-ally, can feel responsibility for US policy in Iraq today. I do not speak of a reporter from Tanzania, or even from India or South Africa, or even, these days, from Russia, because the facts are that the press corps that covers crisis stories has been and is 90 per cent Western, with the important exception, already mentioned, of the local press in the countries concerned, and the local helpers of the international press, often more or less the same people. To these we need to add the new Arab news organisations such as Al Jazeera.

The reporters are there because their countries, like their news organisations, are wealthy and influential, in some cases powerful. Since that is the case, they are reporting not only what is happening in itself, but also the impact of policies that their governments have shaped, or at least the impact of policies over which their governments have some influence.

The policies can be of commission or omission. Reporters can be concerned with the working out of decisions made in the past. They can be justifying or deploring an intervention that has already occurred, asking for it to be reshaped or for it to be brought to an end, or they can be pleading for an intervention. They can be in Vietnam, in other words, or in Bosnia. Or, in southern Africa, they can be arguing for AIDS drugs prices to be cut—the intervention demanded or observed is not always military. Even in situations where the West is ostensibly a third party—an Indo-Pakistani war, for example—the question of whether Western power will or should be brought into play is always important.

In the Middle East now, there are reporters who deplore the intervention in Iraq but demand that the United States put pressure on Israel—in effect to intervene there, or, in another interpretation, to reverse the intervention that, in the shape of support for Israel, has already taken place. There are some who want intervention in both places, but none that I can see who want intervention in neither. Whether it is seen as benign or malign, Western, and particularly American, power, and how it should be used, or whether it should be used, are unavoidable factors in such stories. That is why foreign crisis reporters are, as well as moralists, also interventionists. Intervention, or the lack of it, is a central concern.

Two powerful forces push journalists in these situations towards activism. They come, most of them, from countries with large ideas about how the world should be ordered. Old notions of the white race's right and obligation to govern and decide mingle with newer, and, we think better, ideas about world governance. Second, they make for themselves a narrative and offer to their readers and viewers a narrative, of need and despair, which demands resolution. Journalists in such situations want things done. Or they want them undone. Only rarely, and usually in melancholy retrospect, do they want them not done at all.

The need to reflect

There is a twist to this moral tale that deserves particular examination. I have argued that reporters in international crises collectively embrace broad moral positions and also emphasise the primacy of reporting. But they can fall, and end by sacrificing truth to the cause. The most significant single example of this in my experience is the way in which reporters in Pnomh Penh in 1975, rightly convinced, in my view, of the uselessness and immorality of American policy at that stage, allowed this to influence their reporting of the Khmer Rouge.

That took the form, prior to the fall of Pnomh Penh, of downplaying information—and there was some—about the viciousness of the Khmer Rouge, and, later, of a reluctance to accept refugee accounts of the terrible things that were happening in Cambodia under that regime. In another example, reporters in South Africa had known for a long time what a degenerate and wilful woman Winnie Mandela had become. But they did not report it until it was unavoidable, to avoid giving ammunition to supporters of apartheid.

Again, reporters covering the Middle East knew how corrupt the Palestine authority was becoming. They somehow didn't find time to do the story, until David Hirst, a journalist whose sympathy for the Palestinians was well known, came along and broke it. For Hirst, sympathy didn't mean looking the other way.

It is this area of moral difficulty, morality within morality, that often preoccupies those reporters who carry on thinking over the implications of the stories they have covered for years afterwards. Although this is a case of individuals on a sometimes lonely quest, it also has its collective aspect, for some of the books that result join the journalistic library that influences the whole press corps in future stories. A fine example of this is Neil Sheehan's *A Bright Shining Lie*,[12] because it is an attempt to reconcile the fact that the victory of the Vietnamese communists was the only way to end the suffering in that country with the equally undoubted fact that this victory was a tragedy for many South Vietnamese. In probing the position of the early Vietnam press corps, Sheehan illustrates better than anybody else how the kind of intervention that might have succeeded in Vietnam was beyond what American society, South Vietnamese society and the armies of both were capable of doing. What is more, as William Prochnau's history of the early Vietnam press corps says, 'It would take others to see and ask the most important questions of all. Could the United States win with any South Vietnamese government? Should the United States win?'[13] As Sheehan later said, 'We missed the big one. We surely did.'

The biggest one of all, beyond the rights and wrongs of any particular intervention, is undoubtedly the question of whether the long Western tradition of activism in the world is flawed in principle as well as in application. Tiziano Terzani, the veteran Asia correspondent of *Der Spiegel* and *La Repubblica*, wrote passionately in his later years of the disastrous consequences of always seeking solutions and resolutions,[14] especially by the use of military force. David Rieff, although a journalistic supporter of intervention in the Balkans, has written critically not only of military intervention—that is a relatively easy target—but of the whole idea that things can always be fixed. He told Denise Leith, 'Just saying we came, or we are sorry, or it pains us to see people suffering, does not mean anyone knows what to do without making it worse . . . I think that most of the time we don't know what to do.'[15] Jonathan Steele of *The Guardian* has argued against 'soft' democratic interventions such as that for which he believes Western governments and NGOs were responsible in the Ukraine.

There is a connecting line from Vietnam to Iraq today via the South Asian crises, the Arab–Israeli conflict, the Iranian revolution, the Central American wars, the first Gulf War, the interventions of the 1990s in the Balkans and Africa, and the second Bush administration's invasion of Iraq. It is a story of crisis in the third world, in the Islamic world, in the Russian sphere—often crisis caused in part by earlier intervention; it raises the question of whether the response by the West or, occasionally, by others—Russia, India, Vietnam, Tanzania—should have been intervention or non-intervention; it raises the question of what form intervention should take if it is embarked upon; and it raises the question of what should be done when intervention goes wrong, as it so often does.

The journalistic tussle with the dilemmas of intervention stretches in a long arc from the 'fight a better war' men of an earlier era in Vietnam, to the journalistic supporters of intervention in the Balkans and lamenters of its absence in Africa in the 1990s, to the perplexed and agonised press corps in Iraq today. In Iraq, reporters can't undo the intervention. They must ask the harder question of how Iraqi society is going to be extricated from a terrible situation, given American weaknesses and limitations that are not going to disappear overnight. They face Iraqis who desperately want the democracy the Americans promised, others who are ruthlessly against it and still more who only want security, however achieved. And journalists there cannot even exercise their own trade, but are forced to perform it via Iraqi assistants, who have in truth become the real reporters in the field.

The argument about the moral engagement of crisis reporters runs against the normal radical view of Western journalism, which is that the press corps is largely blind to the structural causes of war and disaster, is subject to continual manipulation, is self-censoring and serves the interests of the powerful—which in the world we live in today, and have lived in for more than half a century, most often is deemed to mean the interests of those who rule the United States. John Pilger charges, in the introduction to his recent book *Tell Me No Lies*,[16] that 'in these days of corporate multimedia in thrall to profit, many journalists have become absorbed into a propaganda apparatus without consciously realising their true role'.

The argument also runs against another view of the modern media, which is that they are essentially purveyors of drama, entertainment and sensation, including the dramas of failed states, starving children and disintegrating nations. But the evidence suggests, at least to me, that the international press corps is to some extent insulated from both these tendencies. Unthinking support of government and the processing of reality as entertainment are not what happens on the ground when reporters see human suffering and despair. This is particularly the case when a big story attracts a semi-permanent body of reporters over a fair amount of time, and the corps develops its internal debate and public opinion.

Some years ago, in an introduction to a collection of pieces by James Cameron,[17] I wrote that Cameron's first instinct on arriving on a story was 'to look for the moral high ground'. If Cameron sometimes erred by being partisan, and he did, his virtue was that he expressed with unusual eloquence the moral instinct of journalists. The message, one of some moral weight and complexity, that a crisis press corps sends out can of course be waylaid. Editors alter, shorten or underplay stories. Proprietors make their views clear to a news organisation's hierarchy and reinforce its tendency to timidity. Influential home-based commentators obscure and overlay the reporting on the ground, and some readers, listeners and viewers don't wholly grasp the difference. Governments pressure news organisations. But something gets through. Crisis reporters have had and continue to have a unique role, above all in testing and reflecting on the interventionist tradition, whether it takes the form of the US Marines or that of debt forgiveness or that of Médecins Sans Frontières. Action, and its consequences—or inaction, and its consequences—are their ultimate subjects.

Notes

1 This chapter is an amended and shortened version of a paper produced during a three-month research fellowship at the Institute of Advanced Study at La Trobe University in Melbourne, Australia, to which institutions and to the Media Studies Department of that university the author wishes to express his gratitude.

2 J. Malcolm, *The Journalist and the Murderer*, Washington, DC, Alfred A. Knopf, 1990.

3 A. Marr, *My Trade: a Short History of British Journalism*, London, Macmillan, 2004.

4 D. Leith, *Bearing Witness: the Lives of War Correspondents and Journalists*, Melbourne, Random House, 2004.

5 M. Pedelty, *War Stories: the Culture of Foreign Correspondents*, London, Routledge, 1995.

6 J. Laurence, *The Cat from Hué: a Vietnam War Story*, New York, Public Affairs Limited, 2002.

7 W. Lippmann, *Liberty and the News*, New York, Transaction, 1995.

8 D. Halberstam, 'Innocents abroad', Nieman Foundation, occasional paper, autumn 1994.

9 Laurence, *The Cat from Hué*.

10 B. Grant, personal communication, 2004.

11 T. Clifton and C. Leroy, *God Cried*, London, Quartet, 1983.
12 N. Sheehan, *A Bright Shining Lie: John Paul Vann and America in Vietnam*, New York, Random House, 1988.
13 W. Prochnau, *Once upon a Distant War: Reporting from Vietnam*, Edinburgh, Mainstream Publishing, 1996.
14 T. Terzani, *Letters against the War*, New Delhi, India Research Press, 2002.
15 Leith, *Bearing Witness*.
16 J. Pilger, ed., *Tell Me No Lies: Investigative Journalism and its Triumphs*, London, Jonathan Cape, 2004.
17 J. Cameron, *Cameron in 'The Guardian' 1974–1984*, London, Hutchinson, 1985.

Lacking a Clear Narrative: Foreign Reporting after the Cold War

SUZANNE FRANKS

GLOBALISATION, the interdependent nature of modern society and the precarious state of international relations post 9/11 make the case for well-explained foreign news coverage more important than ever. We really need to know and understand what is happening beyond our shores. Coincidentally, we also live in a shrinking world in which communications and technological innovations make it easier to report from faraway places. Yet this presents a paradox. For just as it is more vital to understand what is happening across the globe and it is simpler to report the story, we are less inclined to do it. There are several reasons for this. But the root cause is the overall way in which we now perceive certain parts of the world and the changing priorities in news reporting.

Some areas of the globe are bathed in light and regularly reported upon. In particular, the United States features almost daily upon TV news bulletins in the United Kingdom. Yet other countries, indeed whole regions of the world, hardly appear at all. Huge nations such as Brazil or most of the rest of South America rarely make the UK news. Even China, which is of such significance as an emerging economic superpower, receives only the scantiest of coverage. This contrast between areas we hear about and others that we do not raises a distinction between the 'foreign other' and the 'familiar other'. In the former category are those faraway countries of which we know very little, whilst the 'familiar other' refers to places abroad such as the US or those parts of Western Europe that we regularly hear about, and which are more likely to be reported in a rounded, comprehensive fashion.[1]

According to received wisdom, reporters will go to where news is happening. Of course, the reverse is equally true; that news depends upon where there are journalists to report it. The US, for example, is well served by foreign bureaux and correspondents, but much of South America is covered only by stringers. Indeed, the coverage of particular events can depend upon the prior deployment of reporters. The Ethiopian famine in 1984 became a major story because a cameraman and TV reporter happened to be there. However, there were worse disasters, including famines, that led to many more deaths in the second half of the twentieth century, and yet did not make the news. The Chinese famine of 1959–60 is now thought to have killed up to thirty million people, but it never featured as a major news story. The most devastating war since 1945 was the conflict in the Congo in the mid- to late 1990s, sometimes called 'Africa's hidden first world war', in which an estimated three and a half million people were killed. Once again, this

Published by Blackwell Publishing Ltd, 9600 Garsington Road, Oxford OX4 2DQ, UK and 350 Main Street, Malden, MA 02148, USA 91 hardly rated as a news story because, at least for television, no one was there to report it.

A letter smuggled out of Juba in southern Sudan in 1992 summed up poignantly the arbitrary nature of what makes the news: 'Lucky are the people of Yugoslavia and Somalia as the world's eyes rest on them. Condemned are the people of Juba . . . it may be a blessing to die in front of a camera—then at least the world will get to know about it. For it is painful to die or be killed without anyone knowing it.'[2] And the former EU commissioner for humanitarian affairs Emma Bonino posed the question 'What does it take for a humanitarian crisis to make it into prime time slots on radio or television?' She went on to observe that 'Deaths are essential, preferably hundreds of them in places that have not captured media attention before. News is by definition new . . . I became aware that for every humanitarian crisis that made it into the headlines, there were dozens that went unnoticed.'[3]

There is always a capricious element to news coverage and which stories happen to make a bulletin on a particular day, but this is even more pronounced in the case of foreign news reporting. Some stories and some parts of the world will feature whilst others will remain unreported. These wide gaps in foreign coverage are even more obvious on the American networks. Tom Fenton, a CBS foreign news correspondent for thirty-four years, has recently chronicled the decline in international news reporting in the US in his book *Bad News*. One example he cites is that in the first ten months of 2004, CBS Evening News featured only four items on China; a light-hearted look at a phoney version of Clinton's biography, a story on stem cell research and two items on pandas.[4]

An important reason behind the changes in foreign news coverage is the gradual reduction in the numbers of resident correspondents, both for financial and editorial reasons. When a regular reporter is replaced by a casual stringer arrangement, this has implications for the way in which stories are covered. If an institution has invested in a member of staff, there will be good reasons for taking regular material from that person and running his or her stories. In the case of a stringer, there is no longer such an obligation.

It was in the days of Empire and the immediate postcolonial period that foreign news was at its zenith. Faraway places such as Africa and Asia were still covered in a regular, incremental fashion by locally based correspondents. Even middle-market newspapers such as the *Daily Express* or the *Daily Mail* had large foreign news staffs, who covered stories from places such as Kenya, Rhodesia/Zimbabwe or India in a comprehensive fashion. As the end-of-Empire narrative mutated into a Cold War story, the widespread interest continued. Most foreign conflicts could be viewed as part of the global stand-off between the superpowers. It was as the Cold War waned that interest in many remote places began to dissipate. Of course wars and fighting continued, but they were no longer explicable in a colonial or Cold War framework and so were often dismissed as 'tribal' or 'ethnic' conflicts, neither comprehensible nor worthy of much interest.

News saves lives

The distinguished journalist Godfrey Hodgson, writing in 2000 as head of the Reuters Foundation, expressed a pragmatic and interesting view on this development:

Viewers and readers who are less interested in international news than they were before the collapse of the Soviet Union are not stupid . . . they are behaving in a perfectly rational way. From 1914 to 1991 international news was frightening. It could kill you. Now rightly or wrongly, people are not afraid that a new war is going to affect them. Its consequences will be borne by foreigners with ragged clothes . . . or by a small handful of professional soldiers . . . Western readers and viewers have no motive beyond idle curiosity to concern themselves with events abroad.[5]

However, a year after Hodgson wrote that, international news became frightening again. Indeed, the viewers and readers whom he had been describing had been under a misapprehension that news from abroad no longer mattered. Once more it was important to understand foreign parts, but the question is how well we are being served and whether current reporting is good enough. Tom Fenton makes a powerful case for why journalists should be explaining and understanding, and he tells one particularly chilling story on this theme. In May 2001, the infamous Mohammed Atta went to a US Department of Agriculture officer in Florida and tried to get a loan for a 'crop dusting' scheme. He told the loan officer, Johnell Bryant, that he wanted to replace the six seats in a twin-engine passenger aircraft with a chemical tank. She rejected the application as the idea sounded impractical. Atta meanwhile noticed an aerial photograph of Washington on her office wall and offered to buy it. He asked her to identify key landmarks; the White House and Pentagon. As they chatted, Atta enquired if she had ever heard of an organisation of people disillusioned with their governments called Al Qaeda, and of Osama bin Laden, who would one day be known as the 'world's greatest leader'.[6]

None of these details rang any bells with Miss Bryant. But four months later, after 9/11 when she recognised Atta's picture, she went to the FBI. Her recollections confirmed what they already knew from another source; that Al Qaeda had originally intended to use small planes packed with explosives rather than hijacked airliners. Miss Bryant was mortified that she had not been able to alert anyone before the disaster. But as she said to ABC news, 'How could I have known?' Tom Fenton's argument is that if the journalists had been doing their job, then people like Johnell Bryant would have heard of bin Laden and Al Qaeda and lives could have been saved. In the aftermath of 9/11 there was much talk about 'joining up the dots' and news reporting had a key part to play in this.

Saving money

Over the years since the Cold War, news coverage has become subject to ever greater financial pressures. Television has also replaced newspapers as the source of news for most of the population. In a less fragmented market, a classy TV news bulletin in prime time could pull in a large and well-heeled audience for the advertisers. Invariably within a deregulated, commercial environment news has come to be regarded as a cost centre rather than the profit centre, which it had hitherto been. This makes the case for foreign news even more difficult, as it is usually calculated to be at least twice as expensive as home news. ITN has struggled over the past few years to offer adequate coverage of foreign affairs as it has come under ever increasing commercial pressures, just like the US networks.

Cutting back on foreign coverage and shutting foreign bureaux, as the US networks have done, is a quick way to save money. The alternative to well-informed locally based correspondents is fireman-style reporting. An experienced reporter, well attuned to the needs of the various bulletins, is sent to the scene of a far-off disaster and instructed to produce material within a few hours. Given the wide multiplicity of outlets, he is expected to broadcast almost continual reports or 'two-way' interviews. This leaves very little time to go out and find anything about the story, because the reporter, who has probably not been in the country for long, is effectively tethered to the satellite up-link, thus becoming what is known in the trade as a 'dish monkey'. In Kate Adie's words, 'someone stuck next to a dish for hours on end is the last creature on earth to have learned anything new, and probably unaware of a corpse twenty yards away'.[7] The nature of this kind of reporting is completely different from a thoughtful, well-crafted report delivered by a correspondent who has worked and lived in the location, or who at least is highly knowledgeable about the area.

The other way in which international news is now covered involves more use of 'packaging'. Disconnected agency pictures are voiced over by a reporter at base and occasionally intercut with interviews from an expert or pundit. The result is coverage that is authorless and frequently difficult to follow or understand. Very often, this kind of reporting is perceived as boring by the viewer, because it offers such an inadequate level of explanation and understanding. The danger is that this becomes a self-fulfilling prophecy, in that managers who are looking for reasons to reduce foreign coverage will say that audiences find it a turn-off. If international news is reduced to a series of disassociated disasters conveyed in an anchorless way, then it usually will be boring. Broadcasters must acknowledge that to make news interesting and to enable it to fulfil the vital function of informing audiences, it needs to be properly explained, and that requires some investment in the news-gathering process.

One of the most obvious features of contemporary TV news is the vast expansion of outlets. We have an abundance of twenty-four-hour news channels, but the paradox is that this has hardly brought greater comprehension about far-flung places. First, there is the problem that Kate Adie identified: reporters are so busy filing for the voracious bulletins that they have far less time to find out what is going on. Second, there is the question of resources that are spread thinner; and third, there is the tension between speed and understanding. Daya Thussu has written about the tendency towards 'infotainment' in 24/7 live rolling news.[8] And Nik Gowing, a highly experience news reporter, has pointed out the worrying lag between pictures and explanation. News channels are obsessed with 'going live' to wherever there are pictures of something happening, but 'the capacity to broadcast pictures and capability to broadcast real-time pictures from places like the West Bank and the Middle East is now ahead of our ability to do journalism and to find the answer to the question "why, what, where, when and how"'.[9] It is important that editors and producers realise that simply showing the very latest images from somewhere is usually not enough to adequately convey what is happening there. There is no substitute for intelligent reporting.

Surveying the past thirty years, the pattern of reporting developing countries on television is not a consistent one of decline. There were, overall, certain stories and periods where the coverage offered greater understanding and coherence. The BBC's treatment of India provides an example of remarkably well explained and informative reporting over a long period. There were several reasons for this. The existence of a large and vocal expatriate community in the UK meant that the coverage was closely watched and monitored for bias or lack of understanding. Second, there was the presence within the BBC of many people who had once worked and lived in India, and who still had a great interest in the country. Third, the BBC was represented in India for many years by the correspondent Mark Tully, who had developed an extraordinary knowledge of the country. He was the complete opposite of the fireman reporter and he ensured that the profile of India remained high within the BBC; in particular, he was always eager to help film crews and documentary teams wanting to make programmes there. And, fourth, the prominence of the BBC World Service within India meant that Tully was continually kept on his toes, because his material was being heard by millions locally, where he lived. The result was, for many years, a high level of coverage and understanding of India within the UK. So despite all the advances of technology and communication, there was probably greater knowledge and awareness of Indian events some twenty-odd years ago than there is today. Everyone knew that Indira Gandhi was Prime Minister of India. It would be interesting to see how many British viewers could name the current or previous Indian PM.

Current affairs

The most interesting coverage of foreign affairs is often the longer item that is something beyond a basic news report. This enables a journalist to spend some time on location, more than is required for a three-minute news item, and to present a far more nuanced, comprehensive view of a foreign story. With more scope to research and film and a longer slot for transmission, this kind of report gives a far greater opportunity to explain the background to complicated issues. There is a fine tradition of current affairs documentary reporting in the UK: strands such as *World in Action, TV Eye* and *Panorama* have regularly featured peak-time programmes on foreign topics, which have won awards. But in recent years this has become a disappearing genre. ITV is no longer interested in such material and the BBC tends to show it out of peak time or on minority channels.

The Third World and Environment Broadcasting Project has been tracking television coverage of foreign countries, in particular the developing world, since 1989. It was established in that year as a lobbying group in response to the proposed deregulation in the Broadcasting Bill. There was concern that as a result of the lighter regulation of ITV this legislation would precipitate a reduction in the amount of international coverage on television in the UK. 3WE has continued to monitor the level of foreign factual programming since 1989 and its regular reports indicate a steady decline in the amount of airtime devoted to serious coverage of foreign affairs. Its most recent report, *The World on the Box*,[10] which monitored the coverage in 2003, confirms that trend. The total hours may not have changed very much, but at least a third of foreign programming now consists of travel programmes plus TV makeover or reality shows located abroad—programmes such as *Costa Living* or *A Place in the Sun*, or even *I'm a Celebrity, Get Me Out of Here*.

Serious coverage of developing countries on terrestrial channels and anywhere near mainstream viewing hours is slowly disappearing. On ITV in 2003 there was not a single foreign programme under the categories politics, development, environment or human rights. This demonstrates that the concerns expressed by those who started the monitoring project in 1989 were indeed correct,[11] because in that year a quarter of all serious foreign factual programming in the UK appeared on ITV. Over the preceding years there had been excellent examples of foreign current affairs documentaries on ITV, such as John Pilger's work on the Cambodian catastrophe or Charles Stewart and Peter Gills' films on the Ethiopian famine. In their most recent report on public service broadcasting, Ofcom are proposing to remove altogether the obligation on ITV and Five to include programmes on 'matters of international significance and interest'.

Meanwhile, the pattern on the BBC, according to the report on television in 2003, has been to continue to make documentaries on foreign subjects but to relegate them to the digital fringe, instead of the mainstream terrestrial channels. It is only very rarely that a strand such as *Panorama* will tackle a topic on the developing world, and even that will not now appear at peak time. Anecdotally, it seems that 2005 will indicate a different pattern because of the emphasis on the G8 and all the surrounding programmes on Africa, but there is not much evidence to indicate that this is more than a one-season wonder and a coincidental boost to Charter renewal.

News habits

There has certainly been an emphasis upon coverage from Africa to coincide with the twentieth anniversary of Live Aid and the agenda of the UK presidency of the G8. Whilst this has highlighted the issues of poverty and development, there has been a noticeable tendency to rely on an interlocutor in many of these programmes. They have tended to feature a white celebrity such as Rolf Harris or Bob Geldof to tell the story, and in many of them there was hardly an African voice, let alone much sense of African agency (just as the Live8 concert featured hardly any African singers!). This is a pity, as there has been a growing awareness over the past twenty years of the need to use authentic voices and to give agency to people even if they do not speak perfect English. Michael Buerk recalls that when he filmed in Ethiopia in 1984, 'there was no question of interviewing anybody who didn't speak English in those days . . . because our cultural assumption—indeed, our editorial policy—was that we didn't interview anybody who couldn't speak English'. Buerk recalls the notorious story of the journalist who went round Kinshasa airport shouting 'Anyone here been raped and speaks English?': 'we did not have subtitles and we did not have voice-overs in those days; if you did not speak English your voice was not heard. So that if other things have deteriorated (in terms of news coverage) this is one thing that has absolutely improved since those days'.[12]

There has been a gradual shift in broadcasting conventions towards allowing people—whether individuals with learning difficulties or representatives from other cultures—to use their own voice. As Michael Buerk points out, news coverage has followed this pattern too, which gives more agency to those who are the subjects of a report. It would be disappointing if this trend were in any way to be reversed, and there is a need to be vigilant against coverage that appears patronising and condescending.

Another pattern in the way that news is reported is the inexorable move towards what Andrew Marr calls 'an office-based editorial culture'. This is 'the journalism of people sitting in front of screens in airless offices on the outskirts of towns under the lash to be "productive" . . . where "reporting is seen as expensive and the massive global PR industry is available through every national hack's laptop."'[13] Since foreign reporting is regarded as the most expensive, it is especially vulnerable to the 'stay at home' tendency. The whole trend towards 'packaging' other peoples' pictures and material is part of this syndrome. Yet good and enlightened foreign news coverage depends upon reporters leaving the office and really understanding what is going on in other countries. It is not only journalists who need to get out: editors and more senior figures also benefit from travelling out and about to the places where news is happening.

The effect of new technology has changed the whole balance between the reporter and base. The result is more emphasis upon what the desk wants and less autonomy for the reporter in the field. In the past, when communications were less sophisticated, a foreign correspondent could even head off out of range for days on end to bring back a report. Today, he or she is more likely to have to call in on the hour on the satellite phone to discuss the next live insert. More importantly, the correspondent will often be told by the desk what the story is all about, and this distorts the balance of news. Historically, the foreign correspondent was able to offer the editor some new information or opinion. Now he or she is more likely to be fulfilling the pre-ordained views of the news desk back home.

Many veteran foreign correspondents have complained about this shift in the balance of power. The implication is that if well-informed and well-connected foreign correspondents are not listened to, then there will once again be a danger that significant developments will be missed. Of course, after 9/11 everyone poured resources into covering Islamic fundamentalism and Afghanistan. But what are the future stories and issues that we should be paying heed to—developments in the former Soviet Union or relations between China and its neighbours? This is where we should be listening to experienced and knowledgeable voices.

Future stories

The Cold War gave a clear narrative to world events. It was obviously a matter of life and death, and it offered a straightforward comprehensive explanation to what was happening in the world. After the Cold War, many foreign news outlets no longer seemed to know how to tell a story and in some cases they gave up on the plot altogether. There were also inexcusable cases such as the Rwanda genocide and its aftermath in 1994, where they even told the wrong story. In part, this was the fault of the aid agencies, but the journalists were not sufficiently well informed to question the agencies' interpretation and for several days were reporting completely inaccurately on the camps in Zaire.[14]

News depends upon a story, a narrative that has to be seen to be going somewhere. If it just appears to go round endlessly in circles, then people will stop being interested. The problem with much foreign news coverage today is that it appears episodic and sometimes meaningless. Obviously there are plenty of stories to report in a post Cold War order, but they are rather more complicated and internecine than a simple tale of East versus West. They require a far more sophisticated level of understanding and explanation in order to make sense for the reader or viewer. Intelligent and well-researched news reporting is a vital part of that understanding. One clear example of this is the tendency of the news media to report something as a 'humanitarian crisis' and focus on humanitarian solutions, while failing to engage with the underlying and complex political issues.

We do not only need better foreign news for its own sake but also because it is of vital importance, even to our own safety. In an extreme case, this is why the penny-pinching arguments about saving money on foreign reporting sound rather thin. The best way to invest in improved news-gathering is to increase the knowledge base of foreign reporting by recruiting and nurturing people who will be sufficiently well informed to provide good coverage. Even if foreign bureaux are not going to be reopened, it is vital to ensure ways of developing adequate local expertise in important parts of the globe well in advance of an urgent crisis. This is the bedrock for interesting and comprehensible foreign coverage, but there are also other ways in which editors can make improvements, from getting out and about themselves to thinking more carefully about the way in which reporters are deployed abroad. There is also scope for trying to refocus the news agenda. Too often, news from developing countries is the same diet of war, disaster and poverty. This breeds a clichéd view of these countries and leads to image fatigue amongst audiences. Editorial policy should aim consciously to widen this agenda so that poorer countries are covered in a more rounded, normal fashion.

The vital counterpoint to better foreign news reporting is more current affairs and documentary coverage of international topics, preferably at a time when viewers are able to watch it. This is a clear way in which the news agenda can be widened away from the headline coverage of events, which are usually in the category of war and disaster. In a complicated world, well-made current affairs documentaries have a key role to play in providing explanations and setting issues in context, and in providing a more rounded view. NGOs such as the International Broadcasting Trust and 3WE have done much to highlight this deficiency, but this is part of a wider trend within broadcasting away from serious factual material and towards 'lifestyle' or so-called 'reality' programming. They should continue to use every opportunity to make the case to conserve serious current affairs, so that commissioning editors and strand editors will respond. Yet, ultimately, this is an argument that needs to be heard at a higher level. It is a matter for Ofcom and the new BBC regulatory body to embrace the part that international factual programmes have to play in any kind of public service environment. This obligation to include comprehensive coverage of news and current affairs on world issues was made explicit in the 2003 Communications Act, but it is up to the regulators to make sure that it happens in practice.

In a domestic setting, journalism has a key duty to hold institutions and leaders to account. This role is equally important in an international setting, but even more difficult to fulfil. Huge and powerful bureaucracies such as the United Nations and all its associated bodies are rarely investigated; similarly, the activities of multinational corporations in developing countries and their culpability in corruption are extremely important, if difficult, issues. A third area is the explosion in NGOs and international aid organisations. Since the 1980s there has been a transformation in their power and influence, but journalists rarely ever investigate their activities. Most of the media remain in a mind-set that these are simply do-gooding charity outfits, which we have no business to question. All of these and many more are the kinds of subject that foreign current affairs programmes might pursue.

Perhaps the most compelling reason of all for good foreign reporting is that the demarcation between home and abroad is dissolving as never before. This is not simply a matter of globalisation, but the fact that domestic and foreign matters intersect in an ever more complicated way. A London commuter worries about safety on the tube, but this is linked to what is going on in Pakistan and elsewhere. Thirty years ago there were explosions caused by Irish terrorists, and the nature of the threat was essentially a domestic matter stretching only across the Irish Sea. Today, the bombs are the result of far more wide-ranging international forces from Islamic extremism, war in the Middle East and international terrorist networks. More than ever before, we can only make sense of what is happening in our own back yard if we are properly informed about what is happening far away.

In an interdependent world, the problems of inadequate foreign news would be best solved if the powers that be were to recast foreign reporting as an extension of domestic news. Our security and well-being at home depends upon well-explained and informed foreign news. That is the best reason for monitoring and for ensuring that the standard of international coverage remains high. The 3WE report on foreign factual programming on television performs an important role in measuring and recording the levels of inter-national coverage. It would be good if this process could be widened to include an audit of international news, both broadcast and in print. Monitor-ing the coverage is the first step towards maintaining quality. In the US, foreign news reporting has all but disappeared. No one suggests that could happen in the UK, but there is a danger of a continuing trend of disinterest in serious coverage of foreign parts. If too many corners are cut, then the reporting is inadequate and therefore incomprehensible and boring. That becomes a way of justifying further cutbacks.

It is vital for journalists to be able to do an adequate job—to tell the public and opinion formers about the complexity of the world out there, and try to explain to them the ways in which different people and cultures think. If they can only present the simplest of stories or pander to stereotypes, eventually we are all at risk. Therefore, the responsibility for communicating the news from distant places belongs to the reporters. But, equally, there is a much wider responsibility to keep open reasonable spaces in which they can report. News organisations, viewers, lobbyists and regulators should all be on their guard.

Notes

1 E. Michail, 'Foreign news: British media and foreign others as seen in the media coverage of the Balkans in the first half of the 20th century', paper presented to the CCBH *History of the Media* conference, London, June 2005.

2 G. Olsen, N. Carstensen and K. Hoyen, 'Humanitarian crises: testing the "CNN effect"', *Forced Migration Review*, Number 16, 2003, p. 39.

3 'Bringing humanitarian news into prime time', *International Herald Tribune*, 28 June 1996.

4 T. Fenton, *Bad News: the Decline of Reporting the Business of News and the Danger to Us All*, New York, HarperCollins, 2005.

5 G. Hodgson, 'The end of the grand narrative and the death of news', *Historical Journal of Film, Radio and Television*, vol. 20, no. 1, March 2000, p. 27.

6 Fenton, *Bad News*, p. 5.

7 K. Adie, *The Kindness of Strangers*, London, Headline, 2002.

8 D. K. Thussu, 'Live TV and bloodless deaths: war, infotainment and 24/7 news, in D. K. Thussu and D. Freedman, eds, *War and the Media*, London, Sage, 2003.

9 N. Gowing, 'Journalists and war: the troubling new tensions post 9/11', in Thussu and Freedman, *War and the Media*, p. 235.

10 C. Dover and S. Barnett, *The World on the Box: International Issues in News and Factual Programmes on UK Television 1975–2003*, University of Westminster, Communications and Media Research Institute/Report for the Third World and Environment Broadcasting Project.

11 J. Firebrace, ed., *The Future of Television's Coverage of Global Issues*, London, Third World and Environment Broadcasting Project/International Broadcasting Trust, 1990.

12 Interview, November 2004.

13 A. Marr, *My Trade: a Short History of British Journalism*, London, Macmillan, 2004, p. 383.

14 See G. Alagiah, *A Passage to Africa*, London, Little, Brown, 2001, p. 120.

Digitising Democracy

GEORGINA BORN

Introduction

RECENT years have seen attempts to rethink the nature and scope of public service broadcasting and to justify its existence anew. It is uncontroversial that the original conditions—technological, economic, political, social and cultural—that fostered the birth of PSB and sustained it over decades have undergone such radical transformation that the concept and practice of PSB demand to be reconceived.[1] One trigger for such a rethinking is the transition to digital media, a change signalled by the common move to substitute for PSB the phrase 'public service communications'.

But this transition is itself intimately related to wider social and cultural changes. In the words of recent commentators, 'The decay in the old idea of "public service broadcasting" has gone hand in hand with the decay in the old idea of a [national] culture'.[2] On the one hand, contemporary societies have witnessed the growth of an unprecedented and institutionalised individualism;[3] on the other, European democracies aspire to a mature cosmopolitanism encapsulated in the notion of a 'community of communities'.[4] As Ulrich Beck puts it, 'Europe today has been cosmopolitanised from within . . . [It] is if anything in the vanguard of this process.'[5] The moral settlement of the nation-state is affected by both transnational migration and internal restructuring; in consequence, cosmopolitan ideas of citizenship now coexist with new nationalisms and fundamentalisms. In such conditions, the social fabric no longer comprises—if it ever did—a cohesive, unified culture built on shared norms, values and traditions. Instead, it has become pluralistic and culturally heterogeneous to an unprecedented degree—a situation of which, in the age of the 'war on terror' and in the aftermath of the London bombings of July 2005, we need hardly be reminded.

The changing landscape is registered in the Communications Act 2003, which updates the Reithian concept of PSB by stipulating both that television should respond to and stimulate the diversity of cultural activity in Britain, and that it should reflect the lives and concerns of different communities and cultural traditions within the United Kingdom.[6] In a similar vein, the government's 2005 Green Paper on the future of the BBC genuflects to the cosmopolitan present when it lists among the BBC's core purposes 'Making us aware of different cultures and alternative viewpoints, through programmes that reflect the lives of other people and other communities within the UK'. As though acknowledging the recent anxiety over the potentially divisive tensions between social integration and diversity,[7] the Green Paper immediately adds to those purposes 'Reflecting and

 Published by Blackwell Publishing Ltd, 9600 Garsington Road, Oxford OX4 2DQ, UK and 350 Main Street, Malden, MA 02148, USA

strengthening our cultural identity through original programming at UK, national and regional level, on occasion bringing audiences together for shared experiences'.[8] Yet for all the pious principles, in the words of a leading media executive, 'Multicultural Britain continues to be one of the most under-reported areas of British life';[9] while in its survey of contemporary race relations, the Parekh Report concluded that Britain's mainstream media continue to proffer negative, simplistic or stereotyped representations of ethnic minorities, when they are not simply rendered invisible, linking this state of affairs to the perpetuation by media organisations of discriminatory employment and access practices.[10] The reality of social and cultural difference and diversity, then, poses challenges to the media on a scale to which they have only begun to respond, challenges compounded both by contemporary commercial restructuring and by digital technologies.

My intention in this essay is to sketch the contours of current discussions of digitisation and public service communications, and to weigh them against the challenge posed by multi-ethnic and multi-faith Britain. I make two overall criticisms. First, I argue that the discussions have lacked a sufficiently informed, nuanced and imaginative account of the public service power of digital media. In illustration, I outline the BBC's early activities in new media, showing how they exceed the current debates. Second, I argue that attempts to reconceive PSC for the digital age have been weakened by the absence of a grounding in political philosophy—in particular, by lack of attention to well-established debates concerned with reframing democratic theory in terms of the 'democratic politics of difference'[11] that arise in conditions of cultural pluralism and social inequality. I survey aspects of these philosophical debates and draw out central principles. Finally, on the basis of these arguments, I outline some structural proposals that elaborate on the elective affinity between digital media and the politics of difference, proposals with practical implications for how public service communications can utilise digital media radically to enhance and enrich the former mass communications paradigm of PSB.

Digitisation and PSB: policy thinking . . .

In what follows, I take stock of both policy and academic debates on the future of public service broadcasting in light of digitisation. After almost a decade of policy initiatives on digitisation it is striking that, for all the talk of convergence, they have been limited to a focus exclusively on either the Internet or the advent of digital television (DTV). In both directions the same themes repeatedly occur; indeed, there is something of a conceptual lockdown in the way digitisation is framed. Two thematic clusters can be discerned.

First, an economistic discourse has held sway, one that is remarkably continuous with the Peacock Report of 1986[12] and that has been dominant in policy thinking in the last decade. The tenor of this discourse is well analysed by Barnett and Barwise, as it was by Graham and Davies,[13] and their criticisms of its assumptions and arguments need no recapitulation here. Instead, I want to focus on its characteristic preoccupations. Prominent are a linked set of concerns with competition, market failure and the legitimate scope and limits of public intervention via PSB, as well as with the role of digital media in boosting the United Kingdom's prosperity and competitiveness: 'We aim to make the UK a world leader in digital excellence . . . If the UK is to thrive in the future, to succeed in competitive markets and enjoy better and better services, all of us need to be . . . living and working in a digital world'.[14] A key issue is whether market and technological changes imply that PSB should be confined to market failure provision in which it supplies only those services or content that commercial actors tend to under-supply—a debate that has elicited hawkish criticisms of the BBC's entry into digital markets;[15] or, in the more extreme position, whether they imply that public funding should be phased out entirely in favour of subscription funding for PSBs such as the BBC.[16] If the core danger identified in this discourse, in the words of a leading Ofcom figure, is that of 'pre-empting the market',[17] the benefits of digitisation are portrayed repeatedly in terms of growing consumer choice and interactivity. 'Consumers [are enjoying] a gradual but historic act of liberation: the transfer of power into their hands to choose, to select, to schedule and to create, as a result of converging markets and services, powered by the flexibility of digital technology'.[18] Or again, in the Green Paper, 'The increase in channels means more choice . . . Digital technology is likely to provide exciting new opportunities for audiences, who need no longer be so passive . . . [It] may signal the end of broadcasting as we know it, allowing people to watch and listen to whatever they want whenever they want to.'[19]

The second thematic cluster in policy writing concerns political and social matters, specifically the role of digitisation in combating the 'digital divide' and mitigating social exclusion, and the development of e-government—the delivery of government and public services online. In government thinking the two are intimately connected, as they are to DTV policies. A core government 'vision' is that, since 'the market alone will never deliver a fully digital Britain',[20] DTV can be 'a means to provide all citizens with access to e-government services', with the 'expectation that DTV can help to overcome the digital divide . . . DTV can reach those groups who do not have a PC or have difficulties using one. [It] has the potential to deliver much greater participation in the information society—with the attendant social and economic benefits.'[21] DTV is conceived instrumentally as a means of achieving universal digital access, and the Green Paper directs the BBC to add to its purposes 'Building digital Britain'. The government's strongest message on digitisation and PSB therefore amounts to the BBC taking 'a leading role in the process of digital switchover . . . [thereby] helping to bring the benefits of digital services to all households'.[22] Such an intimate yoking of the BBC to what has been a highly controversial policy appears to be considered unproblematic. In reality, it threatens to compromise the BBC's independence by rendering it a proxy for government.[23] A similar point is made by another commentator when querying the potential elision of e-government directives with the BBC's digital strategies for political re-engagement: 'There is a fine line between promoting political [interaction] and delivering government information.'[24]

If the Communications Act and the Green Paper put the creation of a digital Britain high on the agenda, then they have done so in restricted terms, at the expense of imaginative thinking about digitisation's potential political, cultural and social benefits and PSB's role in realising them. There are, however, signs of an incipient shift in the dominant terms of policy debate; it is palpable in the gap between two IPPR publications on digitisation from 2003 and 2005. The 2003 paper dwells on competition-driven issues: whether market failure justifies PSB activities in online markets and whether public subsidy is merited in discussion fora and search functions, in passing posing the protection of 'public service values' against the promotion of innovation.[25] The 2005 paper, in contrast, evidences a different framing. Cautioning that despite the United Kingdom's enviable ICT infrastructure, 'We haven't developed the skills or imagination to use it effectively',[26] it proposes that government must face the complex realities that lie beyond simple universal access, such as psychological and cultural barriers to digital take-up and low morale among public sector staff faced with the digitisation of services.[27] It continues that digital networks enable 'new types of politics . . . [and can support] communities in a way never seen before [through] local and neighbourhood level communication . . . But why only appeal to place-based digital initiatives? Civic- and interest-based online activities' should also be encouraged. It goes on, 'Government will squash intermediary type activities if it endorses them too heavily, or replicates them, but it can offer tacit endorsement by supporting them with grants.' Moreover, the BBC should become a key agent 'in the development of a "multi-tiered public realm"', encouraging grass-roots 'social enterprises' and the local generation of content.[28] A recent Cabinet Office report echoes this endorsement of the importance of public intervention, specifically by an innovative BBC: 'The role of the BBC will be critical in broadband delivery. The BBC has the resources to experiment in ways that the commercial market cannot and to provide support . . . for the nascent broadband content sector. The Graf report into the BBC's online activity set out measures to . . . mitigate any crowding out effect of the BBC in the marketplace.'[29] Critical of narrow policy discourse, the recent IPPR document nudges impatiently at its limits, etching out a larger conceptual space.

. . . And academic thinking

The later IPPR paper undoubtedly owes a debt to academic writings on PSB and digitisation, which have taken thinking further. Academic studies also focus on either the Internet or the future of television. Theoretically, when exploring the democratic potential of digital media, many writers make reference to Jürgen Habermas's concept of the public sphere,[30] which invites reflection on the relations between democracy, communication and the media. For Habermas, the public sphere is a forum in which contending viewpoints come together and, through processes of rational and critical deliberation and debate, scrutinise the workings of public and private powers, forging a consensual public opinion. In his analysis, as in contemporary media theory, the media play a formative role in diffusing diverse opinions and bringing them into dialogue, and PSB has been identified by certain authors as an imperfect embodiment of the public sphere ideal.[31] In his proceduralist account of deliberative democracy, Habermas conceives of a two-level model in which the informal networks of opinion formation of the public sphere and the formal deliberations of political institutions are portrayed as complementary democratic mechanisms.[32] Reformulations of the public sphere idea, and of the media's role in deliberative democracy, then, have become central to scholarly analysis of digitisation and PSB. Just as a key source of contention in relation to Habermas has been the relative status, both normative and empirical, of universal or plural conceptions of the public sphere,[33] so scholars writing on PSB and digitisation tend to divide between those who emphasise the democratic benefits of media that afford a universal public address and those who advocate media systems that enable a pluralistic address among multiple, competing publics, or 'counter-publics'.[34] It is this 'either–or' logic of debate that I want to highlight.

Those writing on the public-sphere potential of the Internet rightly start from its characteristics of networked interactivity, unbounded spatialisation and transcendence of place, and thus its propensity to remove barriers to communicative and political participation—features that afford new, virtual and translocal forms of social identification and political mobilisation. In a period of globalisation and increased migration, the communicative spaces proffered by the Internet and other transnational media, unlike old media systems, are no longer aligned with the geopolitical boundaries and structures of the nation-state. The Internet may be 'particularly conducive for alternative social movements, fringe parties and . . . transnational advocacy networks seeking to organize and mobilize dispersed groups for collective action'.[35] Many political uses of the Internet, therefore, appear to fall outside the political mainstream, reflecting contemporary redefinitions of the 'political' and the Internet's propensity to catalyse new political objects and associations.[36]

Against this background, two writers offer opposed visions of the Internet's public sphere potential. Stephen Coleman, adopting a national–political frame of reference in his concern with Britain's 'crisis of public [political] participation', sees the Internet as a critical vehicle for reinvigorating democracy through its affordance of interactive channels for political mobilisation, governmental accountability, and policy consultation and debate.[37] An advocate of direct representation via the Internet—of the technology's potential to augment politicians' accessibility[38]—Coleman's vision is of an 'online civic commons' hosted by the BBC that would 'inspire and facilitate public participation' in government.[39] It would be charged with eliciting public deliberation on problems facing and proposals made by public bodies—such as local authorities, government departments and Parliament—which would then be expected to react formally to whatever emerged from the public debate. Coleman therefore portrays the 'online commons' as a bridge linking informal and formal aspects of a unified, national public sphere.

In contrast, John Keane rejects the view that public service media have ever been a bulwark of the public sphere. PSB is in decay, he says, suffering from 'self-commercialisation' and a long-term crisis of legitimacy. He chides the 'perilous strategy of [tying] the fortunes of the public sphere ideal to [this] ailing institution',[40] arguing that 'the ideal of a unified public sphere and its corresponding vision of a territorially-bounded republic of citizens . . . are obsolete'.[41] Instead he outlines three tiers of mediated public spheres of different spatial scale—micro-, meso- and macro-public spheres—in which new political forms are facilitated by and articulated with various media. For Keane, meso-public spheres represent the normal business of national politics mediated by the national press and broadcasting; micro-public spheres link new social movements to new media; and macro-public spheres are an outgrowth both of the escalating power of global commercial media and of the Internet.[42] On this basis he advocates a pluralistic, non-foundational account of democratic public life, stating that 'public controversies about power can and should unfold by means of a variety of modes of communication . . . A healthy democratic regime is one in which various types of public spheres are thriving'.[43] Keane slides unsteadily between media-defined and politically defined public sphere processes; his contention that 'the long-term fiscal squeeze [on PSBs rules] out any sustained involvement . . . in the [digital] revolution'[44] has proven in the case of the United Kingdom simply to be wrong. He fails, moreover, to give a convincing analysis of new forms of the political. As Damien Tambini has argued, examining the civic networking movement, the central problem regarding political participation with digital media may not be access to information or voting, 'but the very problem of political organisation in a period of globalisation . . . Whether new media networks can actually be constitutive of interest and identity groups . . . is an open question'.[45] The existence of networked media does not, then, resolve the question of what Habermas has called political will-formation.

Academic debate on multichannel television exhibits a remarkably similar logic: writers either advocate the PSB model in which television is seen as promulgating a unified public sphere; or they welcome the likely demise of PSB, linking it to the rise of digital and narrowcast media, which allow for the articulation of new identities and politics and the growth of plural public spheres. Consider the arguments of Paddy Scannell and John Hartley.

Scannell develops his case around a series of binary terms. Broadcasting is equated with the free dissemination of a universal public good and the creation of a 'general public', an inclusive public sphere—that is, with mass democracy that 'grants formal political equality to all and is (like justice) blind to difference'.[46] Against this he poses narrowcast and digital media, which he aligns with commercialisation, an individualistic consumer address and the personalisation of experience, and which offer 'technologies of self-expression'. Equating the survival of PSB with broadcasting *per se*, Scannell warns that it 'remains an indispensable guarantor of open, democratic forms of public life', and that the expansion of digital media, if accompanied by the attenuation of broadcasting, may have 'catastrophic consequences for . . . democracy'.[47] Hartley, in contrast, writing on the Australian experience, celebrates the development of 'post-broadcast' forms of television, which he links to audiences organised around choice, affinity and decentralised media production, and in particular to the 'trail-blazing' indigenous media sector that, over decades, and with increasing intensity, has engaged in narrating aboriginal experience and an alternative account of nationhood—creating in this way an indigenous public sphere.[48]

Limitations of policy and academic debates

While productively insisting on the varied topological properties of media technologies, often evoked through spatial metaphors, the academic debates share certain striking features with the policy discourse. In four ways, in both their policy and academic incarnations, the early debates are limited in their assessment of the potential evolution of PSB with digitisation. My first two points are 'local' observations applying to the United Kingdom; the latter two are broadly relevant to any account of PSB and digitisation.

First, while scrutiny is directed towards the BBC's new media activities and its fitness to carry forward the mantle of public service communications, the activities and the potential of the commercially funded PSBs—Channel 4, ITV and Five—are less scrutinised, apparently under the assumption that little digital innovation can be expected from them, or that they bear less public service responsibility. Naturally, the BBC's public funding implies the need for rigorous public accountability; but while the regulatory apparatus of PSB remains intact, as it does in the Communications Act, this is a curious omission, reflected directly in Channel 4's lack thus far of a coherent public service rationale for its digital activities.

Second, in both policy and the academy, there is a tendency to project monolithic models of digital transition that ignore both the different media ecologies that pertain in different national contexts, with their distinctive regulatory and funding regimes, and the particular social and political environments in which they operate.[49] There are exceptions: if Keane's account of mediated pluralism is uninformed by the sociological realities outlined at the outset of this essay, Hartley's makes reference to social changes and political developments as they interrelate with transformations in the Australian media. But a notable manifestation of this tendency has occurred in British debates over DTV, which have been marred by the assumption that the American model of transition to a multichannel environment is a universal one. Industry and policy have been drawn to forecasts that appear to reduce uncertainty by conceiving of the American transition as providing a template for the evolution of British markets. Yet recent research portrays clearly divergent patterns in the United States and the United Kingdom. American audiences have fragmented 'almost beyond recognition', with the three US networks now accounting for only 17.3 per cent of all time spent watching television.[50] By contrast, British television does not appear to be undergoing a similar transition. In DTV households, over 70 per cent of peak-time viewing is still taken by the main five networks; in Freeview homes, the figure is 85 per cent. Forecasts of extreme fragmentation along US lines, then, may well be exaggerated,[51] and the eventual balance struck between mass and niche networks in the United Kingdom may be very different to that in the United States. We should therefore resist the temptation to project the American condition as though it was inevitable, and be more attuned to national media ecologies, their propensities and possibilities. The need to avoid conceiving of the United States as a universal model is all the more urgent given that market forecasts are *performative*. They do not so much reflect a pre-given reality; rather, they become the basis for key actors' strategies, in this way powerfully influencing the way new media markets are framed by these actors. In an unstoppable teleology, forecasts can bring about the 'reality' they purport merely to reflect.[52]

Third, the debates have been inhibited in their appreciation of the variety of new media experiences proffered by digitisation that have the potential to be developed for public service ends: in short, they have not attended to the complexity of what is actually going on in digital media. Focused exclusively on under-developed notions of 'interactivity' and 'choice' in relation to the Internet or DTV, the debates have not yet delivered tools for analysing the new content possibilities offered by digitisation. Writers have neglected the importance of emerging cross-media content and services, as well as the need to develop an understanding of entirely new kinds of non-linear content; they have also ignored the continuing significance of linear content, albeit delivered in new ways and on new platforms. To convey the much greater scope and complexity of these possibilities, it is instructive to examine the BBC's digital activities. The BBC sees itself as operating at different scales—international, national, and regional and local—and at each scale its digital services now enhance what is offered. Critical is the way new media extend the range and variety of the BBC's mode of address to its publics, inviting participation. To exemplify, I want to sketch four contrasting initiatives, each utilising digital to innovative ends. The first two are content based; the second two are experiments in which the BBC is attempting to animate interactive connections so as to foster public media spaces.

The first is the use of cross-platform links to populate a thematic event. In 2003 the BBC staged an Asylum Day, in which standard linear factual and fictional programmes on television and radio were linked to online activities and archives, sources of information on charities and NGOs, heated debate and advice. On the website, moving personal testimonies of current and past asylum seekers and migrants—online video diaries—sat side by side with pro- and anti-asylum polemics. Later in 2003 another thematic event, marked by programming on all the BBC's platforms, was Black History Month. A second initiative is the use of interactivity to enhance linear broadcast forms. One such experiment was Radio 4's drama *The Dark House*, which was linked to a website where listeners could opt for alternative narratives and follow the story through the experiences and inner thoughts of any one of the three main characters.

A third initiative forms part of the BBC's response to the crisis in political communication and the widespread disengagement with formal politics. In a departure from Westminster-centred political journalism, and responding to the new modes of political connection engendered by the Internet, a website called iCan was launched in 2003 in the mould of a bulletin board and virtual meeting place for extra-parliamentary issue-based and activist politics. iCan's aim is to animate new political communities and assist campaigning by offering resources such as links to local government and counsellors, information and databases on pressure groups, NGOs and MPs, and the means to create links to like-minded activist individuals and groups. The site encourages user-generated content and is expected to evolve through its use. A productive spin-off envisaged is the generation of local news stories that would enrich the news agenda and boost the relevance of news. Early activities have been locally oriented: one pilot scheme involved links with local radio and television teams in Bristol, Sheffield and other cities; another, in Lincolnshire, developed in cooperation with the local authority, voluntary and community groups, and targeted disabled people. It is early days for iCan; there have been glitches of more and less serious kinds, and the website has recently been extensively redesigned.[53] At its most ambitious, iCan has the potential to become a facilitative online space for political self-representation and self-organisation. The subtext is the reinvigoration of the political culture through political empowerment and reconnection.

The fourth initiative is the BBC's development in Hull, through a public–private partnership and regional and city agencies, of a broadband-based, local-radio backed pilot for a wired city. Named BBC Hull Interactive, the BBC has invested £25 million over five years in the project. It offers unprecedented levels of interactivity and opportunities for local production of content and programmes, a dedicated local television news service, a centre providing free ICT skills and multimedia training, and the delivery of broadband learning packages for schools and home-based adult education. The project also acts as a test site where the BBC can try out and gauge responses to a range of new media services, such as a navigation tool that enables the legitimate downloading of and interaction with audiovisual content from a variety of sources. Research suggests that consumption in the broadband context is polarised between 'apathetic' use and a desire for controls that allow users to rework audiovisual material. Underlying Hull Interactive is a 'micro-community-building' philosophy aimed at enabling users to create their own content, trading technical quality for highly localised, peer-to-peer activities.

In sum, the BBC is pursuing the opportunities afforded by digital media at several complementary levels: platforms (with Freeview), channels (with its four DTV and five digital radio networks), and old (linear) and new (non-linear, interactive and cross-platform) content. It demonstrates an awareness of the need to plan subtly the complementarity between services, essential in an age of convergence, as well as of the public service synergies that can be achieved, enabling innovation to occur across and between different plat-forms. In this way the BBC is forging the architecture of a free-to-air, public service digital media system. Its inspiration has been to see that in digital media it should work across these fronts and at different levels in transform-ing its activities and audience address; and to use digital to try to answer major challenges posed by the coevolving political and media ecology: the need to raise political consciousness and respond to new political forms, to rejuvenate civic cultures, to encourage participation, and to innovate in content. In all these senses, it is making inventive inroads into the reinvention of PSB demanded by digitisation. Yet, to return to the larger picture, both academic and policy writings have yet to rise to the task of assessing this complex landscape of new media activities, whether developed by the BBC or elsewhere.

My final observation on the limits of current debates, and the primary thrust of my essay, is that they have tended not to pay sufficient attention to the profound social and cultural changes associated with pluralism and their implications for contemporary media; at the same time, they have baulked at the challenge of founding ideas for reform on normative rationales. They lack, that is, a sustained attempt to ground reflection on the evolution of PSB in digital conditions in recent currents in democratic theory, specifically in the concerted attempts to provide a normative account of the changing nature of democracy and its discursive and communicative subsystems in multicultural and stratified societies. It is to this that I now turn.

Democracy, diversity and communication

Faced with the upheavals associated with pluralism, a generation of con-temporary political philosophers have re-theorised democracy in the light of diversity and difference. My contention is that productive principles can be found in their work that can translate into new normative thinking about the democratic functions of public service communications.[54] A first preliminary is to make clear that the writers I draw upon come from diverse, and in some instances contending, philosophical currents; but for my purposes this is less important than the commonalities I discern. A second preliminary is to insist that addressing pluralism as a sociological reality does not imply an acceptance of essentialist approaches to multiculturalism that reify ethnic identities and minority cultures as static, bounded and homogeneous. Rather, in the tradition of recent anthropological studies, culture should be understood as fluid and differentiated, fuelled by intercultural contacts that can generate multiple new hybridities.[55] With this as a starting point, it is nonetheless economical to use shorthand terms such as 'minority groups' and 'minorities' in what follows, as do some of the writers whom I discuss.

A first principle centres on self-representation and 'presence'. Anne Phillips addresses the challenge issued to democratic practice by marginalised groups. Rather than conceive of diversity in the liberal terms of diversity of belief and opinion, or the 'politics of ideas', she advocates the 'politics of presence'—the necessity of ensuring the presence within the political process of those most dispossessed from it: 'Political exclusion is increasingly viewed . . . in terms that can be met only by political presence'.[56] Similarly, James Tully insists that disadvantaged groups must be empowered to present their case in their own voice in order for effective dialogue to occur;[57] and Onora O'Neill, reflecting on the communicative ideals called forth by democratic pluralism, proposes the cultivation of a diversity of voices and the protection of 'positions and voices that are in danger of being silenced or marginalised'. She stresses the need for 'practices of toleration that sustain the presuppositions of public communication, in forms from which nobody is excluded'.[57] Taken together, these ideas imply for public service communications that it is not enough to represent a diversity of viewpoints or cultures in terms of content produced, without attending to diversity and inclusion at the level of practice. They point to the need for access to the means of self-representation and self-expression on the part of minority and disadvantaged groups.

A second principle is dialogue: many theorists of democratic pluralism emphasise the role of communication in engendering dialogue and combating social exclusion. Seyla Benhabib, in an influential account of deliberative democracy, elaborates a communicative ethics centred on the cultivation of a 'reciprocity of perspectives' through the provisional adoption by diverse groups of a worldview that may entail a revision of their own, so yielding the 'experience of developing commonality'. In her account, self- and social transformation require a 'politics of complex cultural dialogue' based on public reasoning and exchange.[58] Tully, on the other hand, draws on the experience of aboriginal groups and feminist insights to argue forcefully that 'culture is an irreducible and constitutive aspect of politics'. He calls for a post-imperial citizenship of dialogue and mutual cultural recognition, in which equality entails equity but not uniformity. In this condition, 'one's own identity as a citizen is inseparable from a shared history with other citizens who are irreducibly different . . . The loss or assimilation of any of the other cultures is experienced as an impoverishment of one's own identity.'[59]

If these principles of dialogue and self-representation may seem to imply as their goal the resolution of differences and achievement of consensus, some writers demur from any such assumption. Chantal Mouffe conceives demo-cratic politics as an unending process, arguing that it necessarily entails an agonistic pluralism that 'implies the permanence of conflict and antagonism'. The illusion that a final resolution of conflict is possible, she warns, puts democracy at risk, since it carries 'the desire for a reconciled society where pluralism would have been superseded'.[60] In a similar vein, Iris Marion Young advocates a communicative democracy based on understanding with-out identification, an irreducible plurality, emphasising the way that a variety of language practices can be utilised to maintain that plurality.[61]

A third principle concerns modes of speech, idiom or 'voice'. Criticising liberal theorists' rationalist bias and 'purified' models of political debate, Bhikhu Parekh argues that 'political deliberation is . . . culturally embedded, [and] is never wholly cerebral or based on arguments alone . . . The development of a multiculturally constituted common [public realm] requires [a welcoming of] new conceptual languages, modes of deliberation, forms of speech and political sensibilities [creating conditions] in which their creative interplay could over time lead to a . . . broadbased political culture . . . [and a] richer moral culture.'[62] The theme is also addressed by Nancy Fraser, who writes that the historical bourgeois public sphere was 'governed by protocols of style and decorum that were themselves markers of status inequality [which] functioned informally to marginalize women and members of the plebian classes and to prevent them participating as peers . . . Deliberation can serve as a mask for domination.'[63] 'Universal' public spheres are therefore 'not spaces of zero-degree culture', but 'accommodate some expressive modes and not others'. For Fraser, it follows that public life in multicultural societies cannot consist solely in a single public sphere, since 'that would effectively privilege the expressive norms of one cultural group over others'.[64]

A fourth principle follows on from the concern with idiom or voice: it is that the dialogical mechanisms of democratic pluralism should not be confined to reason and cognition. Support for this proposition is found in writers who address identity and experience in the context of pluralism. Martha Nuss-baum makes the case that emotion is a basic component of ethical reasoning. She contends that a compassionate citizenry depends on cultural forms, by engaging the emotions, to extend its capacity for empathy and, therefore, reason; such processes are essential, she avers, for the well-being and development of the political culture.[65] From another perspective, Moira Gatens and Genevieve Lloyd affirm the critical role of affect and imagination in social identity formation, and the place of the 'social imaginary' in negotiations between diverse groups: 'Identities are determined . . . through processes of emotional and imaginative identification with others, based on relations of partial and shifting similitude and dissimilitude.'[66] It follows that broadcasting's powerful expressive, imaginative and aesthetic potentials, its capacity to engage the emotions, and its mediation of other expressive cultural forms have both cultural and political value. These modes of experience can be a focal means of staging dialogical engagements between diverse groups; as such, they are central to the way that the medium can generate empathy, recognition and toleration in its audiences.[67]

Implicit and explicit in these writings is a realisation of culture's central place in contemporary politics. But the converse must also be taken into account, and is surprisingly absent in the philosophical register of these debates: that is, the critical role that culture, and specifically broadcasting and new media, can play as arenas for staging just those dialogues and reciprocities that are fundamental to sustaining a pluralist democracy. Such reasoning has led some to argue that cultural citizenship is the principal form for the exercise of citizenship in conditions of pluralism.[68] If we take seriously the role of media cultures in influencing audience tastes and conditioning the wider public culture, then, by analogy with the concern in democratic theory with the formation of an educated and informed citizenry, we might add a concern with the formation of a culturally mature and aware, culturally pluralistic citizenry.[69] In this sense, media organisations—both in their social make-up and in their output—can be understood as the primary 'theatres' for contemporary pluralism. It follows that it should be a core function of public service communications to provide such diversity of cultural experience. As Stuart Hall has put it, 'The quality of life for black or ethnic minorities depends on the *whole society* knowing more about the "black experience".'[70] In the contemporary era, public service communications therefore have a vital role to play in fostering the processes of social and cultural development that underlie the general condition of citizenship.

Broadcasting's importance in this context is not only its unequalled reach as a space for exhibiting and experiencing diversity. It is also its inherent power, by virtue of the constant juxtaposition of genres and perspectives on mass channels, to relativise different kinds of knowledge and expression, sensitising its audiences and augmenting their capacity for comparison and critical reflection. In this way broadcasting compounds or 'doubles' a property of cultural diversity itself, as identified by Parekh: 'No culture embodies all that is valuable in human life and develops the full range of human possibilities. Different cultures thus . . . complement each other, [and] expand each other's horizon of thought.' By giving access to other cultures, cultural diversity can enable people to 'step out of their culture', to 'see [its] contingency . . . and relate to it freely rather than as a fate . . . Since [it] fosters such vital preconditions of human freedom as self-knowledge [and] self-criticism, it is an objective good'.[71]

What do these principles and observations contribute in terms of redefining public service broadcasting in the contemporary context? Most of the writers mentioned hold fastidiously to the 'realms of ideal theory' and abjure any 'institutional design'.[72] However, Nancy Fraser, in an astute critical commentary on Habermasian universalism, provides some useful pointers. She offers, between the lines, a kind of normative architecture for public service communications in an age of diversity. It takes the form of a topological discussion of the optimum forms that could be taken and functions that could be fulfilled by democratic deliberation in multicultural and stratified societies. Strikingly, her technique is to shift productively between registers—between normative questions, on the one hand, and history and sociology, on the other. A first step is to argue that any formal ideal that a unitary public sphere could be fully inclusive is a fiction: 'Declaring a deliberative arena to be a space where extant status distinctions are bracketed and neutralised is not sufficient to make it so.'[73] Drawing on the evidence of historians, she notes that 'Contemporaneous with the bourgeois public sphere there arose a host of competing counter-publics' peopled by subordinate social groups (peasants, the working class and elite women). Fraser then counters the view that a single, comprehensive public sphere is preferable to a nexus of multiple public spheres. Rather, 'In stratified societies, arrangements that accommodate contestation among a plurality of competing publics better promote the ideal of participatory parity than does a single, overarching public . . . Subordinate social groups . . . have repeatedly found it advantageous to constitute alternative publics [as] arenas for deliberation among themselves about their needs, objectives and strategies.' She calls such arenas of deliberation 'subaltern counter-publics', and she contends that 'In general, the proliferation of subaltern counter-publics means a widening of discursive contestation, and that is a good thing in stratified societies.'[74] Moreover, only the existence of multiple public spheres allows marginal and subordinate groups to speak in their own voice and engage in their preferred expressive idioms. Multicultural societies, according to Fraser, must allow for a plurality of public arenas in which groups with diverse values and rhetorics participate on their own terms. But—and here is the crux of her normative design—this 'need not preclude the possibility of an additional, more comprehensive arena in which members of different . . . publics talk across lines of cultural diversity', a public in which 'participants can deliberate . . . across lines of difference about policy that concerns them all'.[75]

In this last assertion, Fraser finds an echo in Hall's work when, discussing the imperative of pluralising citizenship in contemporary Britain, he argues that a truly public culture requires that minoritarian cultural practices be brought together and made available for the majority.[76] The goal must be, therefore, to ensure the existence of channels for counter-public to speak to counter-public, and for their integration into an (always imperfect) unitary public culture. The alternative is the extreme segmentation characteristic of commercial media in the United States, where 'the logic of segmentation emphasizes the value of difference over the value of commonality'.[77] Hall's point is that contemporary media politics cannot only be about a proliferation of micro-publics, but should be about achieving a unifying space in which are displayed and in which mutual encounters take place between expressions of the diverse and apparently incommensurable component cultures of the nation.

A normative architecture for pluralist public service communications

How, then, can public service broadcasting be reinvented in digital conditions so as to provide channels for 'mutual cultural recognition'? How can we flesh out the 'politics of complex cultural dialogue' in relation to the future of public service communications? I want finally to sketch a normative typology of the several forms that such a pluralist communicative democracy might take in relation to both digital and 'old' media; I thereby engage in some speculative, if rudimentary, 'institutional design'. My case is that different media—broadcast, niche and narrowcast, networked, point-to-point—have the potential to fulfil different normative purposes; that, as I stated at the outset, something of an elective affinity can be drawn between digital media and the politics of difference; but, emphatically, that the exploitation of digital media for pluralist ends must be supplemented and balanced by a continuation of mass or 'universal' channels. In developing this typology, as well as utilising Fraser's architecture and the principles discussed, I extrapolate conceptually from the inventive variety of the BBC's digital strategies. This is not to suggest that the BBC is alone in developing such initiatives, nor that it is a paragon, nor that it has covered all bases; but simply that in their scope, they are suggestive of the normative functions of dialogical flows between sociocultural majority and minorities, or dominant and subordinate groups. There are five such forms; each is critically important for an extended communicative pluralism. The first three amount to structural variations on the mediated encounter between majority and minorities; they represent three basic vectors of dialogue or reciprocity.

The first is the established form in which the majority hosts divergent and contesting minority perspectives. It is well suited to broadcast networks and comes close to the long-standing liberal orthodoxy in which 'diverse opinions' are presented for debate on current affairs, politics or talk shows—an orthodoxy that, as Hall, Philip Schlesinger and others have shown, was built on now unacceptable political and cultural exclusions.[78] This form can be revivified, after Mouffe and Young, in terms of the staging of more open-ended and inclusive dialogues, and by stressing the necessity of hosting encounters between antagonistic worldviews. For it is only in such a 'universal' media space that the constitutive antagonisms of cosmopolitan societies can confront one another and be worked through, albeit without closure.[79]

A second form is when minority speaks both to majority and to other minorities: *inter*cultural communication. It is well served by both broadcasting and the Internet. This is the core function of cultural diversity-in-unity, of a plural public broadcast culture. As Hall puts it, seen in these terms broadcasting can become 'the open space, the "theatre", in which [Britain's] cultural diversity is produced, displayed and represented, and the "forum" in which the terms of its associative life together are negotiated'.[80] Here, universal channels become the means of exposure to and connection with others' imaginative and expressive worlds, via the self-representation and self-expression of diverse groups in their own voice. It encompasses minority programming on mass channels, such as black and Asian sitcoms, drama or current affairs; access programming, like the BBC's *Video Diary* format on television or the Internet; and cross-platform events engaging the experience of minorities, such as the BBC's Asylum Day.

A third form is when minority speaks to minority (or to itself): *intra*cultural communication. This equates with Fraser's alternative or counter-public spheres, channels that act primarily as arenas for deliberation on the part of minorities about strategies and needs, and that can foster and augment self-expression and self-understanding. Such channels are often also accessible to others, who can thereby gain understanding of minority cultures as well as pleasure from these encounters. Media well suited to the purpose are radio, video, cable and satellite television, DTV and the Internet. Examples are the many diasporic networks and ethnic minority niche media that foster intracultural self-reflection, association and solidarity. The BBC's Asian and black music radio stations approximate these functions. But another powerful model is the innovative Australian network SBS, which offers a continuous series of niche broadcasts serving minority communities.[81]

The last two forms in my structural typology are of a different but complementary order and embody variants of mediated community. The fourth comprises territorially based local and regional community networks; they can be served by all media and by cross-media activities, as exemplified by the BBC's Hull Interactive project or, less elaborately, by experiments in online local democracy. A fifth form is when issue-based politics or associations become the basis for mediated point-to-point networks, a development particularly associated with the Internet. Here, non-territorial thematic communities of interest are constituted by online networks, a potential facilitated by the BBC's iCan website, and exemplified by the countless self-generated, decentred online politicised scenes and activist networks.[82]

Conclusions

Together, these five forms have the potential to populate a new normatively grounded conception of public service communications. In view of this, a first concluding remark in relation to academic perspectives is the need to transcend the sterile assumptions of the 'either–or' polarity: either universal *or* multiple public spheres; either the old, unreconstructed PSB—charged, depending on the orientation of the critique, with being irredeemably elitist,

paternalistic or hegemonic—*or* its inevitable demise. To concretise the arguments given by theorists of democratic pluralism, and to rejuvenate our
collective technological imagination about what digital can bring to public
service communications, I have proposed that we attend to the BBC's
suggestive strategies, which transcend these polarities, rendering them
redundant.

I have also argued that public service broadcasters have an overriding duty
to respond to the redrawing of the social and constitutional contours of the
nation-state, and to developments in the world, and to allow them to inform
and enrich their cultural, political and moral stance.[83] A Britain and a Europe
'cosmopolitanised from within' demand of PSB that it should find a new
engagement with its publics, one that meets head on the formidable
challenges of a progressive pluralism. Such a claim does not amount to a
call for an unthinking multiculturalism, nor for the fixing or exacerbation of
ethnic and cultural differences. It entails two complementary assertions: that
mutual cultural recognition and the expansion of cultural referents, as
opposed to assimilation, are dynamics essential to the well-being of pluralist
societies;[84] but that this does not obviate the need also for integration—for the
provision of common information and experience and the fostering of
common identities, just as it does not gainsay the inevitable syncretisms
and hybridities that will occur across cultural and religious boundaries.

For Britain, a message of this analysis is that the BBC's capacity in pluralist
conditions to reinvent its remit, its institutional shape, and the configuration
and substance of its platforms, services and content is in good health. At
present, the achievement of public media policy in the United Kngdom is
highly dependent on the BBC's initiatives, an assessment that is multiplied
when the success and significance of Freeview as a free-to-air DTV platform is
taken into account.[85] Only the BBC can be expected to monitor the excesses of
the commercial media and on that basis intervene creatively, reorientating the
market under no other imperative than the public interest, orchestrating a
benign media ecology in order to secure democracy's expanded well-being. In
turn, the BBC must expect to engage in self-reforms that respond to the
changing social and cultural contours of contemporary Britain.[86]

For however constructive the BBC's current activities are, they do not
exhaust the possibilities. With much enhanced digital capacity, the corporation should develop its role as the hub of Britain's public culture writ large
through 'public–public partnerships'. More can be done particularly on two
fronts, directions in which the BBC has been surprisingly, perhaps culpably,
inert. First, it should build facilitative connections with other cultural organisations both national and local—at the national level with bodies such as the
UK Film Council and the Arts Councils—as well as with galleries, museums
and universities. Such links would offer means to explore fertile interfaces
between new media and the 'old' arts and culture, and to further develop
some of the products and creative talent nurtured by those organisations. In
parallel, the corporation should take on the responsibility of animating and

offering services to local and community media, aiding the creation of a plural public media space much wider than the BBC, so enabling Britons to benefit from the extraordinary potential offered by the expanding media ecology.[87] As an advocate puts it, such a space must be both local and universal, 'individuated and collective, . . . inclusive, participative and connective'.[88] With digital, as the BBC's early steps imply, there are vast and complex possibilities to be imagined for the future, some of them unprecedented in the history of the BBC. Above all, the opportunities proffered by a new configuration of mass and niche networks fuelled by social and cultural pluralism can enable the BBC to support more spaces for originality and risk, provisions that are central to its remit but that throughout its existence—not least in the past decade—have been under-supplied. Of course these suggestions, while based on observations about the BBC and the United Kingdom, are not limited in their relevance to the United Kingdom.

Finally, a general argument underlying this essay is the need to break down the boundaries between normative theories and the design of democratic institutions, including media systems suited to democratic pluralism. From a policy perspective, we need to take political philosophies seriously—to realise that they offer tangible bases on which to construct institutional arrangements; but also to acknowledge that our existing institutions embody political philosophies that themselves deserve scrutiny and updating. More specifically, Fraser's commentary on Habermas points to the importance of orchestrating a differentiated, multi-tiered public service media system, one that is designed in answer to real sociological complexities and that can be delivered by digitisation. With reference to political theory, I have argued that the challenge for public service communications in an age of diversity is both to develop instantiations of Hall's 'theatre' of the associative life of the nation, as in the universal orientation, the ethical and consensual address of mass channels and impartial news functions; and to offer a rich array of communicative channels for the self-representation, participation and expressive narrativisation of minority and marginalised groups, addressed both to and among those groups and to the majority. In this way, the architecture of public service communications will encompass both practices of toleration and the politics of presence, and will contribute to the formation of a more adequate communicative democracy than we have yet seen.

Notes

1 This, with reference to the BBC, is the theme of my book *Uncertain Vision: Birt, Dyke and the Reinvention of the BBC*, London, Vintage, 2005.
2 P. Dodd and W. Stevenson, 'Creative industries and ''joined-up'' culture', in S. Higdon, ed., *Culture and Communication: Perspectives on Broadcasting and the Information Society*, London, Independent Television Commission, 2001, p. 130.
3 U. Beck and E. Beck-Gernsheim, *Individualization: Institutionalized Individualism and its Social and Political Consequences*, London, Sage, 2001.

4 B. Parekh, ed., *The Parekh Report: The Future of Multi-Ethnic Britain*, London, Profile (in association with The Runnymede Trust), 2000, p. xiii.
5 U. Beck, 'Cosmopolitan Europe', lecture delivered to the London School of Economics (January 2003).
6 *The Communications Act*, London, DCMS, 2003, paras 264(6)(b) and 264(6)(i) (available at http://www.opsi.gov.uk/acts/acts2003/20030021.htm).
7 See, for example, D. Goodhart, 'Discomfort of strangers', *Prospect*, February 2004.
8 *Review of the BBC's Royal Charter: a Strong BBC, Independent of Government* (the Green Paper), London, DCMS, 2005, p. 8 (available at http://www.bbccharterreview.org.uk/publications/cr_pubs/pub_bbcgreenpaper.html).
9 S. Shah, 'Democracy, diversity and television news', in Higdon, *Culture and Communication*, p. 136.
10 Parekh, *The Parekh Report*, chapter 12. Similar findings are given in A. Millwood Hargrave, ed., *Multicultural Broadcasting: Concept and Reality*, London, BBC/Broadcasting Standards Commission/Independent Television Commission, November 2002 (available at http://www.bbc.co.uk/guidelines/editorialguidelines/assets/research/multi1002.pdf). On institutional racism in the BBC, see Born, *Uncertain Vision*, chapter 5.
11 S. Benhabib, 'Introduction: the democratic moment and the problem of difference', in S. Benhabib, ed., *Democracy and Difference: Contesting the Boundaries of the Political*, Princeton, NJ, Princeton University Press, 1996, p. 5.
12 *Report of the Committee on the Financing of the BBC* (The Peacock Report), London, HMSO, Cmnd 9824, 1986; and for an update and discussion of this position, A. Peacock, *Public Service Broadcasting Without the BBC?*, London, Institute for Economic Affairs, 2004.
13 S. Barnett, 'Which end of the telescope? From market failure to cultural value', and P. Barwise, 'What are the real threats to public service broadcasting?', both in D. Tambini and J. Cowling, eds, *From Public Service Broadcasting to Public Service Communications*, London, Institute for Public Policy Research, 2004; A. Graham and G. Davies, *Broadcasting, Society and Policy in the Multimedia Age*, Luton, John Libbey Media, 1997.
14 *Connecting the UK: the Digital Strategy*, Cabinet Office, Strategy Unit, London, March 2005, p. 1 (available at http://www.strategy.gov.uk/downloads/work_areas/digital_strategy/report/index.htm).
15 See, for example, J. Cowling and D. Tambini, eds, *Public Service Broadcasting to Public Service Communications: Choice, Competition and Public Interest on the Internet*—Seminar Summary, London, IPPR, 2003; but also the tenor of the recent reviews commissioned by government of the BBC's digital television and radio services.
16 See, for example, M. Armstrong, 'Public service broadcasting in the digital age' (May 2005) and M. Cave, 'Review of the BBC's Royal Charter: some comments on the DCMS Green Paper' (May 2005), both of them written submissions to the House of Lords Select Committee on the BBC Charter Review.
17 E. Richards, *Ofcom Annual Lecture: Trends in Television, Radio and Telecoms*, London, Westminster Media Forum, July 2005, p. 10 (available at http://www.ofcom.org.uk/media/speeches/2005/07/nr_20050720).
18 Richards, *Trends in Television*, p. 11.
19 *Review of the BBC's Royal Charter*, DCMS, quotes from p. 49, paras 2.5 and 2.6.
20 *Connecting the UK*, Cabinet Office, para 2.9.

21 *Digital Television: a Policy Framework for Accessing E-Government Services*, Cabinet Office, Office of the E-Envoy, London, December 2003, p. 17 (available at http://www.govtalk.gov.uk/policydocs/policydocs_document.asp?docnum=833).

22 *Connecting the UK*, Cabinet Office, pp. 47 and 50.

23 G. Born, Written evidence to the House of Lords Select Committee on BBC Charter Review, in *The Review of the BBC's Royal Charter, Volume 2: Evidence*, London, The Stationery Office, November 2005, pp. 279–84.

24 M. Bracken, 'Seeing the little picture: public service interactivity, investment and a demand-based re-ordering of public service values', in Cowling and Tambini, *Public Service Broadcasting to Public Service Communications*, p. 24.

25 Cowling and Tambini, *Public Service Broadcasting to Public Service Communications*; but see below on Coleman's exceptional contribution to this seminar.

26 W. Davies, *Modernising with Purpose: a Manifesto for Digital Britain*, London, IPPR, 2005, both p. 66.

27 Davies, *Modernising with Purpose*, p. 68.

28 Davies, *Modernising with Purpose*, pp. 70–1.

29 *Connecting the UK*, Cabinet Office, 2005, para 28.

30 J. Habermas, *The Structural Transformation of the Public Sphere*, Cambridge, Polity, 1992.

31 See, *inter alia*, P. Scannell, 'Public service broadcasting and modern public life', *Media, Culture and Society*, vol. 11, no. 2, 1989, and N. Garnham, 'The media and the public sphere', in C. Calhoun, ed., *Habermas and the Public Sphere*, Cambridge, Mass., MIT Press, 1992.

32 J. Habermas, 'Three normative models of democracy', in Benhabib, *Democracy and Difference*.

33 The commentaries are numerous: see the summary in J. B. Thompson, *The Media and Modernity*, Cambridge, Polity, 1995; see also the papers in Calhoun, *Habermas and the Public Sphere*.

34 N. Fraser, 'Rethinking the public sphere: a contribution to the critique of actually existing democracy', in Calhoun, *Habermas and the Public Sphere*.

35 P. Norris, *Digital Divide*, New York, Cambridge University Press, 2001, p. 210.

36 P. Dahlgren, 'The public sphere and the Net: structure, space and communication', in W. L. Bennett and R. M. Entman, eds, *Mediated Politics: Communication in the Future of Democracy*, Cambridge, Cambridge University Press, 2001; N. Marres, 'No issue, no public: democratic deficits after the displacement of politics', PhD thesis, University of Amsterdam, Department of Philosophy, June 2005.

37 S. Coleman, 'From service to commons: re-inventing a space for public communication', in Tambini and Cowling, *From Public Service Broadcasting to Public Service Communications*.

38 S. Coleman, 'New mediation and direct representation: reconceptualising representation in the digital age', *New Media and Society*, vol. 7, no. 2, 2005.

39 Coleman, 'From service to commons', p. 96; see also Coleman's contribution to Cowling and Tambini, *Public Service Broadcasting to Public Service Communications*.

40 J. Keane, 'Structural transformations of the public sphere', *The Communication Review*, vol. 1, no. 1, 1995, p. 4.

41 Keane, 'Structural transformations of the public sphere', p. 8.

42 Keane, 'Structural transformations of the public sphere', p. 15.

43 Keane, 'Structural transformations of the public sphere', p. 18.

44 Keane, 'Structural transformations of the public sphere', p. 5.

45 D. Tambini, 'New media and democracy', *New Media and Society*, vol. 1, no. 3, 1999, p. 325; and see M. Poster, 'Cyberdemocracy: the Internet and the public sphere', 1998 (available at http://www.hnet.uci.edu/mposter/writings/democ.html), and Marres, 'No issue, no public', for additional perspectives on this issue.

46 P. Scannell, 'The meaning of *broadcasting* in the digital era', in G. Ferrell Lowe and P. Jauert, eds, *RIPE@2005: Cultural Dilemmas in Public Service Broadcasting*, Gothenburg: Nordicom, 2005, p. 7.

47 Scannell, 'The meaning of *broadcasting*', p. 8.

48 J. Hartley, 'Television, nation, and indigenous media', *Television and New Media*, vol. 5, no. 1, 2004.

49 See also G. Turner, 'Introduction: global television', *Television and New Media*, vol. 5, no. 1, 2004.

50 J. G. Webster, 'Beneath the veneer of fragmentation: television audience polarization in a multichannel world', *Journal of Communication*, vol. 55, no. 2, 2005, pp. 366 and 378.

51 M. Oliver, 'The UK's public service broadcasting ecology', in *Can the Market Deliver? Funding Public Service Television in the Digital Age*, London, John Libbey, 2005, pp. 39 and 46.

52 See G. Born, 'Strategy, positioning and projection in digital television: Channel Four and the commercialisation of public service broadcasting in the UK', *Media, Culture and Society*, vol. 25, no. 6, 2003; G. Born, *Uncertain Futures: Public Service Television and the Transition to Digital—a Comparative Analysis of the Digital Television Strategies of the BBC and Channel Four*, Media@LSE Working Paper 3, London, LSE, 2003 (available at http://www.lse.ac.uk/collections/media@lse/mediaWorkingPapers/ewpNumber3.htm); A. Barry and D. Slater, *The Technological Economy*, London, Routledge, 2005.

53 See the research report on iCan by the Oxford Internet Institute: S. Coleman and H. Marsh, 'From public service broadcasting to knowledge-sharing commons: an evaluation of the first year of the iCan project', Oxford, Oxford Internet Institute, 2004. The website was relaunched under a new name, Action Network, in July 2005.

54 For a sustained and insightful discussion of normative arguments in favour of cultural diversity as a social condition *per se*, see B. Parekh, *Rethinking Multiculturalism: Cultural Diversity and Political Theory*, London, Macmillan, 2000, chapter 5, especially pp. 165–78.

55 A path-breaking example of this approach is G. Baumann, *Contesting Culture: Discourses of Identity in Multiethnic London*, Cambridge, Cambridge University Press, 1996.

56 A. Phillips, 'Dealing with difference: a politics of ideas, or a politics of presence?', in Benhabib, *Democracy and Difference*, p. 141.

57 O. O'Neill, 'Practices of toleration', in J. Lichtenberg, ed., *Democracy and the Mass Media*, Cambridge, Cambridge University Press, 1990, pp. 173 and 167.

58 S. Benhabib, *The Claims of Culture: Equality and Diversity in the Global Era*, Princeton, NJ, Princeton University Press, 2002, pp. 75, 79 and 115.

59 Tully, *Strange Multiplicity*, pp. 5, 10 and 205.

60 C. Mouffe, 'Democracy, power and the "political"', in Benhabib, *Democracy and Difference*, p. 254.

61 I. M. Young, 'Communication and the other: beyond deliberative democracy', in Benhabib, *Democracy and Difference*.

62 Parekh, *Rethinking Multiculturalism*, pp. 312 and 223.
63 Fraser, 'Rethinking the public sphere', p. 119.
64 Fraser, 'Rethinking the public sphere', p. 126.
65 M. Nussbaum, *Upheavals of Thought: the Intelligence of Emotions*, Cambridge, Cambridge University Press, 2001.
66 M. Gatens and G. Lloyd, *Collective Imaginings: Spinoza, Past and Present*, London, Routledge, 1999, pp. 78–9, 128, 125 and 149.
67 See Born, *Uncertain Vision*, chapter 9.
68 See the discussion in G. Born and T. Prosser, 'Culture and consumerism: citizenship, public service broadcasting and the BBC's fair trading obligations', *Modern Law Review*, vol. 64, no. 5, 2001, pp. 670–5.
69 Born and Prosser, 'Culture and consumerism'; Parekh, *Rethinking Multiculturalism*.
70 S. Hall, 'Which public, whose service?', in W. Stevenson, ed., *All Our Futures: the Changing Role and Purpose of the BBC*, London, BFI, 1993, p. 36.
71 Parekh, *Rethinking Multiculturalism*, p. 167.
72 J. Squires, 'Culture, equality and diversity', in P. Kelly, ed., *Multiculturalism Reconsidered*, Cambridge, Polity, 2002, p. 129; Squires criticises the lack of any 'detailed, practical account of the institutional arrangements required' (p. 130) by deliberative models of democracy in much of the philosophical literature.
73 Fraser, 'Rethinking the public sphere', p. 115.
74 Fraser, 'Rethinking the public sphere', pp. 122–3 and 124.
75 Fraser, 'Rethinking the public sphere', p. 126 and 127.
76 Hall, 'Which public, whose service?'.
77 O. Gandy, 'Dividing practices: segmentation and targeting in the emerging public sphere', in Bennett and Entman, *Mediated Politics*, p. 157; on the segmentation of new media audiences in the United States, see also J. Turow, *Breaking Up America: Advertisers and the New Media World*, Chicago, Ill., University of Chicago Press, 1997.
78 S. Hall et al., 'The "unity" of current affairs television', in T. Bennett et al., eds, *Popular Television and Film*, London, BFI, 1995; P. Schlesinger, *Putting Reality Together*, London, Methuen, 1987.
79 Mouffe, 'Democracy, power and the "political"'; Young, 'Communication and the other'. See my analysis of halting cultural changes in BBC News, including an account of such a confrontation between constitutive antagonisms: a *Newsnight* edition focused on conflicting currents within British Islam (Born, *Uncertain Vision*, chapter 9, pp. 414–30, especially pp. 428–30).
80 Hall, 'Which public, whose service?', pp. 36–7.
81 G. Hawkins,'SBS: minority television', *Culture and Policy*, vol. 7, no. 1, 1996.
82 For insights into new modes of political activism, see Marres, 'No issue, no public'.
83 For a full discussion of this point, see Born, *Uncertain Vision*, Epilogue.
84 Tully, *Strange Multiplicity*; Parekh, *Rethinking Multiculturalism*.
85 On the development of Freeview, see Born, *Uncertain Futures*; Born, *Uncertain Vision*, chapter 10, especially pp. 482–91.
86 See Born, *Uncertain Vision*, chapter 10 and Epilogue.
87 See also Davies, *Modernising with Purpose*, pp. 70–1.
88 D. Redding, 'A vision of a BBC that serves citizens to 2016', in *The Future of the BBC*, London, Westminster Media Forum Projects, April 2004, speaking on behalf of the NGOs 3WE and Public Voice.

Little Citizens: Children, the Media and Politics[1]

JEAN SEATON

What is a child?

CHILDREN are just people, not saints. Equipped with the finely tuned sensitivities of heat-seeking guided missiles in their capacity to find—and exploit—adult weaknesses, they are also entirely vulnerable to the decisions we make for them. Any parent knows that bringing the little beasts up, even in materially comfortable circumstances, is demandingly hard work. It is also enchanting. But the ways in which we privately thrash about trying to manage children and modern lives (and mostly do the best we can) is mirrored at the moment by a large public confusion about children—in which the policies we develop often address our collective fantasies of what a child might be rather than the awkward reality. 'Child centredness', which in many ways has been a benign influence, has been the underlying philosophy of the policy framework for several decades now. Yet it has separated out children's interests from the rest of society—so perhaps it is not surprising that they seem to feel rather distanced from the adults. Moreover, it has unintentionally legitimated an abdication of adult responsibility in many areas that influence children's lives. If they know what they want, goes the rhetoric, then they get what they need. In a moment when social and technological tectonic plates are shifting, we need urgently to reconnect with children. The media are one component of the problem, yet also may be one component of an answer—and certainly one we should bother about more.

Indeed, we should worry particularly about children because there really is a contemporary crisis about audiences. As communication gets increasingly personalised, no one, in any area, feels secure about the response of those they serve, entertain, sell to or inform. The insecurity is shared across every area of public life, from politics to classical music, from news to broadcasting, from comedy through to publishing. Those who produce content are faced with swift-moving changes in the landscape, and have often lost confidence, as well as in some cases markets. The future has just arrived and children, like seals in water, are so comfortable in the new technological waters of communicating that we need to learn from them, but we also need to get some things right for them—fast.

What do children make of the world? What do they use to compose their understanding of how it works and how do they place themselves in it? This active exploring of the map of being a particular person in a particular place must be the first building block of political awareness. The media, whether we

Published by Blackwell Publishing Ltd, 9600 Garsington Road, Oxford OX4 2DQ, UK and 350 Main Street, Malden, MA 02148, USA

like it or not, play an important part in this assembly of a contemporary self. A menacing anxiety that children's childishness is under threat has led us to create increasingly protected spaces for some of them. Meanwhile, we 'diagnose' social disorders in children's behaviour as medical problems requiring treatment, or as proto-criminal behaviour requiring punishment. How do our ideas about the 'child' influence the lives children actually live? One modern answer to the puzzle of the reality of children's experiences is the entertainments (that we are responsible for providing them with) that build a child. The media they consume provide frames of understanding of the real world and provide models of involvement and action to children. But can the media nurture little citizens better?

One way of getting to grips with the characteristics of contemporary childhood is by examining what entertainments absorb and amuse them— increasingly, this means looking at the media. Indeed, by looking at the media that have previously engaged children, one can trace the elusive ghost of the real past of children: not children as we imagine them to have been or as they are now, but children then. Of course, there are also almost universal milestones of development that all children everywhere move through, and books, games, films, cartoons, broadcasting and all of their new life on the Internet and the mobile phone have first of all to tend to these. But, even these apparently rock-like building blocks of becoming a person have been treated differently at different times. Nevertheless, children use what comes their way to make sense of authority, and to sort out how things work. The programmes and entertainments we offer them influence children in any number of ways, both through the obvious issue of content, the overt message that is in the story, and through less considered issues of style and tone and expectation. Attitudes towards what a person can do, how to treat people and images of what a good life might be, the relationship between individuals and social groups—these are all laid down early, and can be derived from the media as much as any other source. Children are in the vanguard of new media use, spending more time with their phones and with games, originating and exchanging material, but these too imply new images of the world, and offer new opportunities to create communities. In a period when the engagement of young people with politics is so low, we need to reconsider the impact of the media on how children think of the world.

Children and politics

Children are born citizens—but they are political actors-in-waiting. We know that despite huge changes in voting behaviour, despite evidence of a distinct generational shift, so that since the 1980s generations neither mature into politics or into news consumers in the way they used to, nevertheless peoples' whole electoral career can still mostly be predicted from their first vote. Indeed, tactical voting, which media-informed voters have taken to enthusiastically, is in a way merely an extension of this. First votes represent values and tactical voters want the closest they can get to reproducing what they care about. If first votes count so much, then it is the interests and understanding of the child that determine the choices of the voter—or, as it perturbingly appears in the contemporary world, the non-voter. But in a far broader sense, the child is the parent of the values and will that politics depends on.

There is, of course, another new and pressing reason to consider children's relation to the world of politics: there is more of the difficult stuff around. Terrorism at home, dire warnings that we may be remaking ghettos, and problems—if not failures—in choosing representative voices all suggest that our democracy is at an interesting stage. Moreover, children are already in the front line of negotiating many of our theories about tolerance, rights, respect, faith, work and life in cities. We are, of course, correct to hope that we can smelt new citizens, fit for a remade nation and world, from our young ones. Cross-community, cross-faith and cross-class friendship and knowledge are best laid down early. Nevertheless, we have the theories—they live the practice. Having it as a mantra is no longer enough; we need to do a bit of listening and understanding. Indeed, the media (and the BBC played a leading role in this) have been good at representing our multitudinous self to ourselves. Over seventy years, children's broadcasting has offered some kind of display of the changing face of Britishness to the young. By the 1970s, an urgent BBC quest at least was 'to get all the divisions out in public: race and creed, colour and class, girl and boy, born here arrived here, difficult as well as easy children . . . we need to get them on screen so that children recognise themselves'.[2] But we need to go beyond this now. The media may often offer a spectacle of inclusion, but what kinds of lives are represented how convincingly to whom? Let's start some of this tricky scrutiny with children.

There is another reason to take children's experience of the media seriously: all of the previous research shows that when there are significant political convulsions children are sensitive to them and may be influenced by how they perceive them for many years—however apparently indifferent to formal politics they are. They pick up their views from the media. The classic study of children's political socialisation by Fred Greenstein in the late 1950s found that even seven year olds knew about the atomic bomb, and sub-sequent research showed how significant Vietnam and Watergate were to generations of American children, while later work argued that 'Political attitudes towards authority, who they respect and trust are established early. Our work shows that children pick up fast on big issues, and that children notice how these are dealt with.'[3] Work for the BBC on nursery-age children during the 1980s showed that even four year olds knew that there was violence in Northern Ireland, which involved weapons and religion.[4] Work done for the Rowntree Foundation in 2005, on what children believe about race, nationality and religion, shows how frighteningly swiftly current events in the Middle East are transmitted through into fears—and prejudices.[5] So now is a moment to re-evaluate how we provide children with the building blocks of political thinking—that is, children live in historical time as well as the mythic world of the child, and we often incorrectly attempt to ignore this.

Young people are apparently estranged from the news. The percentage of those under eighteen who read newspapers or watch television news has declined more steeply than adult consumers. Usually, as people grow older they turn to the news, but for several generations young adults have not followed this pattern: they have not 'matured' into news consumers. Moreover, even on the new media they rarely turn to Internet news: a recent LSE study revealed the limitations of actual navigation of the Internet by those aged between seven and twelve. Despite the cornucopia of sites, they visit very few and are rarely attracted by news or current affairs discussions.[6] David Buckingham has described the dominant attitude of young people to politics as 'cynical chic', and his British and American subjects, aged between ten and twelve, 'most consistently singled out politics for rejection and condemnation. They were very alienated from politics. It was simply seen as irrelevant.'[7] Nevertheless, Buckingham's thoughtful interpretation of his interviews did reveal a more complex underside to this casual contempt. Children, he pointed out, 'pick up knowledge "on the fly"'. They grasped political problems, and related more general issues to the local things that affected their lives directly: but it was the other side of the equation that was missing. They rarely ever understood or believed in the capacity of political structures to do anything at all about the problems they had identified. Of course, the children may be a bit right. In Buckingham's survey, conducted in 1999–2000, children repeatedly pointed out that no one ever took their objections to the dreadful quality of privatised school food seriously. It wasn't a politician who finally listened to them and pushed the agenda on this—but, as we all know, Jamie from telly.

Politics reviled

However, we ought to be concerned about how children come to understand the world, because in so much of the popular youth culture that they value and live within, politics is not merely absent—it is reviled. Much music, comedy, television and computer gaming treats politics, politicians and the structures that deliver services, if it discusses them at all, as corrupt and self-interested. Indeed, the main use of politics is as the object against which you can define your own moral superiority. This is not merely an issue of the general 'decline of deference', but something specific to politics. Indeed, the problem with politics is that we all too often think of it as an issue of information; we believe that if children (people) *knew* more they would have a more positive view of the processes, when knowledge has, at the least, to be combined with rather different attitudes. Indeed, we hardly know whether the indifference to politics is a cause or a consequence of the hostility to it. It is perhaps world-views that matter, and the media paint these in anti-political colours for children.

127

Then we ought to be bothered about how children come to grasp the way in which the world works, because too much of our thinking about the place of politics is so narrow. It may help us think more generously of what politics is about and how to develop it. Just as it is a thrilling discipline to try and answer every question a child asks, however complicated, as clearly as one can, so thinking about how we teach children to get to grips with the issues around them enlarges how we think of politics. Politics is cultural, and is embedded in notions widely dispersed in all sorts of ways of understanding and acting. Of course it matters (although it feels a little like a utopian dream when you look at the evidence about what they know now) whether children have the remotest grasp of why a vote counts, how a party works, what Parliament is and how laws are made. It particularly matters that they have some way of connecting the things they care about—animals, the environment, everyday life in schools and where they live, what it's like on the street—through to the political institutions that actually do affect these things. However, this ought not to be a dry rehearsal of organisations but an issue of argument, cause and effect, and responsibility as well. As Edward Barnes, a former head of Children's Programming at the BBC commented, 'Fairness is the key; all children are passionate about things being fair. That's what you have to build on. There is nothing you can't interest children in. You have to be fair in how you show them the topic of course, but injustice is a direct way to a child's understanding.'[8] Fairness is a pretty profound political value.

But there is something else about the media provision for children—for what we give children for fun also builds an image of childhood, its needs and its possibilities, to which we in the adult world then respond in many different ways. We build schools and eye girls and boys on buses, we build benefit systems and think of ASBOs, think of families and the role of children within them, consider behaviour as appropriate or threatening under the influence of many different institutions, but one important source of ideas is, paradoxically, how we address them for fun. So when we take some care of our children on the sofa after school, we give them a model of their role in life and we build a world for them—for better or for worse. How we talk to children forms how they think of themselves, and how we think of them.

Media images

One way in which the media are powerful—and directly affect the lives of children—is through the relentless churning out of images of children. This has made our culture more 'child centred' in a limited way. In the contemporary news media, childhood is often aggressively sentimentalised. 'Kiddies' are portrayed as sweet, innocent, pretty and coyly preserved in a consumer nirvana, where supplying their every want is an obligation (and a failure to do so shaming). One example of a response to this picture of the child has been, to my entirely biased eye, the truly awful development in the United States (and surely arriving here soon) of enterprises such as The Girl's

Place Empire, which I visited in 2005. This fabulously successful chain of shops (sorry, 'experiences'), utterly blank (like betting shops) to the street, are where long queues of mothers and daughters wait in orderly line to have 'girl's food, girl's gossip, and girl's make-overs'. In these lands of post-feminist delight you can, in a weirdly appealing way (sorry, this is a girl moment), purchase dolls customised to look 'just like you', or—a tad more spookily—you can be helped to look more like the doll of your choice. Not yet surgically. But surely it will come. Finally, you and your doll can be bought identical outfits, 'from sports-wear through school to parties. From jeans to silk . . .'. No chaps of any age are allowed in, and the emporium has a mission statement: 'Girl-power rules!' But the power is that of the mothers to spend, and the power of the child, blackmail (something children, in my experience, are never slouches at). There is also a never-never land promise of cute preservation from the world.

However, as a recent Consumer Council report showed, 'The more "consumerist" children were—the ones who were "brand aware", cared about having things—the more likely they were to be dissatisfied more widely.' Not surprisingly, poorer children, who had the least, wanted the most and, most sadly, felt that they were likely to be disappointed by their birthday presents.[9]

There has also been a tremendous change in the market value of children. Everything from cars to shampoos, computers to holidays, is sold on compelling images of happy children. There has been a doubling of the use of images of children in advertising on television since 1980.[10] Then cunning market researchers discovered that children influenced parental car, holiday and leisure choice more than spouses, and ever since the early 1990s this has had an impact on advertising in general. Indeed, it is one of the forces that have supported the rise of children's cable channels, because advertising time is cheaper on them, but apparently effective. In addition, the market for goods for children fiercely promoted in the media has been explosive. Furthermore, since 1980 the sales of 'children's' toys, clothes, magazines, games and days out, in the United Kingdom have grown twice as fast as those of 'adult' goods. According to the Halifax Building Society pocket money survey, the British child between the ages of three and eleven gets, on average, seventy toys a year. We really do spend on the little darlings. But children also have steadily rising incomes to dispose of themselves. Following on from the US, the connection between films, cable stations, fast-food chains and marketing targeted at children has been a vital new economic link. The cable station Nickelodeon has now overtaken Disney as the most important player in the children's market, by an astute management of this new set of synergies. Indeed, many of the cartoons you like and your children have been fond of (and whose images cover their pyjamas) are really 'loss leaders' for the goods and services that are sold on the basis of their popularity (such as their pyjamas). This is not necessarily a 'bad' thing; it has sometimes financed a higher quality of cartoons, and we need to learn fast how to manage such synergies for public purposes as well as private profit. It was, however, the consequence of a deliberate policy sold to the public as an increase in 'choice', which destroyed the American networks and which consequently led to the disappearance of children's programming on the main channels. Companies such as Nickelodeon found a new market in channels dedicated to children.[11] Indeed, in the new frantic world of communications, just as you may need access to online communities to sell your goods, you also still need the waves of interest pushed by more traditional media. Nickelodeon runs an impressive (and expensive) lobbying machine in the UK, thick around political and media regulators who persistently argue that we do not need public service children's provision because Nickelodeon provides it so well—despite the fact that it spends a fraction of its income on local programmes that reflect the situation and needs of British children.

The ritual lament about the 'commercialisation' of childhood has been a persistent source of criticism of contemporary experience (and one the *Daily Mail* is quite keen on). However, it is usually argued that the 'selling of childhood' corrupts 'innocence', or more infrequently that it reinforces inequality particularly cruelly. These arguments are no less pertinent for being familiar, but there is another less obvious problem, the way in which such a focus on children as commercial opportunities has reduced actual, live, complex children to a fantasy ideal. This means that the problems children face in the stormy waters of the street, school and family life are ignored. Indeed, one less discussed part of the whole rhetoric of 'children's rights' that has developed (and which has had many positive effects—but which is also limited) is that it has been based on the idea of the child as a little, independent, consumer. Such images have in turn had an impact on the media we provide for children. This is an aspect of childhood that children's cable TV channels, for instance, have turned into a kind of credo: Nickelodeon markets itself as 'Giving Children a Voice' and as being concerned with 'empowering' children. But although the station elicits responses from children, these are of a limited kind, and never stray into the contentious. Watching Nickeloden at work is to see a professional and dedicated machine: but for it, children's responses are useful evidence of the station's appeal to children, and they are moderated for 'fun', not representativeness, or indeed for problems. The issues it takes up in the very small public spaces it provides between its professional and international cartoons are typically joking accusations of adult 'silliness'. Nickelodeon, tellingly, has never, ever, caused a row about politics, or about taste, or about children's real lives either here or in the US.

Another side of media concern for children has been an intense fear *for* them. Some of the biggest stories of the past twenty years have been those concerning threats to children: the Jamie Bulger case, repeated failures of social services to protect vulnerable children, sex abuse, satanic abuse and the Soham murders have all pushed circulations and audience figures up. The sensational notion of 'children at risk' is part of one background media narrative that has presumably reflected fears or even constructed an image of the threats to children, and that has had a direct impact on children's lives. In a more general way, there is a fear for childhood itself. Pre-pubescent childhoods are, objectively, getting shorter: choirboys' voices break a year earlier than in the 1950s, and puberty happens for both girls and boys nearly eighteen months earlier than in 1937. Children hit hormonal turmoil earlier than ever before. Perhaps this is marked by the strange contemporary way in which even very small children are now dressed in versions of adult clothing: there is no longer a separate world of children's garments, special easy or comfortable clothes for childhood but, like little Renaissance princes, our children are turned out as mini-adults. In this way, 'childhood' is battered both by markets and biology.

Media coverage of the threats to children concentrates overwhelmingly on the dangers of private life, creating alarm about physical and sexual abuse, with an uneasy ambiguity around the problems posed by modern family patterns. However, there is far less media discussion of the public inadequacies that circumscribe children's lives: bad housing, lack of opportunities for play, poor health—and a fear of the external world that keeps children penned inside, its strange reordering of spaces now making many public territories genuinely threatening; because as fewer children occupy parks and buses, streets and playgrounds, those who do, unaccompanied, may well be at risk.[12] There are solutions to some of these problems (park attendants, for example), but the media are low on interest in answers and high on fear and blame, and always more interested in the salacious danger to individuals rather than the collective solutions to common problems.

We are also predictably anxious about the public spaces to which the media provide access for children. It has long been observed that each new media technology is blamed for corrupting the minds of youth. We often indulge in a thoroughly enjoyable panic about the impact of a movie, television programme, computer game or rap lyric on impressionable minds. Nevertheless, it is, indeed, hard to protect children from some violence and sex on screens, and one puzzles about the effects it presumably has. Most modern nursery school children will have seen the after-effects of a violent death in the news, and any persistently curious twelve year old can find pornography or jihad beheadings on the Internet. All of the evidence on the pin technology designed to protect them is that if they really want to, they can break it. Children watch lots of adult television: *Big Brother*, the soaps and gory thrillers all display the adult world to their beady eyes. Girls between ten and twelve, whose mothers were raised on *Bunty* and *Girl*, now pore over staggeringly explicit sexual advice in modern magazines aimed at their age group. This, for example, has provoked a predictable debate, with the *Daily Mail* railing against 'The media's sick campaign to destroy childhood',[13] while others claim that frank discussion is one of the ways to tackle the UK's uniquely high early teenage pregnancy rates.

Of course, we need some caution here: it may be that what disturbs adults is being made aware of what children actually know. It is also important not to sentimentalise what children once did not know—or perhaps what adults used to be able to believe that children did not know. One representative BBC Children's Broadcasting departmental memo from 1979 pointed out (at a time when nearly 75 per cent of all children aged between four and twelve watched BBC children's programmes) that when the Corporation asked for story ideas in a competition, they were 'almost all totally unusable, being far too blood thirsty, violent and frightening for us to broadcast', while a memo from 1984 (written in defence of frankness) pointed out 'We get an avalanche of letters with jokes in them, about 90% of which are too blue to broadcast. About 20% of them are startlingly blue. I think children know a great deal more about sex than adults like to think they do.'[14] Not even so innocent in the past, perhaps. One of the effects of broadcasting is to expose children to the adult world and adult behaviour in a curiously public way. When I was small my parents used to send me to bed if they thought telly a bit racy; now my youngest son sends me to bed at the juicier moments of *Big Brother*: the embarrassment of shared watching with a parent is the same—though I suppose my ongoing tryst with the bedtime novel says something about a shift in household mores.

Sonia Livingstone's study, *Children Go Online*,[15] shows that children of all ages are apparently upset by 'coming across' material they had not expected; nevertheless, the UK has in fact had some success in clearing at least child-pornography sites from the Internet. The solution has been a collective one, calling on a long institutional history of, and wide public approval for, principled public regulation of broadcasting, and is very different from the American individualist response. The UK has begun to tackle the public spaces of the new media more vigorously, in the interests of all children, but this is again the issue of keeping the illegal and dangerous off, rather than the promoting of the good.

However, these anxieties have fuelled the search for privately controlled safe places—such as cars, and parent-approved 'safe' entertainments—at least for some children. It is part of the familiar modern problem of the secure, ordered, territories of privileged children and the increasingly insecure public spaces of those who are less well off. Combined with the model of the innocent child, the insecurity has produced the huge growth in children's channels on television, and of DVDs for the juvenile market. These are sold because they are unpolluted by disturbing reality, and because it is guaranteed that children will not stumble across anything unexpected—let alone inappropriate—while consuming them. These channels and films vary in intention and quality, but the exclusion of the upsetting is an assumption. They are also children's media for parents to approve of. On the one hand, they exclude the violent and the sexual; on the other, they also exclude the 'nasty' reality of lives as well. What is going on in the world is scrupulously excluded from these spaces, not least because such problems need local and cultural understanding to be aired successfully. A child in Chicago really does live in a different world to one in Newcastle, and even if there are common problems they can only be persuasively explored with the correct (and expensive) local knowledge.

Indeed, there is an ongoing and voluminous discussion of what children ought not to see, with a middle-class fundamentalism on this issue spreading, while anything uncosy is fastidiously removed from the commercial channels (there is an, apparently not apocryphal, story of Angelina Ballerina offending one section of watchful parents—too pink perhaps?). Yet there is little discussion of the good public spaces that the media of all kinds may create for children. We worry about the damage violent media may do to them, but hardly show any concern for what might be valuable. We are very fearful for our children when what we ought to worry about is how to help them to thrive.

The news media do have one alternative image of childhood, and it is not pleasant. The same news media that rail against the 'loss of innocence' also often portray children as undisciplined demons: too 'hoodie', too fat, too unruly, too rude, too unteachable. There may well be a problem. On one day in 2003, the Home Office counted 66,000 reports of anti-social behaviour, of which 60 per cent were caused by young people and children. Is the reality of such children's lives reflected in the media provided for them? Similarly, children are now routinely diagnosed as suffering from a new medically identified illness, 'attention deficit disorder' (ADD)—meaning that they lack the capacity to pay attention (which must surely be a matter of the formation of consciousness, but which we merrily treat with drugs whose long-term effects we understand little of). Of course, the modern child can also alternatively suffer from paying too much (pathological) attention to the wrong things (computer games, for example). These diseases of attention are blamed on the media (when surely parenting and social circumstances must be the cause). Moreover, while we seem afraid of children's disorderly behaviour, we also seem to be oddly divided in our approaches to it, so that while half of the time we oblige schools to include disruptive children, the rest of the time we impose restrictive police orders on (presumably) the same children. These are real issues: anyone who has tried to read stories to a class of five year olds knows that the entire experience can be hijacked and ruined by even one small wild child—while the lives of a whole road or estate can be made a misery by a few children, who bully and terrorise those around them. Nevertheless, the anxious media fretting about these monsters has added to the dominant discussion about the media that children consume— one that concentrates on what they should not see because it will turn them (like victims of a fairy story witch) into the ogres that frighten us so much.

Child centredness revisited

However, our focus on images of childhood has wider consequences. Perhaps in response to the charming image of innocence, a great deal of domestic policy is now built on evocative images of childhood, so that while we rarely talk about redistribution, and almost never about equality, we do talk about 'lifting the nation's children out of poverty', and making 'equality of opportunity meaningful.' Under the present government, a grand political project to transform society has set sail under the flag of childhood, from the comprehensive rethinking of policy in *Every Child Matters*, the National Service Framework for children's health, the Children's Minister and the Youth Green Paper to the appointment of a whole gang of children's commissioners. All of this adds up to an ambitious programme, set going because it is rational—but also precisely because 'the child' is perceived as a popular, politics-free vessel. You can sell progressive policies to a wary public on the image of children. At the same time, we are urged to save Africa from famine and pestilence by the affective power of images of children in want, so that foreign policy is also couched in terms of what we can do to save innocents.

These are all laudable ambitions and it seems right to judge a society by the care it takes of its children, and indeed absolutely right to have the aspiration to transform the lives of future citizens by starting with the tots. Moreover, the government has indeed begun in many ways to improve children's lives. As educational attainment increases, then all of the powerful attendant benefits follow in train: 'You do more for children's health by educating them than the NHS can ever deliver' remarked a professor of paediatrics, 'and we are now on the move.' Nevertheless, it is over competing responsibilities and duties towards the care of children that some of the sharpest conflicts between private individuals and the role of the state occur. The Prime Minister recently observed that he could not bring up each and every one of the nation's children. Yet when and how we should or should not intervene in families on behalf of children is a complex area, where the state and families, and the needs and desires of children themselves, tussle away with each other, locked in an uncomfortable struggle. These are all also political matters, yet we have become very reticent about admitting it. So reforming society in the name of the child is not quite as straightforward as it first seems. And the whole project and its failures are saturated with media images.

The contemporary child is a strange beast: cosseted, yet feared; prized, yet often ignored; conceptually isolated from parents, when in fact you cannot think of a child outside of the relationship that cares for it. Even very recently, families circled around adults. Now there is no doubt who is central, in principle, to the 'ideal' household—the child. The reflective memoirs of writers such as Penelope Lively show how the place of the child has changed. Lively, who has written marvellous books for children as well as adults, was brought up in a period when adults were the hub of households—

and children clearly subsidiary. By contrast, as she observes in her book *A House Unlocked*, 'Today's child is also viewed nervously, seen as a potential time-bomb, an unstable substance requiring the most informed and delicate handling. And thus they have acquired a power of which they must be unconsciously aware of.' As child-raising fashions wash over that most intimate of relationships, we now believe we are more child-centred than in the past. But perhaps we do more in their name, rather than for them.

We also spend much of our time 'giving' children rights. Since Elizabeth Butler Schloss put children at the heart of law making in the Children's Act, we have had a legal revolution in which the interests of the child are treated quite separately in disputes involving families. They are represented separately in courts, and their interests have been distinguished from those of their parents. Yet, at the same time, the 'home', or the place where children and adults actually thrive together, is almost lost as an idea. Then children are the people who must give their 'informed' consent to medical treatments (even if they hurt), and by analogy their consent must be acquired by police, the media, schools and social services in all sorts of circumstances. These developments have all been an expression of a slow, valuable revolution in the official attempt to listen to, and attend to, children's voices and needs. Indeed, if you see this shift as a way of re-educating the institutions that deal with children, it makes a different kind of sense. But the processes may also help us feel good about the respect we give children—and obscure some of the reality. Thus, I am not at all sure that even adults can give 'informed' consent to medical treatment—let alone children. You can discuss consequences and consider alternatives as best you can, and this is important, but nevertheless ultimately patients depend on the professional expertise of the trained medical staff to advise them. With children it is parents in reality, and properly, who have to take responsibility for approving treatment. Children's rights are important, but we should not use them to fool ourselves or abrogate responsibility.

Television and the new media

When I asked my sons—recently-ex-children—who brought them up, they unhesitatingly answered, "Television". Computer games, music, books, videos and the Internet figure—but not as much as television. Games matter especially for boys. It is the ambition of their designers to make games that have the narrative and emotional complexity of action movies, combined with the involvement and interaction of a sport. Games deserve much more scrutiny than they get: they are the fastest-growing, most profitable sector of the media market, and they have been kept discreetly beneath the radar of authorities and institutions, and although they are certificated like films, there is little or no informed public discussion of what is going on in them. To my biased maternal eye, they are mostly shockingly violent (I do not, however, think that my addicted sons have been corrupted by them).

Music matters as a real pleasure, a taste and a first complex badge of tribal identity that may develop into a lifelong passion. The ritual attendance at the first gig (accompanied by massively humiliating father) is just one staging post on the way to teenage independence. Books matter in a house like mine, although my sons have taught me how differently different children read: one reads (like me) fast, furious and avidly, another reads slowly, and very absorbingly—and we are still on tenterhooks to see whether the third will ever read anything at all, except for magazines about football, football leagues, and biographies of footballers and football managers.

Books, from picture books for tiny children (which the UK leads the world in producing) through to the blockbuster Potters or the awesome Pullmans, do deal with the whole range of children's lives. Stories cover everything, from the wonderful ordinary to mad pleasures, as well as the shadows and threats that beset children. Books still deal with the whole range of children's experience and imagination in a way that the newer media are in danger of losing, from the almost mythic fears of fairy stories to the gritty everyday fears and the terrors of growing up. The other useful thing books have often done, that is surely related to the basis of political understanding, is analytic-ally to demolish adult institutions. The wild anarchic world of the incompar-able schoolboy anti-hero Molesworth, and much of the best children's comedy, displays forensically dissected adult institutions, and a comprehen-sive grasp of political power as well as the role of propaganda. Yet it is this range of experience, that stirs the relationship between the world children inhabit and how they make sense of it, which is increasingly deliberately excluded from much of the media we offer children. And surely political understanding is based on ways of thinking about the conditions you and others live in. But the books are also written, illustrated and addressed to children. It is this world made for children—that is also complex and real—that we might all too easily completely lose in other media: after all, it no longer exists in any American broadcast space.

What television provided for my children was a collective entertainment: it was commanding and common. It is no use bemoaning the loss of the hours of creative boredom that I, at least, spent as a child, on my own: drawing, humming, fiddling and playing solitary bossy games with hosts of imaginary companions. If I were a child now, I would be in front of the television, or just possibly some other screen (or texting my friends). Television was, of course, where my children were dumped when I was doing other things. It was what they did after school, before homework, and on Saturday mornings and at any time in between. Once their temperatures were no longer soaring, it nursed them when they were ill. It was used, as all the sociological research shows, to structure their days, folded into the routines of their lives, and they used it to gossip about. It was often rather remote from the adults around them; it was theirs.

They came to the radio later (radio can be influential if children get the habit—exposing eight year olds to the *Today* programme every morning on the run into school may produce a generation with a firm grasp of the role of the World Bank and deep anxieties about the fate of the skylark and, later, they may turn into World Service listeners on their 'gap' years in far-flung continents, up mountains and on projects in poor cities). Nevertheless, television was a currency of experience for them. We also watched (and indeed watch) a good deal of television together, discovering family enthusiasms (for unspeakable comedy, for example—other, better, mothers have often phoned me to complain of the damage I have done to their children by exposing them at a tender age to the grotesque). But much of this (and of course the acres of sport) is family material. There is no doubt that television created the dimensions of much of the world for the children I know well: from news to comedy, from sitcoms to documentaries on other children, science and animals, it structured the limits of what they knew and, indeed, established appropriate attitudes to these things.

What mattered to my children, and what we need to hang on to whatever the technology, were the programmes that they consumed as themselves, not just as interested observers, and which somehow initiated a conversation with them. All of this took place in, comparatively, a stunningly privileged household—the adults hovering anxiously, ever ready to pounce on any nascent infant capacities, ready to stuff them with mind-stretching resources. How much more important this could be for children in houses where the television is simply always on, or for children who live in more complex ethnically and culturally multilingual places, than for my pampered chaps. But the broadcasting that did this best was intended for children in the context of the places and situations they really inhabited.

Broadcasting is changing rapidly, and its role in our lives is mutating. In particular, children are used to personalised communication, and we need to be sure that the opportunities (to make content and share it, as well as consume it) address them personally, not just technologically (which is the bit everybody gets obsessed about), but in terms of the material the technology uses—the content—as well. Children do other things as well, and they use technology for other newer amusements, yet television still interacts and drives tastes and arguments in playgrounds. We need to hang on to the lessons the best broadcasting practice demonstrated, because it offers a set of principles that we need to develop. New media for children will develop differently, and will have more complex purposes, if we use them to nurture the public service tradition. As Alison Sharman, the recently departed Controller of Children's Programmes at the BBC, put it, 'We need new ways of relating to the things children do now, but the values remain the same. We need to preserve trust with children—to provide them with safe and creative spaces that nurture all children's capacities, and that they recognise themselves in.'[16] But even the BBC seems in danger of losing a sense of the best practice of the past in developing new services. Sharman seemed to have little interest in or reflective idea of the past of the service she was the custodian of; which is a shame, because we need to hold on to the

DNA—not the programmes exactly, or how they are delivered, but the range of purposes and meanings.

What can this 'proper' broadcasting do, and what can we learn from it now? Children are already digital, so there are new opportunities to apply some older lessons. Well, it has to include the silly and the entertaining, but it can and should also include drama and perturbing reality—not hidden, but handled for children. Drama is one of the best ways of tackling sensitive issues and engaging children in a conversation. It is this model we need to have in mind as we consider new services for children. 'Proper' broadcasting can worry about children, and attend directly to them and their needs and interests. Monica Sims, another distinguished controller of broadcasting for children, expressed the principles well in 1971: 'There is no question of giving children what parents or teachers believe to be good for them . . . cartoons and adventure series are the ice cream . . . we must also produce the proteins and vitamins and mixed ingredients of the main course. Most of all we want to nourish children so that they can be active, full of enthusiasm to learn and always able to do things for themselves.'[17] In the new digital age, as Sharman argued, this means 'nurturing children's formidable media skills' (less building things from old washing-up bottles; more putting together interactive video diaries), but the underlying principle remains the same.

What we need to preserve from public service children's broadcasting is seeing children as actors, not merely spectators. Indeed, there is a direct line from the attitude towards children's own contributions—the things you can make, the questions you ask that get answered, the notion of the active, valued child—through to encouraging an even wider sense of possibility that has to be the basis of political understanding. As Edward Barnes, a former head of BBC Children's Broadcasting (and the man who invented *Newsround*) wrote in 1981, 'It is not only important to inform children about the plight of people caught up in famine and wars, about the poor, the underprivileged and the disabled but also to demonstrate that children can, by their own efforts, do something positive to help'.[18] There was a commitment to the transforming power of doing something for all children that informed all decisions. The idea was that all children's contributions would be equally valuable (so you never collected money, because this would privilege the well-off). Indeed, such ideas embody an appeal to 'fairness': as Rosemary Gill, another producer from the 1980s, pointed out, 'you show children how to do things so that everyone can do them'.[19]

Such thought and backroom cherished activism could have remarkable results. Recently, I interviewed sixteen people who had shaped BBC children's broadcasting, from presenters and writers, to producers and heads of children's programmes, from animators to those who ran the appeals. There was one unexpected and startling finding. Every single person I saw, all of whom had shaped children's broadcasting for over three decades, had their own, direct experience of a response from broadcasting. They had, as earnest ambitious children, sent a letter, asked a question or sent in a joke, and they had been acknowledged, replied to, answered, known (in one case rather rudely—but it was still a stimulant). If anyone wants to be shown an effect of broadcasting on children, then surely this is novel, but fairly conclusive, evidence that if you get it right you intervene decisively in children's lives.

The public service child

Thus, paradoxically, broadcasting—the mass medium—has been able to talk (just like books in many ways) intimately and directly to individual children. It is this way of addressing children that we also need to consider, because it is the basis of much that is valuable to children. Indeed, the history of public service children's broadcasting is awash with documents emphasising that children are the audience, not parents or teachers. This attitude has produced a whole range of programmes that have explored how children find themselves placed. This is not always the world as adults would like to interpret it. But it has taken a particular commitment to children to do this. It is the rather different history of public service broadcast provision for children, and particularly that of the BBC, that provides the best model.

Thus no niche channel for children in the commercial sector would have produced *Grange Hill*, the soap opera based on life at school—it was too uncomfortable. Indeed, no commercial channel has produced anything at all like it. *Grange Hill* repeatedly got into political trouble, and was often described as 'corrupting'. An articulate and influential minority of campaigners objected to way in which it dealt with teenage pregnancy, drugs, bullying, rules at school, exam pressures, the impact of divorce and unemployment, step-parents, sibling rivalry, dropping out, poverty, racism, illness at home, petty miseries, bad teachers and good teachers, and the way in which institutions ignore the seething under-life of children's life experiences. They did not think it 'appropriate', yet it has been hugely popular with its audience and it has tackled the things that real children and teenagers face out of a well-researched and considered responsibility to them. Incidentally, it was written, when it was started in the 1980s, by men and women who were first-class writers, and whose work has dominated British TV and film screens ever since. The point is not so much whether *Grange Hill* is an ideal or attractive programme, or whether the format is desirable, or whether such slightly dated 'realism' is contemporary. Rather, there is something more fundamental, the conditions that made path-breaking programmes for children possible, which involved a vigorous relationship with children, but not with the authorities who pontificated about them. Edward Barnes commented that he had wanted a watershed, but one that set a time when parents and teachers were not allowed to watch television, so that broadcasters could get on with talking with children free from the prurient adult eye.[20] The greatest temptation that children's broadcasters face, pointed out Biddy Baxter, the redoubtable creator of *Blue Peter*, is that of over-protection.[21]

Then there is the issue of the proper relationship to the fears children may have. As any parent knows, you need to learn to handle children's fears so that they are not overwhelmed by them. You do not do this by pretending they do not have them. But explaining what is happening in a newly turbulent world is the basis of the kind of understanding of events that is a precondition for beginning to appreciate political solutions. As the creator of *Newsround* observed, 'I was concerned that although children may not be watching news, it was going on whilst they were in the room. I was worried that children might be distressed by half understood disasters and strong news stories. Fear and anxiety are often generated by ignorance; if you are given the facts in an understandable form there is a chance you can learn to live with it. There's little to be said for ignorance in either children or adults.'[22] Of course *Newsround* (over, for example, the relationship between Catholic and protestant children in Northern Ireland) ran into just as large, and consequential, political rows as the adult news programmes, so it is risky— but that's the point. It is important to find how to communicate to children what is going on, in ways that (rather counter to normal news values) do not seek to sensationalise and thrill, but do seek to explain what is happening— and, indeed, relate their vision of the world to events. For this to develop, organisations must attend to children as a distinct audience.

The child who makes a difference

Another aspect of 'proper' broadcasting for children has been the image of the child it has elaborated, and this is overwhelmingly one of an active and engaged equal, not a just a passive recipient of amusement. The 'model' child of public service tradition enters into a conversation with the programme providers, in its own voice. Grown-ups complain about or approve of programmes: children have related to them quite differently—they write as if chatting to a friend, occasionally confiding in a voice that they recognise treats them as sensible and sentient. The BBC responds by producing a structure of care, a back-room discussion that produces a front studio tone of address to children, and a view of their true capacities. When it gets it right, the BBC metabolises what a child is at any given moment. But the expectation has, at its best, been of children who could be interested in anything and, perhaps most important of all, who could be active and have an effect. As one BBC memo put it in 1981, 'The aim is to encourage children to do things for themselves at every turn. It means building a model, but it also means taking action to help other people in distress. It means sending in a joke and standing up for people having a tough time at school.'[23]

From writing letters and e-mails to running bring-and-buy sales for charity, the idea has been to elicit action. The public service child is an egalitarian thing, and every child's contribution must count. The model was an engaged child, and one who was an agent. This is a very different way of responding—or in the contemporary argot, 'interacting'—with children, from merely harvesting interest in order to fuel the programmes' success (although it also does that). But it takes care, resources and principles.

What we also need to do is ambitiously to re-imagine children. Perhaps we need to attempt to be more forthcoming with them. In 1940, Commander Stephen King Hall (later a Labour and then rather maverick independent MP) addressed the nation's children on *Children's Hour* in one of his tremendously popular series of talks. At the height of the blitz, he was talking to children who were at risk of being bombed, or had been evacuated and hence separated from their families. There was a very different image of a child at work in how he addressed them—no talk of anxiety or problems here, no talk of trauma or fear, just remarkably straightforward levelling between adult and child: 'We live over here,' he started, 'in what is called a democracy, and that means our government does what the people want it to do and more important than that it cannot do things which the people do not want it to do.' Nor was his message comfortingly indulgent: 'It cannot do wise things if the people are shouting and asking for stupid things. That is why if you and your friends are sensible when you grow up the British government of that time will be sensible.' His prescription for the 'sensible' child was 'taking the trouble to find out the facts about problems yourself . . . train yourself to use your brains' and 'not believing everything you are told, or read or hear. Question everything but be sensible judges.'[24] What a child he is addressing: the responsible, hopeful, restrained, independent-minded democrat child— an image that I find immensely moving. Reminding ourselves of how it is possible to address children is not an issue of comparing our current situation to some lost golden age, but just using the past as a source of new thinking.

Making it better for children and politics

So, what do we need to do to help the media encourage our future citizens to be more engaged with society and more politically articulate? Well lots, but there are some simple things that could begin a new ambitious push, one that makes a genuine difference to a generation. We need broadcasters to engage with children's audiences in any way they can. Broadcasting needs to be obliged to take children seriously: this is the basis of connecting to them, though it does not mean being serious *at* them. They do watch grown-up stuff and there are commercial channels giving them never-never land. It is not enough.

The regulator, Ofcom, has been concerned with delivery of content, and children will be in the vanguard of exploiting any new technology, so it is important to get this right. Ofcom, however, has a misguidedly narrow definition of 'public service broadcasting', which it has reduced to high-rating programmes in prime time. It has also been concerned with maintaining 'creative competition' in commercial television provision for children. Ofcom must learn that the quality of content depends on the care and attention broadcasters (or whatever they are to be called in the future) devote to considering the needs and realities of modern children's lives. It is this 'behind the programme' imagination and principle that needs to be preserved. In the case of children, the ambition for the child of public service providers is unique. Broadcasters are rightly rather shy about mentioning the back-room work they do, and yet it is absolutely vital. In the case of children, the intelligent institutional response to the material sent in (it used to be letters; now it's mobile phone film clips) is key. But so too is the delicately political work of monitoring and auditing responses to issues.

Moreover, we need real vigilance to hold Ofcom to its brief. For example, it has powers over grown-up content that it has simply failed to use: How much more tempted will it be to leave commercial broadcasters to do what they want in this area?

Indeed, we also have to be vigilant that we simply go on regulating. Teaching children to be 'media-literate' sounds fine, but there is a real danger that it is simply a way of legitimating new, 'responsible', 'choice', which could all too easily be a backdoor route to dismantling the regulating that demands quality programming and responsible thinking about children (even if it is quality response to your home-made movie). Surely, as with the food children get in school, the time has come to accept adult prescriptive authority in what is provided for children—'choice' should not be used to dismantle the quality of what children are provided with.

Then, to be blunt, you have to make sure that children's programming stays central to the BBC, because the Corporation has such a powerful tradition of considering children, that can always be built on. But new technology is not enough. New realistic thinking about the experiences of British children is also necessary. We need services that reach out in novel ways to a newly active audience that wants to communicate more personally, that wants to exchange and make its own content, but that also needs to recognise its own world in what is is offered. We need to re-engage with children and the risky world in which they live.

Equally significantly, the BBC's investment in programmes for children is huge and everyone else's is minute by comparison. The BBC's World Service is a world leader, so we ought to expect the Corporation's provision for children to lead a new approach to children's real experiences—and their hopes and dreams. We must protect the public service provision that we are extraordinary lucky to have, learn its lessons, demand that it do more, and make sure that it has enough resources to storm out imaginatively—and that it is managed by people who care about the quality of children's experience. If provision for children is very good and very challenging—as it must be—it will probably run into some political rows, with groups complaining not merely of bias but also (because we are discussing children) of the threat of indoctrination in some form. Of course it is vital that any material is fair, but rows can often be an indication that the work is being done in challenging ways.

What children need (as well as the great programmes and cartoons you can buy in, and the profoundly different cartoons that a public service commissioner can make) is content that is in touch with them, programmes that are local and topical and—however uncomfortable for adults—in which they recognise themselves. It might be worth reconsidering the tone of ruthless, frantic fun that seems to be the dominant mode of address to children. In an exceptionally competitive market, shrieking has become accepted as the only means of capturing wanton childish attention. However, having fun on screen is not the same as engaging children in fun.

Of course there is much to make better for children, but to maintain the pretence that they live in an anodyne world apart is no way to begin. We have a Children's Commissioner, who has the job of producing a cross-departmental National Service Framework for children: 'It has to start,' argues the new commissioner, 'with the most important partnership of all – with children and young people and listening to them.'[25] We are bountifully supplied with institutions that promise to listen to children, but suppose that they say—like the articulate children on a recent BBC series, *Children's Voices*—painfully shrewd things about how their parents and society treat them: then the media that they consume ought also reflect or relate to that. That is, if we aspire to engage citizens by taking what they say seriously, then we ought to start by taking children's fun seriously. The issue is one of making good programmes, not the old chestnut of prohibiting bad ones. We have a vigorous discussion about the bad, but we pay shamefully scant attention to preserving the good. Children are just people—they are not perfect, or nice, and it is real children we have to get to grips with. We need the media for children to reflect and articulate the children's world, not least because this conversation with children is the first step of engagement.

The vanishing conversation

Perhaps we also need to stop being so frightened of the little darlings. Looking at the whole history of broadcasting for children threw up another startling finding. I have listened to radio from the very start and watched television programmes from the whole period, from 1926 to 2005. A terrible mystery appeared: the puzzle of the vanishing adult. In the past, up to about 1985, you could make programmes where adults and children discussed issues, made things and enjoyed each others company—together. You even used to be able to make programmes in which some adults (such as Nobel prize winners), who were actually expert, imparted information to inquisitive children. Now, no one makes programmes in which adults engage with children. Adults are anathema to most programme makers and have been replaced by weird youthful quasi-children (who giggle manically). Adults are caricatured or made fun of, in a mild, faintly cheeky way—but there are no real 'grown-ups' around. Images of adults and children in conversation together have almost completely disappeared from our ways of addressing children in the world of the media that we have provided for them. The tableau of adults and children engaged together seems to be too unlikely, too off-putting, to show.

No wonder children despise the adult world. They simultaneously need a space that is not produced for adult 'approval', but that tends to their needs, interests and predicaments. Surely, from their point of view, the first step to politics is some capacity to identify and articulate your own circumstances. They ought to be able to see their lives mirrored in the media that they consume. This is not an issue of solemn preaching: *Alice in Wonderland* is, after all, just such a document, painfully acutely pinning down the ridiculous capriciousness of the ways in which adults behave—when seen in a child's perspective. But many of our children live uncomfortable lives in unsettling circumstances, and the programme makers need to be charged with using their imaginations to confront these realities. We can only get them to do this if they are free enough to make programmes for children—not programmes for parents—in which case we have to will the policy makers to go on producing material of quality for children.

Then, it is about time we started using the media to have a discussion with our children. A teenager of my acquaintance pointed out to me that Dostoyevsky put it well in *The Idiot*, a book about a perfect man: 'A child can be told everything – everything! I've always been struck by the fact that grown-ups, fathers and mothers, know their children so little. One must never conceal anything from children on the pretext that they are little and it is too early for them to know things. What a lamentable and unfortunate idea . . . Grown-up people do not realize that a child can give extremely good advice even about the most difficult matters.'[26]

Notes

1 The research in this essay is part of the AHRC-funded project on volume VI of the official history of the BBC, *The BBC under Siege: Broadcasting and Thatcherism 1975–1987*. In addition, a number of contemporary broadcasters were also interviewed and time was spent observing children's television production.
2 BBC Written Archive, Monica Sims, Head of Children's Programming, *Report on Children's Broadcasting*, the General Advisory Committee, BS/27, 123 Children's Policy, 12 June 1975.
3 The classic work is F. Greenstein, *Children and Politics*, Yale, Yale University Press, 1957. However, Vietnam and Watergate changed American children's political socialisation dramatically, and a whole load of political 'science' about children had to be reconsidered; see S. Moore, *The Child's Political World*, Praeger, New York, 1986.
4 BBC Written Archive, *Playschool Audiences*, BBC Audience Research Report, T2/315/1, 3 June 1974.
5 See G. Lemon, *The Search for Tolerance*, York, Joseph Rowntree Foundation, 2005. This is an invaluable attempt to get to grips with the racism in children.
6 S. Livingstone, *Children Go Online*, London, LSE, 2005.
7 D. Buckingham, *Young People, the News and Politics*, London, Routledge, 2004.

8 Interview with Edward Barnes, Head of Children's Programmes, BBC, 1978–92.

9 E. Mayo, *Shopping Generation*, London, The National Consumer Council, 2005.

10 J. Peterson and J. Jones, 'The effectiveness of children's images: a historical perspective', *Journal of the Psychology of Advertising*, vol. 32, 2005, p. 21.

11 H. Hendershot, *Nickelodeon Nation*, New York, New York University Press, 2005.

12 See H. Roberts, *Children at Risk*, Buckingham, Open University Press, 1995; and *What Works for Children*, Buckingham, Open University Press, 2002.

13 'The media's sick campaign to destroy childhood', *Daily Mail*, 24 July 2004, p. 1.

14 BBC Written Archive, Policy, *Children's Programmes*, RS1, 2-118, 23 June 1979.

15 Livingstone, *Children Go Online*.

16 Interview with Alison Sharman, BBC, Controller of Children's Programmes, 2005.

17 BBC Written Archive, Monica Sims, *Children's Policy*, RS1-1, May 1971.

18 BBC Written Archive, Policy Document (for the Board of Management and the Board of Governors), Edward Barnes, *Children's Broadcasting*, B213-3, 1981.

19 Interview with Rosemary Gill, Producer of *Blue Peter* and *The Multi-Coloured Swap Shop*, 2005.

20 Interview with Edward Barnes, 2005.

21 Interview with Biddy Baxter, producer, *Blue Peter*, 2005.

22 Edward Barnes, 'John Craven's Newsround,' *EBU Review*, vol. 14, 1984, pp. 118–23.

23 BBC Written Archive, the Director General, *Television Weekly Programme Review*, 14 January 1981.

24 BBC Sound Archive, Commander Stephen King Hall, *Children's Hour*, 15 November 1940.

25 The Children's Commissioner, Ainsley Harriot, 'A Policy for Listening', 2005.

26 Fyodor Dostoyevsky, *The Idiot*, translated by David Magarshack, Harmondsworth, Penguin Classics, 1955, p. 90.

On the Cusp: Finding New Visions for Social Gain from Broadcasting

DON REDDING

Introduction

A new citizens' movement is required, to protect 'our info'. If we want everyone to have access to the highest-quality information and education, through media that serve our interests first and foremost, we will have to fight for it, vigorously and relentlessly.

This new movement would capitalise on the latent demand and desire of the UK public for access to high-quality, independent media. It would mobilise this 'public interest' to defend and promote 'the public interest' in relation to communications services in the information society.

We are now in a true 'convergence' era, where the possibilities for making and using new forms of communications media appear unlimited. But that is only an appearance: markets will not provide all we need for citizenship. If we want to maximise the potential social, cultural and citizenship benefits of this new era, conscious policy decisions must be made—and will only be made if we are strong enough to push for them.

Cultural policy regarding broadcasting and related communications services is escaping from the public, parliamentary and quasi-democratic realm into a non-democratic space, impervious to the needs, rights and demands of civil society. We need to wrest it back.

Is this nirvana?

> The nirvana of convergence is upon us.
> Karen Thomson, head of AOL UK

In the convergence era, all communications platforms and services begin to blur together, based on the shared and 'interoperable' technologies of digitisation. The 'traditional' sectoral divisions begin to break down. Broadcasting, telecommunications and computing cease being separate industrial realms and begin to merge together.

What, then, should happen to their separate and different regulation? For many in the new communications industries, the answer is simple: don't regulate. If all information pipelines can compete to transmit the best information and communications services, free them to do so. Retain a minimum of competition regulation to prevent dominance of the pipelines, use self-regulation to minimise harmful content, and all other special

146 Published by Blackwell Publishing Ltd, 9600 Garsington Road, Oxford OX4 2DQ, UK and 350 Main Street, Malden, MA 02148, USA

provisions can be removed, including the strange social and cultural regulations that applied to traditional TV broadcasting.

Who better to articulate this view than James Murdoch, CEO of BSkyB:

Broadcasting should no longer be regarded as a special case . . . The purpose of broadcasting regulation should be to ensure competition through freedom in pricing, through secure and transferable property rights, and through the removal of genuine barriers to market entry. Full stop.[1]

The United Kingdom appeared not to have chosen this route. The Communications Act 2003,[2] while anticipating convergence and increasing the emphasis on market solutions, nevertheless appeared to protect a special role for broadcasting. And yet convergence is pulling those protective rugs from under our feet. Policy and regulation in the UK is moving rapidly in the 'don't regulate' direction. When the European Commission proposed not rolling back TV regulation, but extending some of its concepts to the new audiovisual industries, Lord Currie, chair of the UK regulator, Ofcom, roundly rebuked them:

We are seeking to achieve a framework for growth and innovation rather than clinging to the past . . . We start from the position that it is doubtful that the best way to create the conditions for growth is through regulation . . . Our view is one of scepticism and concern about the practicalities involved.[3]

Communications convergence has been predicted for a decade, but is now a reality. The crucial impetus has come from the mass digitisation of broadcast-quality audiovisual content. This means that TV-like video pictures can be sent down any digital pipe, in combination with other digital media, to a wide variety of consumer electronics devices in the home, in the office or on the move. What's more, like still pictures, text, graphics and audio before them, they can be 'cut and pasted' on PC by anyone from communications corporations to 'guerrilla video' collectives.[4]

This means that anything audiovisual can be made available to anyone, anywhere, at any time. And take-up is rising as costs and barriers fall. Digital AV is already universally available and actually on tap in the majority of UK homes: 63 per cent have digital TV, and 25 per cent already have broadband Internet.[5] By 2012 all television will be delivered digitally, while BT is planning a new backbone of ultra-fast broadband connectivity.

For established broadcasters, the challenges of this era are especially acute. Audiences can only fall further; their industry can only become less powerful. As Mark Thompson, BBC Director General, put it:

Broadcasting is morphing and the boundaries are becoming indistinct. It's happening much faster than we ever thought. For broadcasters this means virtual re-invention.[6]

The BBC, Channel 4 and others are now adapting to this revolution, deploying new digital channels and online technologies alongside their mainstream TV channels. The BBC is about to launch a media player giving access to TV programmes online for a week after first broadcast, a service already available for radio; and is licensing once-broadcast content to other services for on-demand use, such as Home Choice's video-on-demand service.

Meanwhile telecommunications companies, ISPs and Internet content services are increasingly providing audiovisual content. The UK broadband association expects every serious company to be an 'audio-visual content provider' by 2010. As Damien Reid, Executive Vice President of Orange, noted:

It's all change . . . Established business models are now redundant and new, stable models have yet to emerge.[7]

This is a future in which TV no longer looks like itself; but everything looks like TV. Television broadcasting, *pace* James Murdoch, is losing its 'special place' in society. Public service TV is now one division of a broadcasting sector that itself is a small part of the wider communications market in which it is regulated: broadcasting accounts for only one fifth of retail revenues in this market, compared to over three fifths for telecommunications.[8]

Citizens' interests in the communications market

> . . . a positive cultural and social development.
> Professor Anthony Everitt on community media

Politicians, corporations and regulators are fixated on the issues that communications convergence raises for industry and for markets. Few people are looking at its implications for citizens—both the threats and the opportunities.

The greatest threat would be the loss of public service broadcasting. Already, the old model of public service television—four, then five channels, competing mainly with each other, and highly regulated both 'negatively' (to protect viewers) and 'positively' (obliging them to make certain investments and provide certain types of programmes in the public interest)—is at an end. Broadcasting now competes with everything else, an imperative bearing on the two publicly owned institutions that are the residue of that old 'ecology'. Channel 4 believes its survival is at stake and is pleading for special measures, but so far the government and Ofcom have turned a deaf ear. The BBC looks strong and healthy but, as we shall see, may still be undermined in the near future.

This is a crucial bottom line for citizens. Public service broadcasting has been our guarantee that all of us, no matter who or where we are, can have equal access to the highest quality of information, education and entertainment, free at the point of use, through the media we most use. It is a conscious intervention in a market for information that, otherwise, would not function efficiently in the public interest. As Davies and Graham argued at an earlier stage in the defence of the BBC, high-quality TV content is too expensive for the market to want to provide it; people as 'consumers' buy less information than is in their best interests; there is the danger of market dominance, which is not easily prevented by *post facto* competition regulation; and the mere agglomeration of individual consumer decisions does not take account of citizenship, community and their complex interplay with culture. Finally, the creation and dissemination of 'common knowledge' (that which everyone knows that everyone knows) is indispensable to democracy.[9]

The second threat is that precisely this kind of dysfunctional market will be created. Ofcom has already stated its ideological belief in a consumer TV heaven: 'We believe that, in the future, public service broadcasting will no longer be needed to ensure consumers can buy and watch their own choice of programming', it opined. And since 'the market is likely to produce significant amounts of programming which meet both the purposes and characteristics of psb', we should see how public intervention can be reduced.[10]

Yet Barry Cox, a leading advocate of a freer TV market and of digital switchover, is scathing about the imperfections in the current pay-TV market:

I doubt whether we will ever be able to move to the kind of market . . . where you can buy what television you like in a way that most suits you – without much more serious legislative or regulatory intervention than we have seen hitherto.

Cox recommends three such interventions: to reform 'bundling', where consumers are made to buy channels they don't want in order to get those they do want; 'tighter regulation of pricing structure so that platform operators can't dictate the price of channels'; and forcing Sky to separate carriage from content.[11]

Ofcom has never made such an analysis, and the government refuses to take on Sky. It is precisely this lack of willingness of legislators, policy-makers and regulators to intervene on the side of the public against media market dominance that gives the lie to their 'consumer-empowerment' policy recipes, and indicates how politically and ideologically influenced the contest over the future of the media may be.

A third threat is the obverse of the opportunities; that is, without conscious policy and regulatory intervention in the public interest, the potential gains for citizens from the new communications market will not be realised.

Champions of the new AV media have little time for traditional broadcasters or for regulators. 'They just don't understand what's happening,' a European lobbyist for the broadband industries told me at Liverpool. 'We have a big task of education on our hands.' And this is not surprising: the adopters of the communications revolution are out there creating, sharing and networking their own media, while software companies, Internet portal providers and others give them the tools to create their online communities.

Media consultant Jeff Jarvis, like many others, sees this 'user-generated' content as spelling the end for corporate market dominance: 'It's the audience who will do that [challenge big media's monopoly] for now they – or rather, we – can produce, distribute, and market our own content at a cost media giants cannot beat . . . The one-way pipe that was broadcasting is giving way to an open pool that everyone owns, where anyone can play.'[12]

These benefits to citizens are real. As users of information, we now have available new and varied forms of subversion, free networking and potential control—at a micro-level—over the means of media production. Advocates for freedom of expression may see in these convergence phenomena a welcome 'liberation' from the heavy-handed enforcement of the centralised, top-down, patronising and spuriously objective culture that was mainstream broadcasting. The emergence of weblogs and 'civilian' or 'citizen' journalism is, to some, the great hope for the future.

Yet notes of caution should be sounded. First, these new grassroots user networks will be highly vulnerable, not so much to regulatory as to security action. In October 2004 police in London seized and removed without explanation two Web servers that hosted websites for both the UK and several European branches of the IndyMedia collective. It emerged that the UK authorities had been asked to act by the United States—the ISP being a US-owned company. And the US in turn had been prompted by the Italian authorities. The case illustrates the ease with which 'networked' security authorities, cooperating ever more closely in the 'war against terror', can disrupt alternative media providers.[13]

A wider note of caution, however, relates to one of the very selling points that Jarvis claims for the new media—that 'cost [that] media giants cannot beat'. For the simple fact is that high-quality information is expensive. Broadcast journalism and factual programming are not shoestring operations. The new media or 'citizen' journalism interprets, comments, brings alternative perspectives from those involved and tries to put neglected stories on the agenda. But it rarely breaks news. For information 'essential to citizenship' to be brought to the public domain, with enough reach and impact to influence democratic debate, we need an independent, well-resourced mainstream media. Think of the BBC's exposure of racism in the Manchester police force, or *Panorama's* judicious documentation of the twenty-first century's first genocide, in Darfur, Sudan.

And the terms 'reach' and 'impact' bring us to a third caution: online 'marketing via links', which Jarvis claims as a citizen journalism strength, is a limited means of mass communication. We need also to create *access to audiences* for the new, innovative, plural and diverse forms of AV media that are now possible. Without deliberate intervention for citizens against the market, these access mechanisms will not happen, and we will miss a once-in-a-generation opportunity.

Ofcom's first year included another major review—of the market for spectrum. Apparently a technical issue, good only for nerds, this review in fact had big implications for citizens, and is another key indicator of the way the convergence future is moving.

One reason why convergence can be liberating is that digital spectrum, unlike analogue wavelengths, need not be scarce and rationed. The Communications Act specified that recognised public service channels must be given guaranteed spectrum, but beyond that the way was clear to open a new spectrum market. Ofcom has taken this route to its maximum, guided by its statutory duties to prioritise market efficiency and consumer interests. Its approach, crudely, has so far been that 'all the valuable parts of the spectrum will be marketised for commercial operators . . . but if there are some unattractive bits left over we could give them away'.[14]

A different approach is possible, in which policy-making recognises, first, that new forms of not-for-profit community media can and will emerge, and second, that these should be formally recognised as public service communications. It would consequently involve planning for and responding to those developments by reserving licences, spectrum and other forms of regulatory support for their establishment.

There are already some notable successes. The Community Channel is a national digital TV channel carried on all the main platforms, dedicated to community use: for example, by publicising the information, advocacy and awareness campaigns of the UK's voluntary sector.[15] At the very local level, 'access radio' pilots have demonstrably proven their success, not only in reaching into neighbourhoods and communities to create a new sense of social inclusion and a new level of 'informed-ness' but, moreover, enabling those communities effectively to own and operate their own media stations. Professor Anthony Everitt's evaluation of them led to the recognition of community media in the Communications Act, the creation of a fund to develop them, administered by Ofcom, and the subsequent licensing of many new stations.[16]

But other parts of Everitt's report were less heeded, notably his advice on the level of funding required, and his warning that these radio pilots may be 'a transitional medium-term phenomenon'—that is, paving the way for the emergence of genuinely converged, cross-platform community media, including community TV.

Here is one of the big challenges in the contest over the future of communications: how to enable such virtually penniless, but determinedly public service, new broadcasters to get equal access into people's lives and living rooms. For the market theory of spectrum simply assumes that the costs and barriers to new market entrants will fall. It does not take account of those who cannot meet any cost. It does not provide equal access for community media to those boring-sounding but critically important mechanisms to support PSB—the 'must carry' provisions that oblige the owners of transmission platforms to let the channels on, the length of licence that would give future certainty for the channels to grow, and so on. Every aspect of the potential future for these community media, and others, yet undreamt, that may join them (perhaps growing out of Jarvis' online journalism communities) requires conscious legislative and regulatory promotion.[17]

The anti-democratic regulator

. . . the challenge is to 'maintain and strengthen' public service broadcasting in circumstances very different from those prevailing when the excellent statutory objectives were first penned.

Stephen Carter, CEO, Ofcom

This discussion of the future for community media points to where we need to go to start rethinking questions of cultural and social policy for communications. The old tools of cultural policy are inadequate: positive content regulation, made possible because spectrum was scarce and broadcasters who were licensed to use it would have to take on obligations in return, has a diminishing grip. But now we can try the other tack: content providers who contribute to desirable social and cultural *outcomes* should be rewarded.

The Community Radio Order that permits such stations to exist specifies the 'social gain' they must pursue, including such terms as reaching 'underserved' communities, strengthening community links and facilitating discussion and free expression of opinion. Similarly, the new Charter for the BBC will for the first time contain a set of social and cultural 'purposes' the Corporation must serve, such as stimulating creativity, supporting informed citizenship and showing the world to UK citizens.

This approach of 'social gain' needs to be extended. For example, community TV should be positively encouraged to step forward and fill the huge gaps in local and regional broadcasting that the national broadcasters can't fill. As another example, Ofcom has proposed the creation of a new 'Public Service Publisher' to operate mainly via broadband, with some 'front end' TV, but has rushed down the route of trialling commercial tenders for the licence before deciding what its purposes should be. Like the BBC, it should have a clear set of social purposes, and any provider should be required to network the content with community media and online communities of interest—even internationally.[18]

But in what space can these new social and cultural purposes, and the mechanisms to achieve them, be debated? We have a critical problem: cultural policy is moving out of the public, parliamentary and democratic realm into a non-democratic space.

The Communications Act was the last of its kind. We have left that slow evolution where broadcasting, a special case industry, highly regulated, remained in a stable state between acts of primary legislation that came along once or twice a decade, and could be contested through the democratic system. The Act has created an independent, free-range regulator that can and will make policy as it goes, in response to rapidly changing markets. Ofcom, in short, is the new policy battleground.

And Ofcom is not a democratic space in which to contest policy. Its key 'stakeholders' are the wider communications industries, for whom it looks to provide 'solutions'. Its orientation is industrial and commercial. Unlike Parliament, and indeed previous TV regulators, Ofcom has no imperative to, and no real interest in, listening to civil society voices. Its many consultation processes soak up the scarce time of under-funded civil society groups, without offering hopes of any influence on the outcomes. For example, Public Voice and its constituent groups have repeatedly asked for non-profit community media to be recognised and considered as a part of the public service broadcasting ecology; whereas Ofcom continues to treat them as marginal. Its existing apparatus of (non-independent) advisory panels appears both unrepresentative and toothless.

I would go further. Ofcom is *anti*-democratic. It has felt free to ignore the intent of government and Parliament through a freewheeling approach to the Communications Act and to its own duties. This is a serious charge that I have outlined elsewhere, but the following are some brief examples.

The key battle around the Communications Act was to insert a public interest duty for Ofcom, to balance the set of duties to markets and competition. It took an overwhelming Lords vote against the government to do this, and the resulting Section 3.1 of the Act is worth quoting:

It shall be the principal duty of Ofcom, in carrying out their functions –
a) to further the interests of citizens in relation to communications matters; and
b) to further the interests of consumers in relevant markets, where appropriate by promoting competition

The express purpose of Parliament was to separate citizens' from consumers' interests, to enable Ofcom to weigh one against the other and, when deciding in favour of citizens' interests, to be able to over-ride the competition principle.

Ofcom's first move, however, was to give itself a mission statement that completely confused this wording:

Ofcom exists to further the interests of citizen–consumers through a regulatory regime which, where appropriate, encourages competition.

Not only did Ofcom spit in the face of Parliament—and of all the civil society groups who campaigned for this duty—but when the matter was frequently raised through its own consultations, Ofcom refused to change its wording.

Similarly, Ofcom decided it knew better than Parliament how to look after public service broadcasting. Within a year of the Act having set in law, for the first time, a detailed set of 'purposes' for public service television, Ofcom rewrote them, stripping out the specifics and replacing them with general notions, as a precursor to reducing what it called the 'marginal' public service obligations on the commercial channels. This undermined not only the will of Parliament but also the efforts of civil society groups that had contributed to valuable improvements in the Act's wording.[19]

The example of Ofcom driving forward the public service publisher proposal without first opening a wider policy debate on what it should be *for* has already been cited. Most egregious, however, has been its approach to the BBC. As noted earlier, rather than reforming the dysfunctional pay-TV market, Ofcom has sought to reform public service broadcasting to suit the market. Hence its approach to the BBC has been to edge incrementally towards saying that its days are numbered.

Phase 2 of the PSB review included assertions—based on slim evidence— that in the future 'PSB will be under threat' or 'under increasing pressure', that 'there is a real chance that . . . the provision of PSB will fall substantially', and that support for the licence fee 'may' begin to fall. These conditional assertions—over-riding Ofcom's own public opinion evidence on the desire of the public for PSB and the licence fee to survive—were then hardened into a consultation question baldly stating that 'the existing PSB system will not survive the move to the digital age'.[20]

The review examined a number of consequent policy options for the BBC, but said it was 'for government to decide'. Having listened to this, but also to its own public consultation and to a range of opinions through the Burns advisory panel, the government did decide—to maintain and protect the BBC, via the Green Paper. Immediately, Ofcom responded that the government was simply wrong. It should be moving as soon as possible to take the BBC's governance away, review licence fee funding, make the BBC experiment with subscription, and create mechanisms to share the licence fee with other broadcasters. In so publicly rebuking the dcms, Ofcom cannot have been unaware that it was aligning itself decisively within a political battle. Simultaneously, the commercial broadcasters and other anti-BBC forces were meeting to try to align their positions on precisely the terrain Ofcom described. This was a clear case for a decision under the 'principal duty'—to side with 'competition' and the sovereign 'consumer', and align with the commercial lobbies, or to side with 'citizens' who, in both Ofcom's and the government's surveys and consultations, and not least in the aftermath of Hutton, clearly *want* the BBC.

Ofcom will shortly examine whether there are other, purely commercial TV channels that are providing programming that 'looks like' public service. With the cable and satellite operators arguing that their channels are the only way to reach younger viewers who have deserted the mainstream, we can expect this to be another part of the case for reducing public intervention.

While the BBC *appears* protected by the current Secretary of State, the battle for its future is far from over. Ofcom and the commercial lobbies, together with well-placed government insiders, will push to dismantle slowly the BBC edifice. Their agenda, well prepared by 'radical' (read 'free market') thinkers such as Barry Cox and David Elstein, will involve a capped or reduced licence fee, the sharing of that funding with other broadcasters after removal of the BBC's governing structure, and the introduction of subscription for all but the most mainstream BBC services.

A different vision

Our vision of the 'Information Society' is grounded in the Right to Communicate, as a means to enhance human rights and to strengthen the social, economic and cultural lives of people and communities. Crucial to this is that civil society organisations come together to help build an information society based on principles of transparency, diversity, participation and social and economic justice, and inspired by equitable gender, cultural and regional perspectives.

Prologue to the CRIS Charter[21]

Another media future is possible. But to define it and to achieve it, we will need to mobilise the latent but evident desire of the UK public for high-quality, independent, informative and educative media. We will need to connect the generations—the middle and older generations, for whom public service broadcasting is a key feature of the landscape; and the younger generations, for whom convergence *is* the landscape. The time is ripe. We stand on a cusp between the age of protected PSB and the age of markets and consumerism. The current government has at least extended the life of the former, and allows the notion of public service some continued validity. We may be less lucky with the next government, and we should be organising now.

That there is interest among the public can be seen from various fragments of evidence. *The Daily Telegraph* had to abandon its regular campaign theme against the BBC because of its unpopularity with readers, and this shortly before the post-Hutton surge of 'keep your filthy hands off our filthy BBC' public feeling. More empirically, 5,000 people and organisations responded to the public consultation on the BBC's future in 2004—not a vast figure, and the 60,000 complaints against *Jerry Springer, the Opera* show what a more organised civil society campaign could achieve—but still the largest government consultation ever. Overwhelmingly, the responses were in favour of the BBC and the licence fee. Likewise, in Ofcom's qualitative research for the PSB review, people supported PSB-style programming, 'particularly when asked to view things from the perspective of society as a whole'; and even when faced with a trade-off against 'realistic costs', they wanted a high level of PSB.[22]

In its quantitative research on 6,000 individuals, Ofcom found that 'there was clear and substantial support for the notion that there should be programming that offers something more to society than entertainment alone'. The viewers 'overwhelmingly agreed' that the main TV channels should promote debate and keep us well informed, provide quality UK-made programmes, give us a 'balanced diet' of programmes and meet the needs of a wide range of audiences. The four highest-scoring programme genres 'of importance to me' were news, drama, serious factual programmes and comedy.

In other surveys, too, people show their awareness of the importance of public service broadcasting in the globalised world. In its annual survey on attitudes to development, the Office for National Statistics has found high levels of concern about poverty in developing countries in the years since 1999, together with rising awareness that this may have effects on our own society. In 2004, 82 per cent of people said that they find out what's happening internationally through TV news, while 21 per cent said that they used other TV programmes and radio for additional information.[23]

The problem has been that this public interest in quality broadcast media has been hard to tap. And it could get harder, as we move away from legislative and parliamentary routes to regulation. There will be fewer high-profile processes or landmark events to help galvanise opinion. Neither nation-states nor their regulators can be relied upon to protect and promote the interests of citizens in the hyper-world of communications convergence.

In the (imperfect) democratic space, a small number of civil society groups were able to secure a few significant gains during the progress of the Communications Act and the BBC Charter review. In the non-democratic space, these groups are outnumbered, out-muscled and effectively powerless. As the pace of industry development and regulatory change intensifies, there will be a greater need than ever for us, as citizens, to assert our communications rights, needs and interests; and we will need to be alert, intelligent, fleet of foot, many in number and coherently organised.

Academic insights and inputs are vitally needed to understand the nature of the emerging markets, and their impact on traditional production industries as well as on user behaviour; to help rethink and re-invent notions of 'public service' in the convergence era; and to suggest new forms of positive action and regulation that are appropriate to pursuing cultural goals across these markets.

Above all, however, we need to fashion together new social and producers' coalitions and lobby groups. I am suggesting that we need a new, US-style citizens' movement for public service communications. It could be established and marketed through the Internet, and could tap in both to existing networks in the voluntary sector and to the growing movement of alternative, user-generated media, providing an organising mechanism to influence wider change.

Such a movement—'our.info'—would establish a vision of 'social gain' through new public service communications, imagining and defining the new ways in which public interest communications services can meet our demands. It would:

- protect public service broadcasting against threats while lobbying the key broadcasters to meet their public purposes;
- promote innovation, by campaigning for public policy that promotes new kinds of public service intervention in the emerging communications markets, including positive action to establish, fund, licence and secure spectrum for not-for-profit and community media;
- organise concerted responses to the 'public consultations' that are currently so dominated by industry;

- generate specific active campaigns targeting the regulator, Parliament and the broadcasters; and
- demand a place in the room wherever new regulatory initiatives are under discussion.

What is stopping us? The short answer is resources. 'our.info', along the lines of US Internet campaign groups, could aim to self-fund through the online donations of new members, but it would need some initial backing to get started. Enlightened philanthropists, please call.

Notes

1 J. Murdoch, speech to the EU conference on the TV Without Frontiers Directive, Liverpool, 21 September 2005.
2 See http://www.opsi.gov.uk/acts/acts2003/20030021.htm
3 Lord Currie, speech to the Liverpool Broadcasting Conference, 21 September 2005, available at http://www.ofcom.org.uk/media/speeches/2005/09/liverpool_conf
4 For an example of a downloadable software tool to author video presentations, see http://www.realnetworks.com/products/visualcommunicator/
5 Ofcom, 'The communications market 2005', available at http://www.ofcom. org.uk/research/cm/cm05/#content
6 M. Thompson, speech to the Liverpool Broadcasting Conference, 20 September 2005, available at http://www.bbc.co.uk/pressoffice/speeches/stories/thompson_ presidential.shtml
7 D. Reid, speech to the Liverpool Broadcasting Conference, 20 September 2005.
8 Ofcom, 'The communications market 2005'.
9 A. Graham and G. Davies, *Broadcasting, Society and Policy in the Multimedia Age*, Luton, University of Luton Press, 1997.
10 Ofcom, *Is Television Special?*, Phase 1 report of the public service broadcasting television review, London, Ofcom, 2004.
11 B. Cox, *Free for All? Public Service Television in the Digital Age*, London, Demos, 2004.
12 J. Jarvis, 'A TV revolution from the corner of the living room', *Media Guardian*, 26 September 2005.
13 For more on this case, see http://www.eff.org/Censorship/Indymedia/
14 Since the original drafting of this chapter, Ofcom has produced a report on the future potential for 'local digital content', including local TV. This report does recognise the potential for new forms of local TV to serve public purposes, and notes that they would need to be supported through spectrum provision. Whether this form of indirect subsidy will be allowed, however, will depend on another Ofcom review, during 2007.
15 See http://www.communitychannel.org/
16 See http://www.ofcom.org.uk/static/archive/rau/radio-stations/access/ Evaluation.html; forty-eight community radio licences had been awarded by October 2005.
17 For the campaign manifesto of the Community Media Association, see http:// www.commedia.org.uk/policy-and-campaigns/what-we-stand-for/commedia- manifesto/

18 Public Voice has set out some key principles for the PSP: see its submission to the consultation on Ofcom's second phase report on public service television, on the Public Voice website.
19 For example, my coalition of international charities, 3WE, had successfully had a requirement for TV programming on 'matters of international significance or interest' inserted. This now has no bearing on ITV1 and Five.
20 Ofcom, *Meeting the Digital Challenge*, phase 2 report of the public service broadcasting television review, London, Ofcom, 2004.
21 The Charter for Communication Rights in the Information Society, available at http://www.crisinfo.org/content/view/full/98
22 Ofcom, 'Meeting the digital challenge'.
23 Office of National Statistics for the Department for International Development, 2004; available at www.dfid.gov.uk/pubs/files/omnibus.pdf

Index